A Few

Murphys

From

Brockton

***

Kevin Murphy

Shining Tramp Press

Cover: (l. to r.) Drs. Robert, Edward and T. J. (Joe) Murphy, on the south side of 551 Warren Ave., Brockton, MA c. 1933.

Published by Shining Tramp Press
2114 Harbor View Drive, Rocky Hill, CT 06067

ISBN 978–0–9749352-3-2

Library of Congress Cataloguing-in-Publication Data

Murphy, Kevin J., 1949-

A Few Murphys From Brockton
Kevin Murphy, - 1st ed.

260 p.; 22.75 cm.
Includes author's notes and index.

Ireland – Emigration
United States – Immigration – Biography
United States – Immigration Ports
United States – Steamship Industry
United States – Shoe Industry

Printed by Amazon.
First Edition: February 2014

Dedicated to

My Aunt

Muriel (McCarthy) Murphy

She encouraged me to write.

Table of Contents

Preface

Missouri journalist Frederic J. Haskin wrote these words in 1913. Since the author's ancestors arrived in America just before that, it seems appropriate now to give Haskin's words a reprise.

I am the immigrant. Since the dawn of creation, my restless feet have beaten new paths across the earth. My uneasy bark has tossed on all seas. My wanderlust was born of the craving for more liberty and a better wage for the sweat of my face. I looked towards the United States with eyes kindled by the fire of ambition and heart quickened with a newborn hope. I approached its gates with great expectation. I entered in fine hope. I have shouldered my burden as the American man-of-all-work.

I contribute eighty-five percent of all labor in the slaughtering and meatpacking industries. I do seven-tenths of the bituminous coal mining, I do seventy-eight percent of all the work in the woolen mills. I contribute nine-tenths of all the labor in the cotton mills. I make nineteen-twentieths of all the clothing. I manufacture more than half the shoes. I build four-fifths of all the furniture. I make half of the collars, cuffs and shirts. I turn out four-fifths of all the leather. I make half the gloves. I refine nearly nineteen-twentieths of the sugar. I make half of the tobacco and cigars.

And yet, I am the great American problem. When I pour out my blood on your altar of labor, and lay down my life as a sacrifice to your god of toil, men make no more comment than at the fall of a sparrow. But my brawn is woven into the warp and woof of the fabric of your national being. My children shall be your children and your land shall be my land because my sweat and my blood will cement the foundation of the America of Tomorrow.

Introduction

Clachan . . . (`klax-en) . . . a haphazard cluster of up to 200 houses
(with outhouses), lacking shops, schools, markets or churches.

In the three centuries leading up to 1900, the poor Irish in the
mountain glens of northern and western Ireland found a way to
survive by living in clachans. The members were all related and
engaged in "partnership farming," leasing large tracts of land that
they divided up based on need. Each family got a little arable land
near the clachan, some poor land in the mountains and the use of
some mediocre grazing land in between.

The clachan Irish were Catholic but never went to church.
They loved to name newborns after family members, and spoke
only Irish. Regarding outsiders with suspicion, they prided
themselves on their hospitality within the clachan. They had no
money, so when a crop had to be brought in, relatives helped and
the reward was a night of food and drink, fiddling and dancing.
Self-advancement was frowned on; it brought scorn and ridicule.
Clachan members were wildly superstitious, believing in fairies
(good and bad), banshees who signaled approaching death, and
"Red Willy" who guarded their illegal stills.

The Irish are similar to a long length of rope, consisting of
millions of strands. All parts of the rope have similar traits. By the
end of this text, Irish readers will realize that they descend more
from the clachan Irish than they could have ever imagined.

Now for some tips on nomenclature—

Townland—the Irish equivalent of "village"—is the key to
understanding land divisions in Ireland. The word "town" has no
government function, but is used colloquially in referring to the
more built up areas of Ireland. In this text, *Book One* deals with
Killarney. Consider this—

County Kerry has 87 Civil Parishes; Killarney Civil Parish is one of them. The twelfth century rulers of Ireland created the Civil Parish for their own administrative purposes.

Killarney Civil Parish has 79 townlands, of which the Townland of Killarney is only one. Often, Killarney is referred to as "Killarney town," even though it is a townland.

The emigration of the Murphys from Kerry and the Sullivans from Mayo is the heart and soul of this story. The action spans about 100 years—from just before Ireland's Great Famine (1845-1851) to about 1955 in America. Since the main characters are Drs. Joe, Bob, and Ed Murphy's immediate ancestors, one might say that this is the book they might have written. However, the past isn't always pretty, and it isn't always fun to revisit. Maybe the journey is best left to others.

When sixteen-year-old Mary Ann Sullivan arrived in Brockton in 1908, the city had 100 shoe factories and a like number of "findings" businesses—firms that supplied laces, eyelets, polish, shoehorns, and forty other items. Brockton also had an average daily wage of $3.75—the highest in the world! For a few short decades, Brockton was the shining city on the hill. Today, Brockton is past its prime; all the shoe factories are gone.

Note: There is no written Irish history before 432 A.D. when St. Patrick arrived in Ireland. Therefore almost 85 percent of Ireland's history is unrecorded. Ever cognizant that this is a book about the Murphys and Sullivans, the author has made every effort not to delve too deeply into Ireland's complicated history. The reader will learn a little Irish history along the way, but this text is not meant to be a history book. Enjoy it for what it is; slur it not for what it isn't.

One final tip: The children of the principal characters in this book can be found in the Author's Notes. The footnote corresponds to the first mention of a couple's children in the text.

-KJM

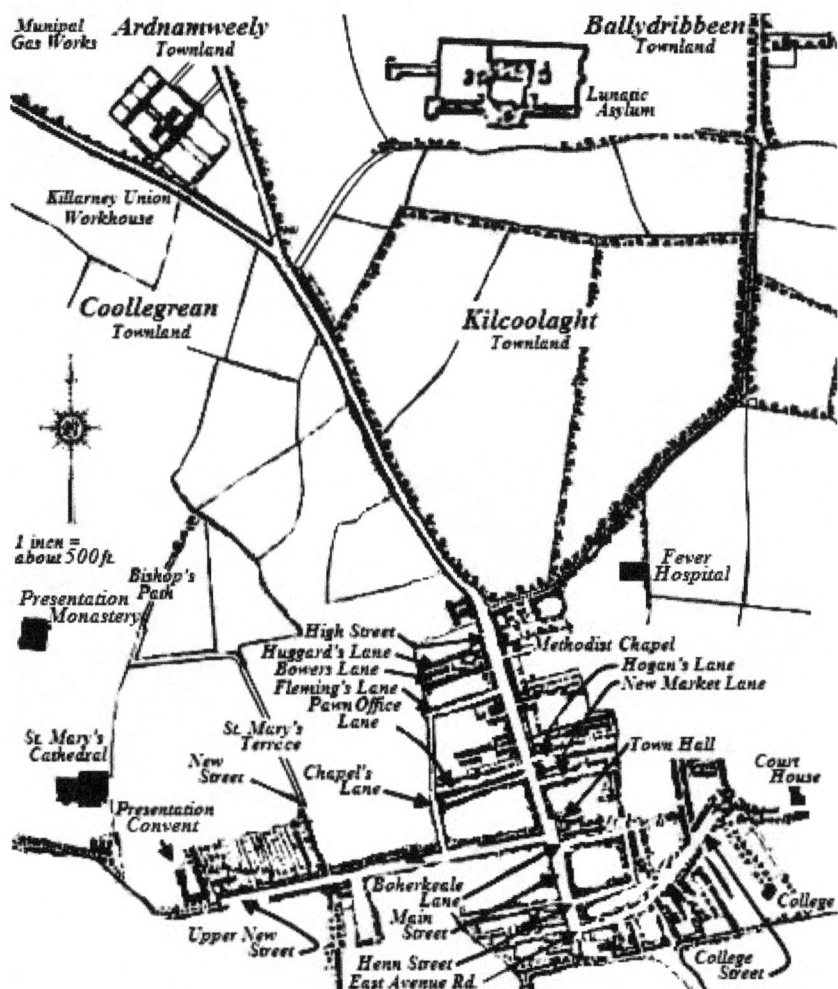

Municipal Gas Works

Ardnamweely Townland

Ballydribbeen Townland

Lunatic Asylum

Killarney Union Workhouse

Coollegrean Townland

Kilcoolaght Townland

1 inch = about 500 ft.

Bishop's Path

Presentation Monastery

Fever Hospital

High Street
Huggard's Lane
Bowers Lane
Fleming's Lane
Pawn Office Lane

Methodist Chapel

Hogan's Lane
New Market Lane

St. Mary's Cathedral

St. Mary's Terrace

New Street

Chapel's Lane

Town Hall

Court House

Presentation Convent

Boherkeale Lane

Main Street

College

Upper New Street

Henn Street
East Avenue Rd.

College Street

KILLARNEY
County Kerry, Ireland

This map of Killarney shows Boherkeale Lane where Maurice Murphy and Honora McCarthy lived. Daniel Murphy and Catherine Sullivan also set up housekeeping on this lane and four of their six children were born there before the family left for America in the early 1890s. At the top are the workhouse and lunatic asylum where Daniel Murphy made shoes.

Book One

The

Murphys

of

Killarney

County Kerry

Ireland

Chapter 1

Killarney

Maurice Murphy was born in Killarney, County Kerry, Ireland on February 17, 1820. The oldest of six children born to Cornelius Murphy and Catherine Lyne, Maurice did his part to add to Ireland's baby boom that didn't end until just before the Great Hunger in 1845. Cornelius and Catherine Murphy moved from the Townland of Ross Island to Killarney and married in 1819, just ten months before Maurice made his appearance.[1]

Ross Island—actually a townland peninsula about a half-mile south of Killarney—had substantial copper deposits. Large shipments of Ross Island copper fueled England's Industrial Revolution during the 1700s and 1800s. However by 1819, when Cornelius Murphy and Catherine Lyne left Ross Island, the copper mines were flooding and production had fallen off appreciably. Soon enough, Ross Island copper mining would end.[2]

Cornelius Murphy labored as a merchant tailor in a small shop on Main Street in Killarney, but winning over customers from established tailors in a small town offered very hard work—coupled with bad feelings. After five marginal years, Cornelius and Catherine Murphy moved to Teernaboul townland. Teernaboul sits a mile east of Killarney on the main Cork-Killarney road—still within Killarney Civil Parish. For more than a decade, the Murphys tried to make a go of it in this townland, but with no lasting success. They returned to Killarney in 1836. Presumably finding business better this time, Catherine had two more children and the couple remained in Killarney for the remainder of their lives.[3]

Though Maurice and his brother Timothy were born in Killarney, the next two children, John and Cornelius, were born in Teernaboul. Maurice's last two siblings, Mary and Thomas, were born in Killarney. With the hubris of hindsight, one can say that Maurice became hobbled by his father's inability to grow roots. In towns and villages all over the world, the men who build sizable estates are the ones who remain in one place and work hard. It takes time to build relationships and recognize opportunities within any given city, town or village. Those who stay in one place have the best chance of sending down a strong taproot and setting themselves up for a comfortable life.[4]

Cornelius Murphy and Catherine Lyne, while searching for a better life, inadvertently ensured that some of their children would not blossom in Killarney. While lifelong friendships were being forged in the small schoolhouses of Killarney, Maurice Murphy lived in Teernaboul, a townland that had two national schools of its own.[5]

Between the ages of four and fourteen, Maurice Murphy saw no one from his birthplace. Beyond that, since the English government would not allow Irish children any education beyond sixth grade, he met no one from Killarney during his school days. Absent extraordinary brains and ambition, Maurice Murphy, and his sons, were given tough hands to play. They may have applied themselves assiduously in the trades, but never rose to positions of prominence in Killarney.

Pigot's 1824 *Provincial Directory of Ireland* described Killarney as "a market, post and fair town . . . a handsome, well-paved, thriving town, and during the summer is the resort of a great assemblage of visitors, who come from all quarters to view the unrivaled scenery of its romantic lakes. . . .The town has three clubs and reading rooms . . . . Saturday is market-day and fairs are held on the 1st of July and the 11th of November."[6]

While the physicians, solicitors, grocers, milliners, linen dealers, iron mongers, and hardware men rented—or in a few cases, owned—property on Main, High, and New Streets in Killarney, tradesmen rented houses on the small lanes off these thoroughfares. From time out of mind, tradesmen—especially shoe and boot makers—rented masonry hovels on Boherkeale (narrow road) Lane. *Slater's Directory* (1881) showed twenty-seven shoe and boot makers in Killarney, with 25 percent of them living on Boherkeale Lane. In the few directories still available, Boherkeale Lane shows itself as the home to the Spillanes, one of the biggest independent shoe and boot makers in Killarney. Shoemakers John, James and Patrick Spillane, all rented houses close to Maurice Murphy's family. In the 1880s and 1890s, when Dan, Tom, and Dinny Murphy emigrated, the Spillanes of Boherkeale Lane were birthing large families who continued the family shoe and boot business well into the 1900s.[7]

In Killarney, the housing stock appeared better than that in the countryside, and the layout of the town led to a more stable way of life. There were two principal roads—High and New Streets, which formed a right angle. Main Street extended from High street, running south of New Street. The narrow lanes that ran off these major roads were churning urns of activity. For example, tradesmen ran forges in eight different places—College Street, Pig Lane, Walsh's Lane, Hogan's Lane, Huggard's Lane, Barry's Lane, Dodd's Lane, and Boherkeale Glebe. (This last lane runs perpendicular to Boherkeale Lane and "Glebe" refers to property lent to a cleric to build a house. His residence then became known as Glebe House.) There were also a couple of tradesmen who ran bark mills—on Bower's Lane and on Well-Lane North. (Bark mills ground branches and bark into a fine powder that more efficiently released the tannin needed in tanning leather.) Lastly, John Donovan kept horses stabled at two separate locations in Killarney—Tuohill's Lane and Ball-Alley Lane. (An Irish "ball-alley" in the 1800s referred to a handball court.)[8]

There were also many leather tanneries, timber stores, coal yards, stores and plenty of offices, almost all on the narrow, secondary lanes off of High, Main and New Streets. As a general rule, townspeople in Ireland lived barely above subsistence level in filthy slums. Killarney's general appearance put other Irish towns to shame. However, any population growth around the time of the Great Hunger occurred primarily due to influxes of evicted, unemployed paupers from nearby farms and estates.[9]

Killarney's population did increase, but its economy declined. The new arrivals didn't have any money, but they did have hunger and the fevers spawned by the famine (mostly typhus). During the Great Hunger, the uncompleted St. Mary's Cathedral functioned as a fever hospital. Another Fever Hospital, just north of Killarney proper and dedicated in 1853, was operated by the Sisters of Mercy.

BOHERKEALE LANE, KILLARNEY

After the Famine, a long slide in the fortunes of Ireland ensued. As one writer noted, "For sixty years, the younger and better element have been leaving Ireland . . . . Since 1850, the most roseate dream of the young Irish mind has been a home and a chance beyond the Atlantic."[10]

Ireland seemed moribund. Even in areas with the best soil, all that met the eye were endlessly rolling meadows. Farming stood at a standstill and a visitor caught no indication of life about the deserted, thatched cottages. In the countryside and in the squalid villages, there were no young or middle-aged people. Cooking took place in the most primitive way on open fireplaces, and the production of potatoes, wheat, and turnips fell off sharply.

Beggars in Killarney, Cork, Limerick, Galway, Dublin and a hundred other townlands, hounded starngers for a few coins. The children wore rags, as did some of the able-bodied workmen and laborers.

Far too many sections of the numerous townlands sat in ruins. "Third-class" dwellings were everywhre. Even the poorest people in America would not tolerate these shacks for a day, yet 1.5 million Irish people never knew better; and, 50,000 of the desperately poor lived in "fourth class" structures—huts that were unfit for human beings.[11]

Ireland's harbors were fine, but they sat stagnant except those in Queenstown, Belfast and Dublin. Queenstown especially bustled with activity as quayside workers helped young Irish men and women onto steamships headed for America.

Ireland's rivers offered superior mill seats, but lacked takers. Cork had a few tweed mills, Limerick some fishing tackle factories, Blarney a tweed mill, and Dublin a number of manufacturing establishments; but these industries counted for little in the entire life of the southern Irish people. [12]

Ireland seemed like a beaten dog and the age-old question nagged: How did the Irish lose their land? The simple answer came in two parts: The Norman Invasion (twelfth century) and Oliver Cromwell (seventeenth century). By the end of the 1100s, the Normans were in control of more than 60 percent of Ireland. Thanks to the conquerors, farming improved and castles, manorial villages, and monasteries rose from the land. Much like the feudal system, manors and baronies were established. Town-building followed as the invaders reclaimed old Viking settlements and established villages predominated by a church and the local lord's castle. However, the Norman conquerors were spread out too thin to rule the conquered people, causing the Normans to eventually adopt the Irish language, laws and customs. Many Irish chieftains reoccupied some of their tribal lands. By 1500, the conquerors controlled only a small section of Ireland around Dublin.[13]

Henry VIII's break with Rome in 1534 ushered in a new chapter for Ireland, as he had become the ruler of the Church of Ireland in 1536. Five years later, the Irish Parliament in Dublin made Henry "King" of Ireland. But this did little to calm the Irish. When Henry died in 1547, the collective Irish mind felt that royal rule meant confiscation of their lands. The developing Church of England and Church of Ireland (Protestant) did not do well under Henry VIII, but blossomed under his successors. Under Elizabeth I, English laws were instituted in Ireland, thereby supplanting Irish *brehon* law, and of course, the Church of Ireland (Protestant) was continually forced on the Irish people. Recently situated English landlords established market, fairs, and industries. Despite careful attempts to Anglicize the Irish, Roman Catholic priests proved intractable. Their belligerence offered the perfect excuse to confiscate land and enact harsh Penal Laws.[14]

England and Ireland continued at loggerheads. By 1607, large-scale English plantations peopled by Protestants rose, as James I confiscated six of the nine counties in northeast Ireland (Ulster). The land was given to English and Scottish "undertakers," who agreed to populate the land with Protestants. The Irish rebelled in 1641, killing several thousand. A ten years' war followed, capped with the bloodthirsty siege of Oliver Cromwell. When Cromwell arrived in 1649, his 20,000 Ironsides stormed Drogheda and Wexford, killing about 5,000 townspeople, mostly Roman Catholics. Cromwell exalted in the slaughter, seeing the bloodletting as apt punishment for the Irish uprising of 1641. The sheer depravity of Oliver Cromwell's massacres at Drogheda and Wexford earned him universal hatred among the Irish. Cromwell departed Ireland in 1650, leaving behind devastation coupled with widespread famine and disease—including bubonic plague. Meanwhile, Cromwell's remaining soldiers continued their work. By 1658, Irish Catholics were left with only 20 percent of Ireland, mostly in the far west.[15]

Cromwell expected that Ireland would remain under English rule, but other events intervened. In 1660, the restoration of the Stuart monarchy—in the form of Charles II—allowed Irish Catholics to once again practice their religion openly, but Cromwell's land confiscations stood. When the Catholic King, James I, ascended to the English throne in 1685, he appointed Catholics to all Irish civil and military posts, which alarmed the English Protestants. Ireland teetered in the balance.[16]

James I was deposed and fled to France. In 1690, James' Irish and French forces fought William of Orange at the Battle of the Boyne. After two weeks of desultory fighting at Londonderry, on

July 12, 1690, William of Orange defeated James I at the Boyne River. The Irish battled on for a year—without James I—until a final surrender at Limerick. More land fell into British hands. By 1700, Irish Catholics had only 14 percent of Ireland. In the meantime, the Penal Laws did their work. By 1750, only 5 percent of Ireland belonged to the Irish. The new Penal Laws of the early 1700s, while sometimes described as unenforceable and ineffective, were devastating to Ireland. However, the ten years' war (1841-1851) has always been considered the war that finished Ireland. The subsequent Penal Laws were salt in the wound.[17]

The toughest of the Penal Laws, passed in 1703-1704 by an Irish Parliament at Dublin—almost completely composed of Protestansts—were comprised of an odious collection of statutes that forbade Catholics either to purchase land or to lease it for more than thirty-one years. Moreover, at death, the land had to be equally divided among all heirs (hopelessly fragmenting larger estates, and diminishing Irish political power). The land and inheritance provisions of the Penal Laws were strictly to strip the Catholics of their property and political power, but further measures were taken to completely demean the Irish Catholics.

Protestants were the only ones who could raise Catholic orphans. Catholic children couldn't be educated in Catholic schools. The Irish children had to be educated in Ireland and only at institutions belonging to the Church of Ireland (Protestant). Neither could Irish Catholics vote or hold public office. They were barred from service in the military, entrance into the legal profession and the civil service. The Catholic clergy was forbidden to say mass, and the Catholic hierarchy were virtually banished from Ireland. To enforce these laws, informers were offered lavish rewards.[18]

The counties in western Ireland—in truth, anything west of the Shannon River—suffered less thanks to the distances involved. However, it cannot be said that the people living in Mayo, Galway, Clare, Kerry, or western Limerick were unaffected because disposed land owners in the east had no choice but to relocate. Their hopes lay in leases west of the Shannon River.

In southwestern Ireland, the years before the Great Hunger were still not comfortable times. In the pre-Famine decades, thousands upon thousands of tenant farmers were evicted in

County Kerry alone, as strong farmers and landlords of all sorts consolidated common lands into large grazing farms. Many of these evicted farmers had no choice but to descend on Killarney, looking for work or handouts. The town, like much of Ireland in the first half of the 1800s, exhibited a curious mix of laudable improvements aligned cheek-by-jowl with great swarms of people living in the most heartrending poverty and gnawing hunger.

Even with all the dislocations and land confiscations, a town like Killarney wasn't of much interest to the English. Most of the rentable lands were confiscated from the O'Donoghue-MacCarthy families and awarded to Sir Vincent Browne in 1583. The Brownes ultimately became Viscounts Kenmare. About 1750, Thomas Browne, a Catholic and Fourth Viscount Kenmare, decided to improve Killarney, with the idea of turning it into a tourist destination. He wrote in his diary, "There were not six slate-roofed houses in the village, but mostly mud cabins, low and ill-thatched. As well for neatness, as that my own house was situated in it, and would have otherwise run a constant risk in respect of fire, I studied to get them slated and better built, and to that purpose offered such of the owners as were capable of taking them, leases . . . at five shillings each . . . for 31 years . . . .My reason for taking such trivial rent was . . . by giving them such a property . . . it was a sure means to keep so many families on my estate; besides, they would require the neighboring grounds for dairy, etc. . . ."[19] Slowly, Killarney gained a reputation for charm and in 1780, even the Bishop of Kerry, Francis Moylan, settled there, rather than in Tralee, the capital of County Kerry.[20]

When the Great Hunger commenced in 1845, Lord Kenmare's dream came to a grinding halt, as tourism dried up and subsistence farmers all over Ireland fought to stay alive. By 1847, the Killarney Union (workhouse)—designed to hold 800 workers—ballooned to 1200. The local landlords were active in Famine relief, remaining on their estates throughout the crisis. They cut estate expenditures drastically to supply food to their tenants. Nevertheless, during the Great Hunger, at least a fifth of the people of Killarney died or emigrated. As a perfect indicator of the devastating effect of the Potato Famine on Ireland, from 1845 to 1926, the country's population plummeted continuously from a pre-Famine high of 8.175 million to a record low of 4.228 million.

This single fact alone shows how long Ireland remained devastated—and how relentlessly emigration continued—after the Great Hunger.

Lord Kenmare had polished Killarney nicely, but by the time Maurice Murphy and Honora McCarthy wed in 1855, very little had changed in the town's economy. Killarney remained small— only 5,187 people—and quite distant from the political and commercial center of Ireland—in the northeast. However, even if you lived in the poorest part of town, Killarney seemed always to maintain an even keel.[21] Railroads came on the scene in the 1850s as tracks were laid all over the Irish countryside. In 1853, a rail extension connected Killarney to the main Dublin-Cork line at Mallow—seventeen miles north of Cork and Queenstown.

A TYPICAL IRISH VILLAGE ALLEY—"GREEN LANE," KILLARNEY

Alongside Cornelius Murphy's peripatetic existence loomed Ireland's long-term losses as an agricultural state. The Great Famine was only one of a long string of crop failures in Ireland. In 1816-1818, the grain and potato crops were lost; Ireland escaped famine in 1825-30 only by the importation of large stockpiles of Indian corn meal from America; again in the early 1830s and early

23

1840s, the potato crop failed a number of times. Even after the Great Hunger of 1845-51, the famines reappeared. In 1879, still another failure of the potato crop caused a crisis, but it didn't reach panic stage because money poured in from America and large supplies of foodstuffs arrived from England.

The cause of the Great Hunger was a fungus—phytophthora infestans. It rotted the potatoes and caused a sickening stench. Ireland's gross overpopulation, as well as its complete dependence on the potato for subsistence, culminated in disaster. Even the Catholic Church comes in for some blame, for it made a fortune from the burgeoning Irish population in the pre-Famine 1800s. The church encouraged big families and the subdivision of farms well beyond reason. As farms became less and less productive, farm laborers were paid with a few acres, adding new members to the lowest class of subsistence farmers (cottiers).

The Famine set patterns that prevailed over the next seven decades. By 1847, nearly 250,000 Irish citizens were emigrating annually, often robbing Ireland of the most promising members of the population. The old landscape and customs were replaced by deserted villages, the bachelor farm, and the late marriage. The loss of the subsistance farmers meant the loss of the farm laborer.

After 1850, farms under fifteen acres declined as the assemblage of larger farms increased and more land came under grazing. Pasturage resulted from depopulation, and in high emigration counties like Mayo, grazing replaced tillage.

Just before the Great Hunger, more than 50 percent of the Irish were working farms that were so small, they could only offer subsistance. Too late, everyone realized that "partible inheritance"—where a farmer continually subdivided his farm so that each son got something—was the road to hell paved with good intentions. The second half of the 1800s brought changes with "impartible inheritance" now the rule. But of course impartible inheritance led to even more emigration. The sons who did not get their own farms were unmarriageable and forced to emigrate. Ironically, on the same steamships to America, were plenty of young Irishwomen who couldn't find marriageable men.

Though Cornelius Murphy's family lived their adult lives in Killarney, they were not much removed from the rough clachan Irish who were so predominant in the west and the north of

Ireland. These clachans or communal settlements—run under the system of rundale—reached their peak in the 1830s while the population of Ireland built to its summit. So said, during the long process of clachan decay, some of them lasted past 1900.[22]

The whole rundale system offered poor tenant farmers acccess to land by "communal farming." Each homeowner in the clachan received arable land near their homes (infield), grazing land in the mountainous areas (outfield), and use of the community grazing land near the settlement.

The largest clachans were in the west, with some approaching 200 houses. The clachans were characterized by desperate poverty, close kinship, and ongoing disintegration of the community because of emigration.

The members of a clachan arranged their cottages and huts—with attendant outhouses—in random, hugger-mugger fashion—without churches, shops or schools. They rarely used money and repaid favors with their own labor, music, food, drink, and dance. Wed to wild superstitions, they believed in herding their livestock through bonfires built atop hills and they delighted in naming newborns after close relatives and ancestors. Beyond that, it fell into the category of unthinkable that a member of the clachan would not care for destitute relatives and aged parents.[23]

The clachan Irish frowned on individualism and self-aggrandizement. The interdependence of community life ensured survival. And though the members of the clachan viewed the outside world with suspicion, its residents prided themselves on their hospitality within the group. In short, the clachan Irish were bound together by custom and tradition—for purely practical reasons. As we shall see, the Murphys of Killarney were removed from the clachan Irish, but their worldview differed little from that of their ancestors.[24]

Maurice Murphy followed in Cornelius Murphy's footsteps and became a merchant tailor. He learned the business in his father's small shop at 3 Main Street, Killarney—just around the corner from Boherkeale Lane.[25] Cornelius Murphy had no trouble taking his oldest son in as an apprentise because he didn't have to pay him much, but as Maurice became a skilled tailor, tension arose between the two men. Deciding what perentage of the profits should go to the son has been the bugbear of many a father-son business and the Cornelius Murphy-Maurice Murphy arrangement was no exception. Unless a business threw off copious amounts of money, no easy solutions surfaced and the fractious denoument often estranged family members.

When Maurice Murphy finally married at thirty-five, Cornelius Murphy was sixty-five—had been a merchant tailor for almost fifty years—and probably longed for the day when he could assume a diminished role in the business. Judging the situation as optimistically as possible, the transfer of this little merchant-tailor business may have been one of the smoothest transitions in the history of father-son businesses. Even so, the distribution of profits must have been a quandary that really left an impression. After all, Maurice did not take his oldest son Dan into the tailoring business. Dan Murphy had to make his own way in the world.

Killarney Sheep Fair

When Maurice Murphy married, he chose an attractive young girl, Honora McCarthy, from the Townland of Ballagh (Ballaghcommane) three miles to the east of Killarney. Honora was one of eleven children—ten girls then finally a boy—and her family suffered through the Great Hunger by renting one farm after another in Ballagh townland. The birth certificates of the children highlight the family's travels: first Ballagh; then East Ballagh; followed by West Ballagh, and finally, back to Ballagh, as they fought to keep body and soul together.

One suspects that Maurice Murphy did not marry earlier because his position in his father's tailor shop netted him so little money. But when he met eighteen-year-old Honora McCarthy—who *might* have been the cutest girl to ever grace the sidewalks of Killarney—Maurice fell madly in love and the two got married apace. The Famine taught Honora two things: Stay away from farms and marry a reliable breadwinner. Killarney was no farm and even a lowly merchant-tailor like Maurice Murphy, seventeen years her senior, met the "reliable breadwinner" part of the bill nicely.

Maurice Murphy may have felt like an outsider in Killarney, but Honora McCarthy was the ultimate outsider. Her growing up years were grindingly poor. The eighth of eleven children, Honora had precious little time for education, manners, ettiquette or anything else. The quest for daily bread completely consumed the McCarthy clan of Ballaghcommane townland.

Maurice Murphy probably lived with his parents in Killarney until he married Honora McCarthy on November 29, 1855 at St. Mary's Cathedral. (In the spring of 1855, the Bishop of Kerry, Rt. Rev. Dr. William Egan, dedicated St. Mary's Cathedral. Services officially began on April 5, 1855.)[26]

St. Mary's Cathedral—often called Killarney Cathedral—demonstrates an important point about the Irish and the Roman Catholic Church. Due to the Penal Laws, Irish Catholics were driven underground. The Penal Laws were designed to eliminate Catholic land ownership, and the accompanying strictures were harsh. From the start, the Penal Laws were selectively ignored—with priests saying Mass in private homes, outdoors, and even in caves. The Penal Laws were eventually abandoned and in 1829, the Catholic Emancipation allowed Catholic priests to once again say mass in public. Only thirteen years after the Catholic Emancipation, in 1842 the foundation stones of St. Mary's were laid. Of course, the hierarchy of the Catholic Church did not want the Catholic Emancipation to be reconsidered, repealed, or changed in any way. Building massive cathedrals across Ireland literally cast the matter in stone.

That said, Killarney, for all the religious shrines and devotion to tourism, still qualified as a small town when Maurice Murphy and Honora McCarthy began housekeeping. Besides Catholics,

Killarney housed Methodists, Presbyterians and members of the Church of Ireland (Protestant). A Friary had been constructed for the Franciscan Fathers, a Monastery (and school) for the Presentation Brothers and their young male pupils, plus a convent (and school) for the Presentation Sisters and their young female students. The remaining Catholics crowded into the old Roman Catholic Chapel on Upper High Street, until St. Mary's Cathedral opened its doors.

The "R. C. Chapel"—the Chapel of Saint Joseph—sat originally on Chapel's Lane, but the small quarters became a burden as time passed. The relocation to Upper New Street was an interim move. While construction progressed on St. Mary's Cathedral, the alter and double baptismal font were taken to the new cruciform cathedral and installed in the Chapel of St. Joseph in the north transept. From early 1855, Killarney's Roman Catholics worshipped at the impressive new cathedral.[27]

Since the nave at St. Mary's Cathedral seated about 1,900 worshipers, small marriages and funerals were held in the Chapel of St. Joseph in the north transept. Baptisms obviously were performed there because that's where the baptismal font from the "R. C. Chapel" came to rest.

The magnetism of the Roman Catholic Church in the lives of the Murphys of Killarney cannot be overstated. All of the people of western Ireland were deeply religious. Keeping in mind that there are thirty-two counties in Ireland, in 1900 County Kerry was one of only seven counties in the country composed of more than 95 percent Catholics.[28] That's why the Murphy children went to Catholic schools and remained devoutly Roman Catholic all their lives.

Honora McCarthy's father and mother, John McCarthy and Mary Connor, were at the wedding ceremony, though as we shall see, the union wasn't the most popular marriage ever held in Killarney.

Many of Honora's eleven siblings were present—although eleven-year-old Dermot McCarthy surely wondered about all the exitement. The witnesses were John Coffee, a shoemaker friend of the Murphy family, and Denis McCarthy, an uncle of Honora McCarthy. Father Michael J. McDonnell—one of a number of priests at St. Mary's—performed the ceremony.[29]

Neither Maurice Murphy's father, Cornelius, nor any of his three brothers, Timothy, John, or Cornelius, acted as witnesses at the marriage. Obviously, Maurice had not asked them. Reading between the lines, the Murphys family may have thought of the marriage as a mésalliance, with the groom seventeen years older than the bride. Along the same lines, perhaps Cornelius and Catherine Murphy perceived young Honora McCarthy as an opportunist? Compounding all these suspicions, Maurice Murphy could be a really hard case. One suspects that regardless of the thick air and thin smiles, Maurice couldn't have cared less if his father or brothers were even there.[30]

Although, we will never know the exact reason for all the uncertainties in the union between Maurice Murphy and Honora McCarthy, it's fair to say that the groom seems to have been an unusual person. Maurice Murphy married late (at thirty-five) and died early (at fifty-one)—though his father, Cornelius Murphy, lived to eighty. In sixteen years of marriage, Maurice fathered eight children. He tried to feed them by working in his father's tailor shop on Main Street. Whether or not this business provided enough money for Maurice's big family is questionable. The struggle may have put him in an early grave. The bright side of Maurice Murphy's untimely death was that it acted as the catalyst for his sons' emigration. After all, it is not the wealthy and successful who seek greener pastures; it is the malcontents, pinched by hunger, and burning with ambition, who risk so much because they have so little to lose.

The rocky relationship between Cornelius and Maurice should be examined a tiny bit further. The Murphys and McCarthys of Killarney were a sentimental bunch, who often named their children after other family members. This harkens back to the clachan Irish—although it could just as easily be dismissed as arrantly unimmaginative behavior. In any event, when it came to naming their children, the same names pop up with astounding regularity. For the males, Thomas, Denis, Daniel, and Michael were the favorites; the females were overwhelmingly named Mary, Mary Ann, Ellen, Honora, Bridget and Dehlia (a nickname for Bridget).

Maurice and Honora Murphy's family size raised no eyebrows. Eight children wasn't remarkable in Killarney or the

Irish countryside, for couples averaged six children throughout the 1800s in Ireland.[31] The Murphys had four daughters and four sons. The daughters were Mary, Mary, Mary Ellen and Mary Ann. (Honora Murphy determined to have a baby named after her mother, Mary Connor McCarthy, or die trying!) The sons were Daniel, Thomas, Denis and Maurice. Since Maurice Murphy failed to name any of his sons after his father Cornelius, the name, as a recurring entry in the Maurice Murphy genealogical line, died forever. Maurice had four brothers. One remained single, but three married and dutifully named one of their sons after their father Cornelius. Maurice Murphy remained the outlier.

A honeymoon wasn't part of wedding packages for the poorer classes of Ireland. Usually a house party followed. After that, the newlyweds, Maurice and Honora Murphy, set about filling their small rented house on Boherkeale Lane with children. A few more Murphys in County Kerry wouldn't hurt anything. In the middle of the 1800s, Kerry had only 6 percent of the Murphy households in Ireland, but twice the percentage of the average county.[32]

Maurice and Honora's first child Daniel "Dan" Murphy was born on October 9 and baptized at St. Mary's Cathedral on October 12, 1856, with the Rev. William Horgan officiating. Sponsors at a baptism don't mean much, but Margaret McCarthy—Honora McCarthy's aunt—stood in with John Coffee—the same shoemaker who witnessed Maurice and Honora's wedding the year before.[33]

While Maurice Murphy engaged in the tailoring business, Honora kept house, cooked meals, and birthed children between 1856 and 1870. When he started school, Dan Murphy attended the "Monstry of the Brothers," as he called it.[34] The old monastery was built in 1838 on College Street, but a new monastery rose in 1861 on a five-acre site just north of St. Mary's Cathedral. Dan Murphy walked a quarter of a mile to the new school each day. Since the annual temperature in Ireland swung between thirty-five and sixty-five degrees Fahrenheit, this walk to school never qualified as a hardship.

Upon completion of the sixth grade, Dan "worked 4 years to have xpenses [sic] of one year off."[35] He was now fifteen.

Sadly, Maurice Murphy died in 1871 at fifty-one. The details of his death are lost to history; he didn't even leave a will. Like the other Catholics of Killarney, Maurice Murphy was buried in a cemetery in Aghadoe, a quiet Civil Parish just to the northwest of Killarney. There are no cemeteries in Killarney. This arrangement has particularly suited those who separate tourists from their money. Vacationers flock to Killarney—the gateway to the most beautiful lakes region in Ireland—and thanks to the Great Hunger, no one wanted to see another cemetery.[36]

Daniel was only fifteen when Maurice died. It is impossible to know how Daniel felt about his father or the older man's death, but it is certainly possible that he resented Maurice for saddling him with a wide variety of responsibilities that he never saw coming. When the time arrived, Daniel did not name any of his children after his father, but then again, Dan only had two sons and naming them after his two brothers, Tom and Denis (Dinny)—who together constituted his only hope of getting to America—looks like familial capital better spent. Worth considering is that Maurice and Daniel were both first-born sons, who tend to be more aggressive than their younger siblings. That said, Alfred Adler's belief in birth order as a significant factor in the development of personality has never been supported by any scientific work, so maybe we should leave this matter to the pop-psychologists among us.

Since Dan Murphy left school at eleven, he had been a part of Killarney's workforce for four years already. When Maurice Murphy died, Dan became the man of the family. This is a cliché, but Dan's story is vastly more complex as he eventually attempted to care for his mother and siblings while moving his own wife and four children to America.

Dan Murphy next "went a work Killarney Union . . . .," the workhouse a half-mile north of Killarney proper.[37] Walking along Main, then High Streets, the lane turned into the Road of Rocks (later Rock Road), which led to the workhouse.

The Killarney Union served an important purpose, but it wasn't to Dan's liking and he only stayed a year. Afterwards, he tried freelance shoemaking only to return to the Killarney Union a short while later. This time, he stayed six years. Toward the end of this hitch, in July 1877, Dan was recommended as shoemaker to the administrators of the Lunatic Asylum, just east of the Killarney Union. Making shoes for the mentally ill could only have been entrusted to a highly skilled worker with a gentle personality. Not surprisingly, relatives mentioned much later Dan's extraordinary kindness.[38]

Ireland had workhouses before the Irish Poor Law Act passed Parliament in 1838, but there were only a few in use. Killarney Union—on eight acres of land—started operations in 1840 and catered to the poor of all the townlands over a 395-square-mile area. A board of guardians ran the colossal stone complex. Killarney Union housed 800, but also had plenty of day workers, like Dan Murphy, who made their way to the huge structure each morning to earn a day's pay.

The meals in the workhouses were right out of a Dickens novel. Breakfast featured some combination of broth, bread and cheese. Dinner could be pease porridge, hasty pudding, or frumety (boiled, cracked wheat bolstered by eggs, cheese, broth or currants). Supper reverted to bread, broth and cheese.

By 1877, at twenty-one, Dan left the Killarney Union to work on his own account for the next eight years. Part of that time, most likely intertwined with his other orders, he made shoes for the sisters at the Presentation Convent on Upper New Street and sandals for the Franciscans at the Friary on Fair Hill in Killarney.[39]

There are no records of any training in the boot and shoe business for Dan's young brothers, Tom and Dinny, but it seems logical that Dan shared his knowledge of the trade and that the two younger brother also earned money at the Killarney Union when necessary. The family's circumstances were difficult and none of the children enjoyed the privilege of sitting idle. Everyone had to contribute money to the household in whatever way they could.

Before Dan took leave of the Killarney Union and the Lunatic Asylum, he secured letters of recommendation from the master of the workhouse, the presiding chairman of the board of guardians, the clerk of the union, and the chaplain. He also garnered a recommendation from Dr. Oscar Woods, the superintendent of the Lunatic Asylum. Lastly, he received favorable *bona fides* from the Bishop of Kerry, who lived at The Palace in Killarney. (The Bishop's Palace, also designed by Augustus Pugin in 1849, sat in the northern shadow of St. Mary's Cathedral.) Information traveled freely among the tradesmen of Killarney, as it does everywhere else, and the dream of going to America never left Dan Murphy. He planned continuously for the day when he could make it happen.

Still, Dan wasn't alone in his thoughts of emigration. His younger brothers, Tom and Dinny were also keen on emigration. As evictions resumed, almost at the pace of those during the years of the Great Hunger, tenant farmers traveled to the cities looking for work and dragged down the wage scale of the region. Jobs became fewer in Killarney and, worse still, pay continually slid. The relentless belt-tightening became endemic to the region and emigration emerged as the only option for many. Twenty-one-year-old Thomas Murphy finally decided to emigrate in the spring of 1881.

Dan, Tom and Dinny had different visions, skills and responsibilities, but the two younger brothers had more options. For Ireland's emigrants, the most popular destinations were England, Australia, Canada, and America, with the United States offering the greatest opportunities. In 1881, the U.S. had a population hovering around fifty million—ten times that of Ireland. However, the United States had a hundred times the square mileage of Ireland, and thanks to the continental railroad, a young man had unfettered access to the whole country.

For a family of shoe and boot makers from Killarney, North Bridgewater (Brockton), Massachusetts represented the biggest rising star in the shoe industry worldwide—bigger than Lynn and bigger than Haverhill. Simply put, the Murphys didn't have to waste time choosing their final destination.

The "American wake" had become a staple when a young man or woman emigrated from Ireland because only 10 percent ever returned. In all likelihood, Tom Murphy would never see his friends again and the streets and lanes of his youth would soon enough be nothing more than the stuff of errant dreams. Friends and family gathered at the home of Maurice and Honora Murphy for a drink and a bite to eat. On a pleasant spring morning in early April 1881, Tom Murphy took his cloth satchel and headed for the Killarney Depot, just a few blocks east of Boherkeale Lane.

The Irish have been in America since before the American Revolution, especially in Maryland, Pennsylvania, New Hampshire, Virginia and the Carolinas. In colonial times, the

United States government did not keep immigration records, so it is difficult to find reliable numbers on Irish immigrants. From 1820—when record keeping began—until 1872, the number of Irish emigrants tallies about four million. Not surprisingly, the largest numbers fled Ireland as a result of the Potato Famine.

During the Great Famine, 1 million Irish died of starvation and the fevers spawned by it—mostly typhus. Another 1.5 million emigrated. Most emigrants were peasants and laborers. While there were always Irish leaving from Dublin, Galway, Cobh, Limerick, Belfast, Londonderry, Waterford, and Sligo, approximately 65 percent of the Irish, traveling to North America, made their way across the Irish Sea and booked passage from Liverpool. About 25 percent went no farther. For some, lack of funds created a roadblock; for others, after three hours on the Irish Sea, they reasoned that eight days on the North Atlantic would kill them. Either way, Liverpool became their new home. (That is why so many Liverpudlians, like Paul McCartney, have Irish roots.) By 1870, the Irish harbors at Queenstown and Moville (Londonderry) overshadowed Liverpool when it came to emigrant steamship passage to North America.[40]

The age of steam brought big changes to the Port of Cobh (pronounced Cove). In 1838, the side-wheel, wooden hulled *Sirius* became the first steamship to sail from Cobh to America. Owing to Queen Victoria's visit in 1849, Cobh was renamed Queenstown. By 1881, steamships were the only passenger vessels plying the North Atlantic, and most of the Irish never looked beyond the Port of Queenstown for passage to America.

Booking passage wasn't a problem for Tom Murphy, as travel agencies—specializing in emigration—existed in every part of Ireland. Cunard Lines gained a fabulous reputation for having sales agents in every major city in the world.

Tom Murphy rode the train sixty miles due east to Mallow and then a much shorter distance south to Cork and Queenstown. About the size of Killarney, Queenstown sat in the shadow of a massive Roman Catholic cathedral. Completed in 1879, St. Colman's Cathedral commanded a bluff overlooking the harbor.

The Deepwater Quay lay at the edge of the harbor right behind the train station. Tenders, in constant motion, ferried passengers and cargo out to the different steamships. The water alongside

Deepwater Quay measured only twenty feet deep, while Tom Murphy's carrier, the six-year-old Cunard liner *SS Scythia*, drew almost thirty feet of water. (The SS stood for screw steamer; RMS, royal mail ship; and HMS, her/his majesty's ship). Because of the weather, the North Atlantic steamer season ran from the first week of April to early October. Passengers loved trans-Atlantic travel during the good months, as breathtaking views and balmy ocean breezes, made the crossing a dream. Conversely, a winter crossing—when passengers sailed strictly out of necessity—could be a thoroughly unpleasant experience.

Samuel Cunard was born in Halifax, Nova Scotia. His father built ships, but young Samuel removed to Boston to learn the ship brokerage business. In 1839, he traveled to England to enlist backers for securing a Royal Mail contract. (The wooden brigs of the Admiralty were such tubs, even Samuel Cunard referred to them as 'coffin ships.' The negotiations with the Admiralty lasted two years, but finally Cunard won the right to transport the mails between Liverpool and Canada.[41]

Samuel Cunard had no interest in passengers. As long as he held the Royal Mail contract, passengers were superfluous to his business and the emigrant trade, to put it bluntly, was beneath him.[42]

While the tall-masted sailing ships offered service to Irish emigrants at the Cove of Cork before 1859, passage to America could not have been more dangerous. Passengers died regularly. However, when Inman Lines decided to stopover at Queenstown in 1859, the firm enjoyed the sweetest of monopolies, making enormous profits from Irish emigrants who were driven from the Emerald Isle. But Samuel Cunard's Royal Mail contract wasn't producing the profits of earlier days and he eyed Inman's Irish franchise greedily.[43] Soon enough Cunard, National, Guion, and White Star Lines were making port at Queenstown. The iron-hulled steamships of these major carriers soon enough put the wooden sailing ships out of business, but the steamers fought fiercely for passengers. Inman's original £8 8s ($40) steerage fare dropped to £6 6s ($30) by 1863—briefly plummeted to £2 ($7.74)—but eventually stabilized at £5 ($24.33). That was the rate that Tom Murphy paid when he sailed on the *SS Servia* in 1881.[44]

Cunard Lines earned a fabulous reputation for safety by default. While Cunard held the Royal Mail contract, the Lords of the Admiralty would not allow the liner to experiment with steamship improvements. Therefore, when it came to twin screws (Cunard didn't build a twin-screw steamer until 1893), triple jacketed boilers, and number of other improvements, all the bad luck fell to Cunard's competitors; thus, Cunard's reputation for safety. But this reputation did not completely still the anxieties of the historically superstitious Irish.[45]

In Ireland, superstition goes back thousands of years. For example, livestock were considered linked to their owners' health. With so much at stake, pigs, donkeys and horses were allowed into the peasants' huts. Irish Catholics believed in the existence of fairies, who inhabited abandoned farmhouses and ancient ruins. Some fairies enjoyed good reputations, but others were decidedly malevolent. They could bring disease to the crops, sicken livestock, and steal healthy infants, leaving "changelings" in their places. Irish women dressed young boys in girls' outfits to disguise and protect them from the fairies.[46]

With steamships, the Irish suspected that Cunard ran the safest carriers, but vaguely linked this to the number of engines built into the company's vessels. For this reason, they counted the number of funnels of a steamer to determine its seaworthiness. Three funnels were better than two; two were better than one. The Irish emigrants booked passage accordingly. To beat the Irish at their own game—and to corner the market on third-class passengers—the owners of the White Star Line designed the *Titanic*—and her sister ship the *Oceanic*—with four funnels, the last of which was a hollow dummy—capable of absolutely nothing.[47]

Tom Murphy, as the first of the Killarney Murphys to get a shoemaking job in Brockton, was undoubtedly the first to send money back to Killarney, with his brother Dinny running a close second. Not to put too fine a point on it, but Daniel and Dinny Murphy—and the rest of the Killarney Murphys—might never have gotten to America without Tom's help. Dinny's emigration wasn't difficult because he was still single. If anything, it gave Honora and Dinny's siblings some breathing room on Boherkeale Lane when he emigrated.

On the other hand, the difficulty of Dan Murphy's relocation of six people to America—while still meeting his obligations to his siblings and widowed mother in Killarney—should not be underestimated. Without help from his brothers in Brockton, Dan's emigration might never have come to fruition. Truth told, Dan Murphy's emigration dream was so complicated that it languished for more than a decade and a half. Dan started collecting recommendations in 1877 and left to take a shoemakers job at S. B. Grover in Brockton in 1893—sixteen years later! When Tom Murphy left for America in 1881, Honora Murphy was forty-four and her youngest child, Mary Ann (Annie), was only eleven. Dan could not possibly have emigrated at that time.

While life continued as usual in Killarney, Tom Murphy began to build a whole new world for himself in Massachusetts. At South Station in Boston, he took the Old Colony Street Railroad south to Mattapan (a section of Dorchester), switched trolleys and continued south to Brockton—a total trek of twenty miles. Then Tom Murphy followed written directions that he had received from a friend to the home of Mrs. Dora Murphy (no relation). She was the widow of John Murphy, another shoe worker. Mrs. Murphy lived in a huge triple-decker at 75 Forest Avenue (northwest corner of Track Street). For $1.25 a week, Tom Murphy received a room and an evening meal. His first order of business was to find a job, and toward that end, the day after his arrival, he began visiting the shoe factories. Almost all of them were within walking distance of Mrs. Murphy's boarding house and Tom Murphy made good use of his time.

There were more than fifty shoe manufacturers in Brockton and a like number of firms in the "findings" end of the trade. The number of firms fluctuated wildly as companies were lured away with inducements, competitors folded due to poor management, and still others went belly up during periodic recessions. Beyond that, economies of scale reduced the number of factories, while increasing the size of the average firm.

The "findings" industry didn't interest Tom Murphy. The shoe industry broke into two different segments—manufacturers who assembled and then shipped shoes all over the world and a lesser contingent that supplied all of the components for making shoes.

37

The findings industry produced everything from the lasts (the wooden forms on which shoes were constructed), to leather hides, to the boxes in which the finished shoes were shipped. They also supplied dyes, polishes, shanks, heels, buckles, eyelets, lacings, buttons, tacks, thread and about forty other items used in the manufacture of shoes. These firms served a vital purpose, but generally speaking, they were small. Owing to the lightness of buttons, shoehorns, laces and polish, the work lent itself well to female workers. For example, women exclusively made laces. Determined not to waste his opportunities, Tom Murphy dismissed the findings end of the shoe business to concentrate on landing a job making shoes and boots.

Within a mile and a half of his lodgings in the Irish "Foster Street" section of town sat all of Brockton's enormous shoe factories, including the two giants—W.L. Douglas, only about a dozen blocks north on Pleasant Street, and George E. Keith on Perkins Avenue in Campello, the southern section of the city. Negotiating the business waters—as if caught between Scylla and Charybdis—the other shoe factories ranged from the tiny shops with a few dozen employees and a handful of machines, to factories itching to give Douglas and Keith a run for their money.

Douglas entered the business convinced that he could make an inexpensive—but high quality—shoe and still turn a good profit. With a borrowed $800, he introduced two market beaters—the $3.00 shoe and the $3.50 shoe. George E. Keith descended from one of the founding families of Brockton and chose the opposite course. Keith made the finest shoes money could buy and sold them to upscale buyers all over the world.

North Bridgewater (Brockton) had an agricultural past matching any other highly productive town in Massachusetts, but the land proved so well watered that mills were added to homesteads as if by divine planning.[48]

When Tom Murphy got to Brockton, he stood there awestruck. Brockton was a city of 15,000 people and more than 1,200 were Irish immigrants. Some of the Irish worked in the shoe factories, while many more were laborers.[49]

Among the immigrant groups, the Irish were the first to arrive in North Bridgewater around 1825. Still, the Irish didn't really flood into North Bridgewater until the Great Famine in Ireland forced 1.5 million downtrodden farmers to emigrate. When they did arrive, they settled on the east side of Main Street, at the northern end of Campello. The Famine Irish did not choose to live near the center of town.

When Tom Murphy sought lodging at Dora Murphy's boardinghouse on Forest Avenue, there were many Irish families living near the center. Because they were so close to the businesses on Main Street, they did not need their own neighborhood markets and taverns. This changed, however, as the area became overwhelmingly Irish. By 1910, the Irish section of Centerville encompassed a fair number of streets running east and west off of Warren Avenue, between Lawrence Street on the north and Florence Street on the south.

The Irish were of course discriminated against in Brockton, but not as much as might be imagined. As early as the 1880s, discrimination became counterproductive. Protestant businessmen vigorously raised money for factories where much of the workforce would be Irish. Beyond that, the shoe manufactories were owned and operated by men of various religious faiths— Protestants, Catholics and Jews from a multitude of different backgrounds. At first, the majority of the factories were owned by the descendents of the original founders of Bridgewater—such as the Keiths and the Packards. Later, the owners were as diverse as a group could get. This held true with Massachusetts' whole shoe industry. The factories that assembled the greatest collection of ladies footwear for the world in Lynn, and the many firms turning out slippers in Haverhill, were owned and operated by the same cross-section of the American populace as Brockton.

Still, for Tom Murphy, Brockton remained a wonder. In 1878, the Brockton Telephone Company strung its first 1.5 miles of lines from Centerville to Campello. Thomas Edison had chosen Brockton as his "experimental laboratory" and wired the town like a mad professor. Brockton became the first city in the world to light its streets with electricity after the Edison Electric Illuminating Station came on line in 1883.[50]

The city had a water works (with indoor plumbing and fire hydrants), a city sewage system, cobblestone streets, and every other modern convenience of the day. A year before Tom Murphy arrived, the Brockton Street Railway offered the first horse-drawn trolleys on Main Street. In 1887, the East Side Railway won a charter, and two years later, electric trolleys supplanted the "old" horse-drawn models.

Main Street struck everyone as a profusion of stores, trolleys, horses, buggies, and of course, people. Among the smaller shops, groceries and restaurants developed the first retail attempt of the "The P.T. Barnum of Dry Goods Men," James Edgar. With a partner, he opened the Boston Store in 1878. After a couple of fires—and with "Uncle Jim" now acting as a sole proprietor—he opened Edgar's department store. It won the hearts of Brocktonians and continued as the biggest store in the city for a century.

As with so many other industries, eastern Massachusetts birthed the leather tanning and shoemaking businesses in America. It all began with itinerant shoemakers, working alone, traveling the countryside, and taking orders. After enough work had been assembled, they returned to their small shops and fabricated the shoes.

This began to change in the middle of the 1700s, when shoemakers began to hire other men to work in their shops. Soon enough, this small collection of shoe workers became large enough to qualify as a factory. In North Bridgewater (Brockton), shoe factories began to spring up in the 1830s, 1840s, and 1850s, due to the numerous leather tanneries in the area. In the 1860s, the Civil War—coupled with the development of the McKay sewing machine—gave the shoe business a huge boost. Soldiers needed boots and the McKay machine—the biggest mechanical improvement the industry had seen to date—revolutionized the business of attaching shoe soles to fancy uppers.[51]

By the 1870s, the Town of North Bridgewater had become so prosperous that the public demanded a new name. Oddly enough, the final choice in 1874, Brockton, had nothing to do with shoes, history, religion, geography, government—or anything else. People's minds came to rest there—and that's all. In 1881, Brockton became an incorporated city, with a descendant of an old Bridgewater family, Ziba Keith, as mayor.

When it came to Brockton's biggest shoe and boot manufactories, George E. Keith built his factory in 1870; Preston B. Keith in 1871; W.L. Douglas in 1876; and M. A. Packard in

1877. These are the names of the biggest men in the business, but there were plenty of other shoe manufacturers. By 1884, Brockton had 75 shoe factories, with 60 findings businesses to support them. Tom Murphy could never have imagined it in 1881, but the number of shoe factories in Brockton would crest at 100 by 1900 and then return to 75 by 1922. From there, the industry began a long death spiral. It gave Tom Murphy, and his brothers, a good living, but would break the hearts of their children if they chose to follow in their fathers' footsteps.

Tom Murphy's mind spun. When he left Killarney, it was a sleepy town of a little over 5,000, where people thought it impolite not to stop and carry on a bit of conversation with friends on the street. Brockton ran by the clock, with workers parading like soldiers into the shoe factories early in the morning and emerging late in the afternoon. Brockton offered little time for casual conversation during the work week. Beyond the Irish immigrants, there were large communities of Swedes, Poles, Lithuanians, Italians and a smattering of Armenians, Russians and Czechs. They were all exactly like him, forced by conditions beyond their control to leave their homelands and start lives anew in a foreign land. Brockton wasn't much of a melting pot in the 1880s. Immigrants commandeered large enclaves for themselves and clannishly stuck together. The shoe factories were the great commonalities, where men and women worked side by side earning healthy paychecks—some of which they spent in the markets and taverns of their own neighborhoods—and some they sent back to their people in the old country.

By 1910, the average wage paid in Brockton was $3.75 a day, the highest wage in the world. Prosperity abounded. The shoe workers lived well, supported the church, and educated their children. The Boot and Shoe Union had done an estimable job. So said, in order to pay such high wages Brockton had to turn out the highest-grade shoes and boots produced anywhere. A more delicate truth hid just beneath the surface: The Boot and Shoe Union had priced Brockton's workforce out of the shoe industry. Owners began looking for cities with cheaper labor and the Brockton shoe franchise continued a slide that didn't end until the late 1980s when Footjoy and Etonic were the only two shoe companies left. By 2009, there were none.

With all the Irish Catholic immigrants wafting into Brockton, one would think that St. Crispin, the patron saint of shoemakers, would be mentioned once in a while, but the name never came up—and for good reason. In 1864, Newell Daniels of Milford, Massachusetts, formed the Knights of St. Crispin, a labor organization and the forerunner of the Boot and Shoe Union. By 1870, there were 70,000 members of the Knights of St. Crispin. The formation of the Bureau of Labor Statistics in 1884 stood as one of the union's biggest successes. As a division within the Department of the Interior, the Bureau of Labor Statistics kept accurate numbers relating to employment, wages, production, and dozens of other industrial and economic issues. Just when it seemed that the Knights of St. Crispin had an unlimited future, it got into a nasty tussle with shoe factory owners, who blacklisted its members and slashed wages. In the 1870s, the factory owners had the power to crush a union. Three decades later, they were powerless to suppress the Boot and Shoe Union. In Brockton, the prosperity slowly killed everyone.

Tom Murphy usually brimmed with optimism and self-confidence, but there were concerns. As he made his way from one shoe factory's bulletin board to another's hiring office, his meager skills became glaring. Shoemaking had many specialized divisions. Some of these units, such as the simpler operations in the boxing and shipping rooms were distinctly unskilled trades. Others, like those in the cutting room and the sole-edging room, were highly skilled callings.

In spite of what the average person thought, shoemaking required a wide range of very specific skills acquired only with time, patience and application. Tom Murphy's only real hope lay with the many company bullitin boards. Maybe one of them had something for a novice. With any kind of luck, he might be able to find an entry-level job, just something to get his foot in the door. A hard worker and a self-starter from early on, he knew that once he got a foot in the plant, survival was practically ensured.

The huge factories of W.L. Douglas and George E. Keith were out of the question because they had their pick of both skilled and unskilled workers. Persons skilled in one particular branch of shoe manufacture quite often entered the large factories as experienced operators. Since their skills were in such high demand—and the competition between factories constantly simmered—these skilled operatives moved from factory to factory, trying to better their hourly wage.

The concept of job security was not especially meaningful to shoe workers. The shoe industry was a fickle mistress, with the owners constantly accepting lucrative tax breaks to relocate. Another gambit called for owners to lower the quality of their shoes and then demand wage concessions from the workers. Fierce competition, labor-management hostility, rising material costs, and uneven demand, made the shoe business unstable.

As early as the 1870s, unemployment had become a part of shoe workers lives. Although ". . . a relatively small percentage of Brockton's shoemakers may be out of work at any one time, over a third [35 percent] of them faced unemployment at some time during the [average] year."[52]

Nonetheless, Brockton, with its concentration of skilled workers, state-of-the-art factories, energetic findings businesses, and good transportation infrastructure, represented a winning combination for the large-scale boot and shoe manufacturers of the Gilded Age.

In a small shoe establishment, newcomers like Tom Murphy could get a start. In a major shoe center like Brockton, assuming that economic conditions were in stasis, unskilled workers were customarily hired and, more often than not, began their apprenticeships in the stitching room.

Eliminating the other huge companies, Tom Murphy still had a sizable list of prospects. Eventually, he landed a job with the Brockton Ideal Shoe Company on Franklin Street. Now that he had his foot in the door, Tom Murphy took stock.

Physically, he measured a couple of inches shorter than his brothers, but his size masked a surprising physical strength. Accordingly, he worked hard for Brockton Ideal Shoe and became a sewer in two years and a hand sewer in six, muscling the 3/8" leather welts into a position where they could be sewn to the upper shoe leather. The welt would then be sewn to the sole leather—all around the outside of the shoe—with the Goodyear welter machine. The job required a certain amount of brute strength and was the only stitching job that did not fall under the auspices of the stitchery room. A difficult and frustrating job, powerful machines eventually took it over.

Brockton Ideal did business at 63 Franklin Street, a little less than a mile from Mrs. Murphy's home. Tom Murphy did his hand stitchery in the "makings" room, the place where the upper parts of the shoe was joined with the lowers. As mentioned earlier, the most common means of entry into the shoe business was through the stitching room, but if a company employed the Goodyear welt method—as did Brockton Ideal—the makings department ran a close second.

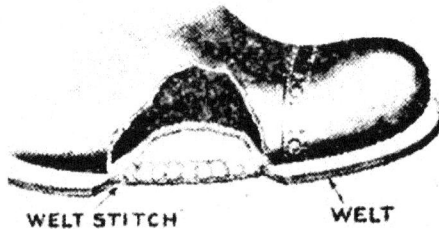

WELT STITCH   WELT

Ordinarily, Tom Murphy's new job would be cause for celebration, but he had learned enough about the shoe business from fellow Irishmen. An entry level job was only a chance to prove you could take orders and work hard when asked. It wasn't anything special. It would be a while before Tom Murphy became a skilled enough operator to use the Goodyear welting machine. In the meantime, he would do all of the small and irksome jobs that no one else wanted. In the best sense of the word, Tom Murphy was a hustler.

Shoe factories employed about 200 different leathers for the "uppers" of shoes and stitching together the soft pieces of calfskin, pigskin, or goatskin went to women. Time consuming, the work demanded great concentration. One slip with the needle and the finished shoe would go into the company's outlet store, where a quick sale at half price would benefit the company exactly nothing—no profit, no loss. After the women completed their work, the upper sections of the shoe were delivered to the makings department where the Goodyear welts were attached. Next the

Goodyear welter machines attached the uppers to the lowers, and the shoes went to the finishing department.

Typically, an average style shoe passed through 100 different pairs of hands and about 150 different machines, involving over 200 separate processes. But Brockton Ideal Shoe didn't have 100 pairs of hands. In order to make even a single pair of shoes, each worker had to master many more skills than their counterparts at the Douglas and Keith factories. In time, the knowledge that comes with a multiplicity of skills would pay off for Tom Murphy.

The opportunities were there. He could stay in the makings room and wind up a hand sewer, attaching the welt to the uppers or he could become a hand cutter and take home one of the best paychecks in the industry as a sorter, marker, or cutter. The hides used for the uppers of the shoes were terribly expensive. (Hides could always be found on Brockton's black market.) The men in the cutting rooms of the different factories had to lay out the patterns on the skins in such a way as to avoid waste. An inept or dishonest cutter could bankrupt a small firm and that was why these workers were so highly prized and paid accordingly.

Owing to Brockton Ideal's size, their different divisions were laid out in a somewhat looser fashion than the rooms at the W. L. Douglas or George E. Keith plants. The stitching rooms at Douglas and Keith were all-women operations and composed about 27 percent of the workforce. Adding in all of the other women in shoemaking—secretaries, boxers, shippers and so forth—the total percentage of women was usually around 31 percent.

At a small factory like Brockton Ideal, men worked with women in the stitching room. This allowed the men to tackle all of the heavier stitching jobs while the women concentrated on perforated toe pieces or decorative foxing strips (which ran up both sides of the shoe near the ankle).

In the makings room, Tom Murphy came to his bosses attention early, for he took to hand sewing the Goodyear welts with alacrity. He possessed a natural ability with a shoe needle and the cumbersome waxed thread ("waxed ends"). The ability to assemble shoes with perfectly spaced, neat rows of stitches came naturally to almost no one, and therefore, did not go unnoticed by the foreman of the makings room at Brockton Ideal. Probably ahead of a typical worker, Tom Murphy became a "hand sewer." Although the job of hand sewer did not sound like much to someone outside the shoe industry, these workers were in great demand and, like the hand cutters, were well paid.

Much like all Irish immigrants, Tom Murphy was a member of a number of Brockton's fraternal organizations and a frequent visitor at the local Irish club. The Ancient Order of Hibernians held a dance every Saturday night at their hall on Ward Street. For 25¢, young people could dance the night away. After about six years in Brockton, Tom Murphy met a first generation American, Ellen "Nel" Kelley. Nel was born in Hopkinton, Massachusetts, and was the fifth of ten children. Her parents were both born in Ireland, but married and emigrated in 1862 so that all their children enjoyed the status of natural born Americans. Nel's father, like so many other men, searched endlessly for a better job. He labored in an iron works and later a copper mill, before he finally landed in the shoe business and settled his large family into a house on Oak Street in Brockton. Thomas and Nel fell in love and married in 1888, when she was only eighteen.[53]

Tom and Nel Murphy rented apartments for the first twelve years of their marriage, but finally in 1900—with seven small children and Nel's widowed aunt, Mary Cragen, living with them—they couldn't last another day in an apartment in a triple-decker. They bought a non-descript two-and-a-half story house at 8 Track Street. It was a boxy-looking structure with the steep gable end of the roof fronting the street. It sat half way between Forest Avenue and Foster Street. As if it could have been otherwise, Tom and Nel's large and energetic family became the "Track Street Murphys."

Tom Murphy had amassed twenty years with Brockton Ideal Shoe, but fierce competition and tired management greased the skids for a gentle slide into bankruptcy. By nature, Tom Murphy was provident and kept a close eye on unfolding events. Naturally, he chose not to stay for the funeral. In the early 1900s, he was in his mid-forties and had a wife, nine children, and Mary Cragen to feed. He wasted no time finding the best paying job in the trade.

As stated, there was a predictable amount of attrition among shoe workers, but even more so with foremen. The promotion to foreman was still a most conspicuous move. A foreman could come from the bench or the machine, but he had to understand the work of a whole department intimately and possess the ability to direct others. In the shoe journals, there were constant advertisements for foremen. The advertisements might read: "POSITION WANTED as foreman of sole leather room. Experience on Goodyear welts, turns, and McKays; and can operate all machines. Also, expert on new economy insole. Best of references. American Shoemaking, Brockton."

Tom Murphy may well have seen an ad like this. Conversely, an owner, who kept his ear to the ground for foremen, may have approached him. Still other owners had bulletin boards in their shops on which they listed the exact type of worker or operator they needed. Presumably these bulletin boards kept the departments in their factories filled.

As for pay, the wages in the shoe industry moved up an imaginary ladder, from jobs like shoe worker and button fastener all the way up to hand sewers and hand cutters. A button fastener earned only 80 percent of what a hand cutter made. At the top of the heap was the foreman, who made about the same as the best operator in his department.

Not only did the shoe foreman need copious knowledge of systems, he needed to be able to train employees in them. He also had to be able to select operators for his department and teach them efficiency. Lastly, he had to maintain discipline in his department. He had to be tactful, firm, friendly to all, yet not so friendly as to lose the obedience of those under his command. The foreman stood between the superintendent and the operator and was responsible for the work in his department. He had to keep every employee occupied and make sure the work passed through on schedule.

At length, Tom Murphy landed a job as a foreman at Kelley-Evans Shoes. By 1910—after Brockton Ideal Show disappeared—the Kelly-Evans partnership changed to Kelly-Buckley Shoes of Herrod Avenue (later, Court Street). One interesting sidebar: John C. Buckley of Sandwich married Katie Reilly of "Paddy Lane" (Centerville in Brockton). Later, John Buckley teamed up with John Kelly of Brockton to form the Kelly-Buckley Shoe Company. Brockton operated as a highly industrialized, manufacturing Mecca, but it behaved like a small town. Was it possible that Katie Buckley knew Nel Murphy through one of the women's groups at St. Patrick's Church? Or maybe Tom Murphy knew John Buckley or John Kelly before he even applied for the job? These are imponderables, but it is very often how things work in small towns. Regardless of the back-story, luck was with Tom Murphy.

Very few people knew it, but Tom Murphy also offered his free time as a Christian Missionary, helping people where he could. Perhaps watching him in this endeavor convinced his youngest boy Tom to become a priest. God only knows what makes big impressions on the little ones.

Tom Murphy was a diligent worker and well-liked foreman at Kelly-Buckley. Sadly he passed away on March 27, 1922 at sixty-two. Many of the descendants of Maurice Murphy and Honora McCarthy owe a special debt of gratitude to their second son, Tom Murphy. Without his hard work and providence, Dan Murphy—and maybe even Dinny—might still be back in Ireland.[54]

In 1883, the third of Maurice and Honora Murphy's boys, Denis (Dinny)," now twenty-one, sailed for America. Although three years younger than his brother Tom, "itchy feet" were part of his inheritance as well. Business in Killarney showed no sign of improving in the two years since Tom Murphy emigrated and his letters made Brockton sound like paradise—which, for a shoemaker, it was. Just imagine a town of 15,000 people with 75 shoe factories. Does it get any better than that?

In April 1883, Dinny said goodbye to everyone in Killarney and boarded the Cunard liner *SS Scythia* for the voyage to America. Dinny had an easier go of it than most, for Tom not only paid for his passage, but set Dinny up in a job at Brockton Ideal Shoe Company. Moreover, he got Mrs. Dora Murphy to take Dinny into her boarding house on Forest Avenue. The following year, Mrs. Murphy passed away and Dinny moved to the home of John T. Murphy—also on Forest Avenue—but didn't stay long. He left to rent a small apartment closer to the center of town—at 44 Bartlett Street. Finally, this bramble bush from Killarney came to rest at 30 Foster Street.

As happens, he met and married an Irish girl, Ellen (Nellie) Sullivan, who had emigrated a year ahead of him. Her parents,

48

Maurice and Mary Sullivan, lived on Crescent Street in Brockton. Dinny and Nellie were married in St. Patrick's Church on November 24, 1885.[55] Together they had five children, one of whom, Maurice "Beeshie" Murphy became an attorney and a special justice on the District Court of Brockton. The oldest child Nora was a saleslady at Edgar's on Main Street, while the youngest, Ellen, worked in the shoe factories.[56]

Following closely in the footsteps of his brother, Dinny became a hand sewer. Monotonous work and tiring too, Dinny called it quits after four years. He needed a change.

For a year, Dinny drove a delivery truck for John S. Conley, who had a small bakery on Pleasant Street. Conley made the complete line of baked goods—bread, pastry, crackers, cakes and confectionery items—albeit on a small scale. Truth told, delivering these goods around Brockton didn't qualify as skilled employment, but it did give Dinny time to hatch a plan. By watching closely, he picked up the rudiments of running a small retail store, and at the end of a year, handed in his notice.

Dinny was no baker and had not even considered opening up an operation like Conley's. A neighborhood grocery was more what Dinny had in mind. In a small little shack next to his home at 30 Foster Street (corner of Track Street), Dinny pieced together a grocery store. A combination five-and-dime and mini-grocery store, it sold a wide assortment of household items, produce, baked goods and just about anything else that his neighbors might need on short notice. Fairly typical of neighborhood markets at the turn of the century, Dinny's store was open from 6 o'clock in the morning until 11 at night, coming in handy for a family who needed some soda bread or a yeast cake for unexpected company. At a time when people walked everywhere, these little markets were sprinkled all over Brockton, each serving no more than the immediate neighbors.

Fortunately for his wife, Nellie, and their five children, the little store was a success and, by the turn of the century, "Dinny's" moved to larger quarters at 69 Forest Avenue (corner of Track Street). Dinny, Nellie and their children lived next door. Many of the neighborhood kids learned the value of a dollar at Dinny's store, including his own kids. Also putting in time at the store were Tom and Nel's nine children.

"Dinny's" catered to the Foster Street Gang, his store acting as a meeting place as much as a grocery. Young people met and hung out at the store and it served as an informal town hall for the older members of the neighborhood. Preferring to call the place "The Old School," the senior patrons met there to iron out the smaller problems of their little corner of Brockton as well as the weightier issues worldwide. The older visitors met in a small alcove in the back of Dinny's store and usually managed to finish their business by 9 o'clock at night.

Dinny, a likeable soul, sat behind the counter during the day in a rocker and smoked a pipe as he tallied the delivery invoices and tried to figure a way to feed, clothe and educate five children. Dinny was a deeply religious man who sometimes read a prayer book while he chewed on his pipe and rocked away the hours. Proud of his Irish heritage, Dinny always remained active in the Ancient Order of Hibernians.

Dinny's wife, Nellie, died in 1935 and, in poor health himself, he decided to retire. The store was demolished the same year and the lot sold. Dinny lived another three years, passing away on November 17, 1938. Depending on your point of view, his death certificate was the answer sheet to a medical school exam or a textbook on pathology. Among his other ailments, Dinny had a hypertrophied prostate, chronic nephritis, arteriosclerosis and chronic myocarditis. Dinny struck everyone as a very tired seventy-seven when they lowered him away.

The Irish immigrants of Brockton settled into three distinct areas of town: the "Bush," in the south end, was bordered by Grove and Clinton Streets and included all the small roads to the southeast; "Tipperary" was in the north end. The "Tip" spread east of the Old Colony Railroad, south of East Ashland and north of Elliott Streets. "Paddy Lane," a disgusting throwback to the impoverished streets of Ireland's poorer towns, sat at the lower end of the Tip. Officially named Alton Street, Paddy Lane took on the new designation in 1870, and it ran north from the top of High Street until it connected to Kimball's Court. After turning easterly toward Main Street, it formed a semi-circle around H. W. Robinson's dry goods store. Paddy's Lane housed the dirt poor Irish, true descendents of the Famine Irish.

Lastly, the Foster Street Gang—the Murphys, O'Reillys, O'Connors, McBrides, Kellys, Brennans—filled the streets west of the downtown shopping area. This Centerville clachan had Main Street on the east, Florence on the south, Lawrence on the north, and Grafton on the west. At its center, it included Warren Avenue and Track Street. In a word, the homes made up the clachan in which all the Murphys from Killarney settled. First they rented from relatives and friends—always in or very close to the clachan. Later, they bought houses in the clachan and raised large families there.[57]

The Irishmen from the "Tip" had a reputation as tough bar fighters, while the Irish who settled closer to Centerville belonged to families that valued education above all else. The number of first generation Irish lawyers, judges, priests, and doctors astounded even the Irish themselves. It is especially noteworthy because these families rarely had any extra money. They did what they could; relatives, hard work, and blind luck did the rest. It is too soon to tell, but this America may be gone forever.

The shoe industry resembled a huge tree lying across a flood-ravaged stream. It allowed the Murphys of Killarney, the Sullivans from Mayo and many others, to scramble to higher ground. As these folks built new lives in America, year-by-year pieces of the tree broke away. Finally it disappeared altogether. Indeed, shortly after the Murphys and Sullivans arrived in America, Brockton reached the top of its manufacturing prowess in the shoe industry. With financial incentives and cheaper labor, one by one the great, churning, smoking behemoths that shod the world, left for Maine, St. Louis, Rochester and Chicago. Later, they moved again—to disparate foreign cities in third-world countries. In the larger picture, the window for immigrant shoemakers was open only briefly. In the blink of an eye, it was closed forever.

In Brockton, Tom Murphy watched as Dinny and Nellie tied the knot in 1883 and the newlyweds attended Tom Murphy's marriage to Nel Kelley in 1888. St. Patrick's Church on Main Street was the spiritual home of all of the transplanted Murphys and remained that way for a century. It must be noted that St. Patrick's Church, where Dinny and his brother Tom Murphy took brides, was the "old" St. Patrick's Church on the east side of Main

Street–south of City Hall. Father Thomas McNulty built this church in 1856. The "new" St. Patrick's Church (Main and Bartlett Streets) was completed in 1912. The "old" St. Patrick's Elementary School was located on the corner of Lawrence and Perkins Streets—roughly behind the old St. Patrick's Church. The "new" Saint Patrick's School was built on Bartlett Street in 1924.

In the early 1880s, Dan Murphy met a girl in Killarney, Catherine Sullivan, and the two dated for longer than usual simply because Dan had the responsibilities of two men. Finally, Dan and Catherine wed on January 27, 1883 at St. Mary's Cathedral. Dan was twenty-five; Catherine, two years younger. The priest who performed the ceremony was none other than the chaplain of the Killarney Union, Father Michael Dillon. He had given Dan a letter of reference six years earlier and now he performed his wedding ceremony. One wonders how many Irish men and women put all the recommendation letters together, but in the end were unable to emigrate. Perhaps they lost the courage or maybe their family circumstances barred such a seismic change in their lives. We'll never know.

At the ceremony, Denis McCarthy—Honora's uncle, who lived on Boherkeale Lane—and Patrick Sullivan—the bride's oldest sibling—acted as witnesses.

Owing possibly to Dan and Catherine's emigration plans, they were slow to start a family. Their first child, Mary, wasn't born until August 27, 1885—two and a half years after the wedding. Since Catherine died at fifty-four of "chronic valvular heart disease," one wonders if her heart circumscribed her life from early on or whether this reluctance to start a family did indeed have to do entirely with the couple's complex emigration plans.[58]

Since Catherine's father, Denis Sullivan, lived in roughly the same neighborhood as the Murphys, it's a reasonable assumption that he worked in the trades too. Catherine's mother, Mary (Herlihey) Sullivan took care of their rented house on Park Lane and raised the couples' six children.[59]

Dan Murphy wasn't merely watching the parade go by. Apparently, Tom Murphy convinced Dan by mail that the owners of the shoe factories were loath to hire Irish immigrants from letters of inquiry, recommendations, and other submissions. They had specific needs and insisted on vetting possible employees in person. So in early 1890, Dan sailed to America alone.

He sailed on the *SS Cephalonia* to visit Tom and Dinny and scout Brockton's shoe factories for his own account. The ironclad *Cephalonia,* running on a single propeller—first saw service a decade earlier. Laird Brothers of Birkinhead, England built the ship for Cunard Lines, but never built another. Cammell Laird had an excellent reputation as a shipbuilder, but the Scottish steamship builders could underbid the English every time. Just as in the shoe business, labor costs dictated everything. Also, the 1890s became the great era of conversion from iron to steel ships and Scottish builders like J. & G. Thompson and J. Elder & Company were in a better position to take the conversion gamble.

SS Cephalonia

The *Cephalonia* was indeed a dinosaur because the following year Cunard committed completely to steel-hulled, twin-screw vessels. They did commission smaller single-screw ships for specific routes, but these ships serviced ports almost exclusively in the Mediterranean.

Conditions in steerage invited no joy. Boredom seemed the biggest complaint. With little to do but eat and sleep, the seven days at sea might as well have been seven months. Cunard recognized this shortcoming and tried—with mixed results—to introduce a regimen that would chew up time.

Each steerage passenger was assigned a numbered metal berth, a canvas or burlap mattress stuffed with hay or dried seaweed, a life preserver which doubled as a pillow, and a tin pail and utensils for meals—served from huge tanks. Not much could be said about the food at seas except that it filled everyone up. The bunks were stacked two high and sat in a compartment accommodating anywhere from 100 to 500 passengers. Yet these conditions, at the close of the 1800s were positively luxurious compared to the great sailing barks that had pursued the emigrant trade from before the Famine and right up into the 1870s. Those were desperate times when the ancient, dilapidated wooden vessels could reasonably be tagged 'coffin ships.'

Once he arrived in Brockton, Dan Murphy not only made a good impression on the people at R. B. Grover Shoes, but also was completely energized by the city itself. Still, he kept Grover on hold until he could figure a way to get Catherine and the children to America. According to his own autobiographical sketch, he didn't start working for R. B. Grover until 1893.[60]

The Irishmen from the west of Ireland, especially those with families, often had to leave home for long periods of time to make money. Typically, they went to England, worked for six- or eight-month stretches on farms or in construction and then returned home.

In 1890, while Dan was in Brockton, his mother Honora and his youngest sister Mary Ann (Annie) caught the *Cephalonia* to America. (Honora also took the *Catalonia* to America in April 1892.) The putative reason for Honora's trips to America was to visit Dan, Tom, and Dinny, and to see how everyone was getting along. Also, it gave her a chance to meet her sons' wives as well as her six American grandchildren—and counting. The youngest generation always called her Gramma Murphy. Catherine couldn't leave Ireland because her three children were too small and kept her a virtual prisoner on Boherkeale Lane in Killarney.

The real reason for Honora's visit was a little subtler. The wives of Tom and Dinny were both from Massachusetts and were perfectly happy with the "shoe city." Conversely, Catherine had to move to Brockton sight unseen. Honora realized that she could lessen the chances of trouble by spending months—years as it turned out—telling Catherine everything about Brockton, while continually reassuring her that she would love the place. So, as mother and sons huddled conspiratorially around Tom Murphy's kitchen table in Brockton, a plan emerged for Dan to bring his family to Brockton in April 1893. As we shall see though, Mother Nature had plans of her own.

From 1877—when Dan first began collecting references—to the end of 1894—when his wife and kids finally descended the gangplank on Noodle's Island in East Boston—everyone went through hell, and it cost a fortune. When Tom and Dinny emigrated, it cost each of them only $25 for a steamship ticket and a couple of extra dollars for train fares. But with Dan, Honora, Catherine and the children, their steamship tickets alone, between 1890 and 1894, came to more than $500. Add in the cost of train fares and the grand total came to almost the annual pay of a Brockton shoemaker. Clearly this money didn't come from Dan, Honora or anyone else in Killarney. Tom and Dinny supplied it.

This brings up an imponderable question: When Dan's brothers Tom and Dinny were in Brockton making more money than they knew existed, did Dan name his two sons Tom and Denis in keeping with the traditions of the clachan Irish, or did he do it because his brothers were such fine shoemakers? Let's face it, Dan, Catherine, Honora, Mary Ellen (Nellie), and Mary Ann (Annie) knew that Tom and Dinny were their only hope of emigration? In the final analysis, the Murphy brothers in Brockton made enormous financial sacrifices to get their mother, brother, sisters, sister-in-law, nephews, and nieces to America. And, in all the many conversations about Dan, Tom and Dinny—and their families—the matter has never been mentioned.[61]

Dan and Catherine's emigration machinations depended largely on the children. If one of them was too young or too ill to make the trip, everything moved to a later date. Dan had gotten into the habit of sailing back to Killarney for Christmas with the expectation of returning to Brockton in April. In 1891, he went home to Killarney, but returned to Brockton alone the following April. (For five years, Dan and Catherine had no children, as they tried desperately to relocate.) At the end of that year, Dan returned to Killarney, and sailing plans were put in place for early 1893. Of course, the last thing Dan and Catherine wanted was for her to become pregnant again, but without Dan's knowledge, that's exactly what happened.

Dan made an unusual winter voyage on the Cunard liner *SS Pavonia,* departing Queenstown on February 21, 1893. As he walked up the gangway, he could not possibly have known that he had impregnated Catherine within the past fortnight. (Nonie was born on November 3, 1893—or 8 months and 17 days after Dan sailed for America.) Why did Dan leave before the others, *when he did not know that Catherine was pregnant?* Perhaps Catherine— or one of the children—was sick?

Dan constantly collected references. All immigrants reasoned that if five recommendations would open the door, then ten might get them the job. Too, immigrants have always had a constant fear that they wouldn't be smart enough to make it in America. With these anxieties in mind, Dan arranged for his old friend Charles Meagher to write a recommendation for him even though Dan probably never worked for Meagher. Dan bought leather supplies from Meagher, but that appears to be their only connection.

Charles Meagher & Son sold hardware, timber, coal, oil and seeds. The firm also maintained a leather and shoe findings warehouse, which is obviously how Dan knew the Meaghers. Considering what the famine did to the psyche of the Irish people, Meagher & Sons stationary featured an interesting warning: "NB: All our seeds are selected with the greatest care, but in consequence of the tendency in late years of some varieties, like the Swede turnip, to "sport" or change in character, we don't guarantee any of them, nor will we be responsible for the crop."[62]

With constant, moist ocean breezes and 250 days a year of rain (in western Ireland), one can see that potatoes rotting and turnips sporting are fairly logical outcomes.[63]

Charles Meagher's letter of recommendation—dated July 8, 1893—states, "Daniel Murphy has been working for us for the past six months during which time we found him attentive to the business and inclined to give satisfaction in every way; he leaves at his own request and we wish him every success."[64] Catherine collected the letter of recommendation and forwarded it to Dan.

The new baby, Nonie, wasn't born until November 3, 1893, and she finally plumped up enough to make the North Atlantic voyage in late September 1894—at the tail end of the normal steamship season. Passage was booked for Honora Murphy, Catherine, and the four children—Mary, Thomas, Denis and Nonie—on one of the last runs of the *Cephalonia* that year. They planned to leave Queenstown on September 7 and arrive in Boston eight days later. They were cutting it close and they knew it.

By mail, Dan and Catherine kept in touch throughout the spring and summer months of 1894. In the end, all worked out well as Nonie added weight nicely. Honora, Catherine and the children would finally be sailing for America.

Oddly enough, Honora Murphy didn't like the word *widow,* preferring to travel as a *matron.* Moreover, Honora lied about her age as usual. She claimed to be 52, when she was really 57. (Author's note: At least about their ages, women lied shamelessly in the 1800s. Even up to the middle of the 1900s, it was considered *de rigueur* for women to lie about their ages on birth certificates, marriage licenses, census reports, and so forth. In fact, the more sacred the document, the more reason to dissemble.)

As an example of how safe and regular the North Atlantic passage had become, it is interesting to note that, at different times, Daniel, Catherine, Honora, and the children traipsed back and forth to America in the early 1890s, and they almost always sailed on the *Cephalonia* with Captain William S. Seccombe at the helm. Seccombe (1847-1910) was a well-read man, who made his home in Peterborough, New Hampshire after 1895. He became fast friends with the writers aboard his ships, and loved to quote his favorite authors. Although Captain Seccombe died in New Hampshire peacefully in 1910, two of his children, seventeen-year-olds Percy and Elizabeth, died when the *Lusitania* was sunk in 1915.)[65]

When Catherine and the children sailed for America, the *Cephalonia's* route resembled that of its competitors in that it started the voyage at Liverpool, laid over at Queenstown for a day, and then proceeded to the United States. The *Cephalonia* had 127 passengers in saloon, 148 in second-class and 585 in steerage—a total of 860. (Judging by the number of poor passengers in the hold of the ship, it's easy to see why the steamship owners were so galvanized by the steerage trade.) It was around the turn of the century that steerage morphed into third-class, but for an odd reason.

After their ham fisted behavior of the early 1860s, the owners of the major steamship companies—Cunard, Guion, Inman, White Star, National, and Hamburg America—developed enough enlightened self-interest to avoid fare wars. They met before the season got underway and fixed the ticket prices. It was agreed that the owners could do whatever they wanted to attract passengers, but the ticket price was cast in stone. Therefore, in 1900, when Cunard built the *SS Ivernia* and her sister ship, the *SS Saxonia,* these vessels were designed so that 70 percent of the passengers in steerage traveled in staterooms. Making the most of this new luxury afforded steerage passengers, Cunard trumpeted the new accommodations as third-class.

Among the Irish who boarded at Queenstown, were 12 children under 15 years old, 215 people between the ages of 15 and 40, and lastly 21 people over the age of 40. In addition, of the 248 Irish passengers, there were 16 spinners, 15 dressmakers, 8 machinists, and 7 domestics. There were a half dozen clerks and an equal number of cooks. Additionally, there were 3 each of teachers, artists, weavers, tailors, and painters. Traveling that day as well were 2 each of blacksmiths, engineers, gardeners and masons. Lastly, there was a lawyer, an architect, a priest, a jeweler, a farmer and a shoemaker.

Of the 248 Irish passengers, 180 listed no occupation or called themselves laborers, highlighting a thorny issue. Manufacturers in America were quick to exploit the emigrant trade and, in the past, had arranged for the passage of large numbers of emigrants to work in their factories at miserable wages. Naturally, this displeased their competitors and soon enough the government stepped in. As a result, when steerage or third-class passengers were asked if they had a job waiting for them, the safest answer was "No." Indeed, the surest way to get deported immediately was to announce that you already had a job waiting for you. Under these circumstances—and though clearly most of the emigrants from Ireland were raised on farms and needed to emigrate more than anyone else—judging strictly by the passenger lists at the Port of Boston, almost none of the Emerald Isle's farmers ended up in America.

Accompanying thirty-year-old Catherine were six-year-old Mary A., four-year-old Thomas J., two-year-old Denis P. and the infant, Nonie. At least that's what the ship's manifest said. Tickets for children cost about half of those for adults, so immigrants—always short of money—fibbed as needed. Since there were only twelve children on the *Cephalonia*, the personnel on the ship chose not to contest the matter. Mary was actually nine; Thomas, seven; Denis P., five; and Nonie was indeed ten months. There were plenty of reasons for the paperwork of immigrants to vary from the facts. This is just one example.[66]

Catherine and Honora were undoubtedly busier than a rescue squad caring for four young children on the voyage, but in truth, the only immutable fact from this period is that Catherine, Honora, and the four Murphy children left Queenstown aboard the *Cephalonia* near the end of September, and after eight days at sea, arrived in the Port of Boston on Thursday, October 4, 1894.

Dan Murphy met the *Cephalonia* at the Cunard dock on Noodle's Island (East Boston) and helped Honora, Catherine, and the children get through the Port of Boston Immigration Facility on Marginal Street. After the usual physical exams and a recheck of the passenger list information, they all took the Old Colony Street Railroad from Boston's South Station to Brockton. They settled into a five-room apartment on the second floor of a home at 537 Montello Street, one block east of Main Street in the Centerville area. By American standards, it was small and cold; by Irish standards, it was deluxe.

Between 1898 and 1916, Dan, Catherine, Honora and the children lived at 557 Montello Street (between Union and Arch Streets) and 364 Montello (near Allen Street). A few years after Honora returned to Ireland, Dan and Catherine rented the second floor of another triple-decker at 172 Forest Avenue (corner of Blaine Street). They remained there for the duration.

Dan started work as a simple shoemaker, at R. B. Grover Shoes, but thanks to his brother Tom, he quickly found a better job at Brockton Ideal Shoe and worked his way up to hand-sewer. This was fortuitous because R. G. Grover Shoes turned out to be a fabulous place to start, but a miserable place to linger.

Grover built the famous "Emerson Shoe" at its quarters on the corner of Main and Calmar Streets. The building was wooden, four stories tall, and one of the biggest shoe factories in the city. At 7:50 on Monday morning, March 20, 1905, R. B. Grover suffered a massive boiler explosion. The blast destroyed the whole building and then a massive conflagration reduced the whole block to a small pile of ashes. In addition, the explosion leveled the adjoining Dahlberg block—the old Drake Tavern, two storehouses, a blacksmith shop and seven dwelling houses. The boiler rocketed through the roof of the four-story wooden factory and—after destroying two more houses—came to rest about 200 feet north of its original location.[67]

The company employed 450 workers, and that morning, 360 were in the building. Of these shoe workers, 58 died instantly and 150 were seriously injured. Other factories closed down. People were in shock and couldn't work. A relief fund started up almost immediately and a large communal service was held at the City Theatre and another at the Porter Congregational Church. The Grover Factory Fire turned out to be the largest factory explosion ever witnessed in Brockton.[68]

Dan Murphy was spared for the most mundane reason. R. B. Grover sat at the corner of Main and Calmar Streets in the south end of the city. Dan and Catherine Murphy preferred to rent apartments close to their relatives, St. Patrick's Church, and the shopping district. The move to 364 Montello Street put them only a couple of blocks from Tom Murphy on Track Street and Dinny on Forest Avenue. Since R. B. Grover was almost twenty blocks to the south of Centerville, the move to Brockton Ideal Shoe on Franklin Street made Dan's life easier.

Dan was not as quick as his brother to appreciate the problems at Brockton Ideal Shoe and stayed there a few years after Tom Murphy became a foreman at Kelly-Buckley Shoes. But by 1907, with Brockton Ideal Shoe teetering on the edge of bankruptcy, Dan joined his brother at Kelly-Buckley. If Dan Murphy had come to America alone, it's very possible that he would still have been working at R. B. Grover Shoes when the place was blown to smithereens.

Finally nestled in the bosom of Brockton, Dan and Catherine had two more children: Helena (Lena) in 1897 and Annie C. in 1902. Sadly, Annie died of capillary bronchitis on March 31, 1902. She was interred in the family plot at Calvary Cemetery after a funeral mass at St. Patrick's Church.[69]

Co Kerry Ireland
Born in Killarney Parish
baptized in Cathedral
of St Joseph that Rev W.
Horgan 12th day October
1868 Sponser John Coffey &
Margret McCarthy
Went to school to
the Monastery of the
Brothers & went to
grade Sch 6 [illegible]
I after [illegible] school
serve 4 years to have
for him one year off.
Then I went a work
Killarney Union one
Year & came to
work to after one
year more & a
worked in Killarney Union
again for six years
aft that went a work
for myself for 3 years
I worked for the Sisters
myself the last 4 Years
as a contract. Came to
America in 93. got a
job at R.B. Grover
Shoes as Worker.

Dan Murphy's Autobiographical Resume – c. 1894

Helena grew up the youngest in the family and according to the psychoanalyst Alfred Adler, that's unfortunate. Lena's behavior bordered on *brathood*, although clearly her future husband, Ray Girard, would have disagreed.

Two years after the family relocated to 172 Forest Avenue, on Monday, June 7, 1915 Catherine Murphy died from heart disease. She was only fifty-four. After a mass at St. Patrick's Church, she was interred at Calvary Cemetery. Dan Murphy couldn't even remember Catherine's birth date while volunteering the information for her death certificate. Undoubtedly this owes to the fact that birthdays were not uniformly celebrated in Irish households—even as late as the Second World War. The clachan Irish would have reasoned: What credit accrues to a newborn, the handiwork of others?

Dan Murphy outlasted Catherine by thirteen years, passing away of heart disease on Thursday, May 24, 1928. He still resided at 172 Forest Avenue, and was buried next to Catherine in Calvary Cemetery.[70]

Dan Murphy never owned a house or a car, but he took good care of his widowed mother, and brought his children to America where they—and their children—would enjoy far better lives than he did back in Killarney. When one considers the burdens that were thrust upon Dan by Maurice Murphy's early death—and how well Dan shouldered those responsibilities—it's a little sad that Dan Murphy is barely remembered at all. Father Tom Murphy S. J., and his two maiden sisters, Theresa and Peg, once answered some questions on tape for Dr. Ed Murphy and the girls kept repeating that Dan was the "kindest man."[71]

Beyond his burdens, through his son, Denis P. Murphy, Dan fathered a branch of the Murphy clan that surpassed the dreams of the most starry-eyed immigrants and contributed handsomely to life in America. Safe home, Dan!

Lost in the emigration commotion of Daniel, Thomas, and Dinny are their remaining siblings—Mary Ellen, Mary Ann, and Maurice. The oldest of these three, Mary Ellen (Nellie), also emigrated and settled in Brockton. She married a Brocktonian, John Clifford, who worked as a hand trimmer in a shoe factory. Unfortunately John died just before 1910, leaving Nellie Clifford with seven children between the ages of five and twenty-four. By

1910, the four oldest were all working as trimmers in the shoe factories.[72]

Her sister Mary Ann (Annie) married Patrick Lucey, a shoe worker originally from Abington. They were wed at St. Patrick's Church in Brockton on June 22, 1901. From that day forward, Annie Lucey was her mellifluous name. She and her husband Patrick lived in Quincy, but were unable to have children. Annie Lucey spent a great deal of her free time visiting her sister, her brothers, plus nephews and nieces in Brockton.[73]

Maurice Murphy emigrated in 1890 when he was twenty-two. Maurice was only fourteen when his brother Tom sailed for America, so clearly some separation existed between Maurice and Dan, Tom and Dinny. So said, it is not surprising that when Maurice emigrated in 1890, he chose to cut his own path. In Lawrence, Massachusetts, Maurice worked as a weaver in a worsted mill. Family members recall Maurice as an "unfortunate soul," a "floater," a person with a serious drinking problem that robbed him of any stability.[74]

After eight years in Lawrence, Maurice Murphy met and married Annie O'Keefe, an Irish immigrant eight years his junior. Together they had a son, Maurice, in 1903. Unfortunately by 1910, the marriage had breached so badly that seven-year-old Maurice went to live with his elderly O'Keefe grandparents in Revere. Later, Maurice (the elder) lived in a boarding house in Boston, while working as a laborer in a rubber mill. After Patrick Lucey passed away, sixty-three-year-old Maurice Murphy moved in with his sister, Annie Lucey, in Quincy. The final details of Maurice Murphy's chaotic life are best left to the imagination.[75]

With all that has been said about Dan, Tom and Dinny Murphy—together with Nellie Clifford and Annie Lucey—it is obvious that they tried to help their brother Maurice. This is especially the case since Annie Lucey took him in toward the end of his life. Sometimes though, there is a divine irreverence for our plans.

When Dan Murphy left Ireland in the winter of 1893, his sisters Nellie and Annie had already emigrated and were settled in Brockton and Quincy, respectively. Dan's mother Honora Murphy was fifty-six. Honora lived with Dan and Catherine from 1894, when she sailed over with Catherine and the children, until a little after 1900. Ultimately, she decided America wasn't for her and she returned to Ireland. She died in Killarney in 1919 at eighty-two.[76]

Chapter 2

Daniel & Catherine's Children

The oldest of Dan and Catherine Murphy's children, Mary, worked as a hand-sewer in the shoe factories, never married, and kept her own counsel. In truth, Mary had great native intelligence, but came across as mentally deficient or eccentric—depending on the source. Denis's sister, Nonie, was quiet too. She worked as a sales clerk in the children's department of Edgar's, never married, but never stopped thinking about those she loved. Nonie always had her feelers out for a crib or high chair missing a couple of screws. This allowed her to discount it savagely, set it aside for herself, and later to take it home for repairs. She eventually gave it to one of the Murphy families in her orbit. Nonie would never take money, and kept her brother Denis and assorted cousins, nephews and nieces in baby furniture and clothing when she was making less than half of what Brockton paid her brother, Denis, the fireman.[77]

From 1938 on, Mary and her sister Nonie rented the third floor of 551 Warren Avenue from their brother Denis. They paid $20 a month when rents in the neighborhood ranged from $24 to $30. Even after Denis' widow, Mary Murphy, sold the house in 1958, Mary and Nonie stayed put until their deaths. Mary died in 1972 at eighty-six; Nonie died in 1975 at eighty-one.[78]

Dan and Catherine's oldest son, Thomas, had a vocation to the priesthood and graduated from Niagara University. Moreover, he was president of the Class of 1910. He then successfully passed the examination for the seminary. Father Bartholomew Killilea at St. Patrick's in Brockton wrote the same year, "Mr. Thomas Murphy, a member of this parish, who passed a successful examination for the seminary, belongs to a very religious family. He was graduated from our school with high honors, and this year finished his College Course at Niagara."[79]

Of particular interest are Thomas Murphy's grades. He consistently scored in the high 90s in English, History, and Elocution, while he received grades between 45 and 65 in Algebra and Chemistry. Strong in the sciences, he was not.

Thomas Murphy entered St. John's Seminary and wrote to his mother on May 27, 1915. "Dear Mother, At last I am a Deacon and a Sub-deacon, thanks be to God. I have the vow of perpetual chastity, must read my office every day of my life, and have the privilege of taking the Blessed Sacrament from the Tabernacle."

On May 12, 1916, soon-to-be Father Thomas Murphy bought a chalice, paten and case at Shreve, Crump & Low jewelers in Boston for $175. Rev. Thomas Joseph Murphy was ordained on June 2, 1916 at Holy Cross Cathedral in Boston. He was scheduled to say his first solemn mass at St. Patrick's Church in Brockton on Sunday, June 4, 1916. For an Irish Catholic family directly from the old sod, no higher honor could come their way. Sadly, his mother Catherine died on June 7, 1915, a year before Tom Murphy was ordained. She never got to see "her son, the priest" say mass. When Tom Murphy said his first mass at St. Patrick's in Brockton, Dan Murphy, Denis and his three sisters were the only immediate family members in the pew at St. Patrick's.[80]

Father Thomas Murphy's ordination took place on a Friday and Dan Murphy threw a huge party that Sunday at his home on Forest Avenue. The party ran from 3 to 5 P.M. and Father Tom Murphy S. J. of Fairfield remembered the party well, even though he was only ten at the time.[81]

On September 23, 1916, William Cardinal O'Connell reassigned Father Thomas Murphy to assist Rev. Francis X. Dolan at St. Gregory's Church in Dorchester Lower Mills, another working class enclave.

Father Thomas Murphy worked hard at St. Gregory's Church unaware that just as his religious life took wing, his death warrant hung fire in far off Fort Riley, Kansas.

Books, magazines, and documentaries have steadily contributed to our knowledge of the Spanish Influenza of 1918, yet scientists still are not convinced of its origins. Many believe that it began in the spring of 1918, when soldiers at Camp Funston—a part of the military installation at Fort Riley in Kansas—burned tons of pig manure. By and by, a storm enveloped the whole area in a huge dust cloud, impregnated with particles from the smoke of the manure fire. A few days later, a soldier reported to the camp dispensary with a fever, sore throat, and headache. A seemingly routine matter, except that in a week, the hospital had 500 similar cases. That spring, 48 young, healthy Fort Riley soldiers died. The deaths were attributed to complications from pneumonia. Meanwhile, the influenza pathogen disappeared as quickly as it arrived. Diabolically, it had slipped into a dormant state, hiding within the bodies of thousands of unwitting young soldiers.

World War I was at its zenith in the summer of 1918 and more than 1.5 million American soldiers sailed across the Atlantic to fight in Europe. Some were from Fort Riley and they carried with them the dormant virus. Disembarking in Europe, the soldiers spread the disease all over the continent. In the meantime, the virus had mutated into a more virulent strain. As it spread throughout Europe, people suspected falsely that it had originated in Spain; thus Spanish Influenza.

In September 2001, *Science* magazine reported that a recent reanalysis of the gene sequences of the Spanish Influenza virus indicated that it combined swine-lineage flu with human-lineage influenzas. The article states that, "Phylogenetic analyses showed that this combination, which probably changed the virulence of the virus, occurred at the start of, or immediately before, the pandemic and thus may have triggered it."[82]

In Europe, people died by the tens of millions and then, as the troops returned to the U.S., the pathogen traveled back to America with them. In September 1918, soldiers at Camp Devens—near Brockton—suddenly began to die, ostensibly from Spanish

Influenza. Unlike other killers, the influenza favored healthy, young men between the ages of 21 and 30.

After a typical hot summer, Brockton rested peacefully, as the factories continued to make rugged boots for the soldiers and fancy shoes for everyone else. Children were in school and, in the late afternoon, playgrounds were full.

In the middle of September, the influenza struck Brockton. The incidence of infection escalated so wildly that Brockton Hospital—built twenty years before—had to erect field facilities, where canvas tents and a limited staff of doctors and nurses, treated the sick. October was the deadliest month of all. The contagion spiraled out of control, to the point where the Spanish Influenza accounted for 50 percent of deaths in Brockton. Children stayed home now.[83]

While Brockton suffered, the epidemic headed west. Hospitals overflowed, body wagons were filled to overflowing and laws were quickly enacted in a futile effort to contain the pandemic. In a few weeks, the flu hit the west coast. The Spanish Influenza halted when it ran out of victims. By early November, the flu had vanished from Brockton and it quickly deserted other cities across the country. At final count, Brockton reported 2800 cases of influenza, resulting in 265 deaths.

Father Thomas Murphy saw it as his duty to administer Last Rites to the dying victims of influenza in hospitals and homes, making him one of the most vulnerable. While administering to the sick, he came down with influenza. He fought it at his father's home on Forest Avenue, but died on Wednesday, October 16, 1918. He was thirty-one.[84] Daniel and Catherine had a total of six children, but after Father Thomas Murphy's death, only four remained—Mary A., Denis P., Honora (Nonie) and Helena (Lena).

When one considers the gauntlet of troubles the Emerald Isle presented poor Irishmen like Dan Murphy, the trials he suffered while relocating his family to America, and the woes he lived through in a factory town in America, it is heartrending to tally the body blows Dan took as he negotiated the new century.

His youngest brother Maurice suffered from the "Irish disease." In 1915, his wife Catherine passed away. Three years later, his pride and joy, Rev. Thomas Murphy, died an agonizing death from influenza. Mary and Nonie were not destined to marry and clung to each other, while Helena married Ray Girard and moved to Plymouth. After all Dan had been through, the only person left to carry on the Murphy name along his branch of the family tree was his son Denis.

Denis Philip Murphy didn't have the social deftness, the mental acuity or the ambition of Thomas J. Murphy. He completed grammar school at St. Patrick's and then attended Brockton High School where he graduated in 1907. With little thought of college, Denis went directly to work at M.A. Packard Shoes. Though he wasn't the smartest shoemaker at Packard's, he quickly worked his way up to hand cutter. He had a natural affinity for tools, but like his brother Thomas, he wasn't inclined at all toward the sciences or mathematics. He stayed at M. A. Packard until he got an appointment to the Brockton Fire Department in 1918.[85]

Denis Murphy

Denis P. Murphy got married in 1920 to Mary Ann Sullivan, originally of Derrylea in County Mayo, Ireland, and was a father a year later. His first child, Thomas Joseph Murphy, was named after his older brother, Father Thomas J. Murphy. Denis Murphy was one of the quiet Irish. He never said much, but in his own way, the death of his older brother devastated him. For Irish immigrants, whose friends and families suffered through ordeals that the average person did not, death never masqueraded as an unrecognizable stranger. As U.S. Senator Daniel Patrick Moynihan once quipped, "You're not Irish if you don't know that life's going to break your heart." That said, grief is an involuntary emotion. Regardless of our personal preferences, people grieve according to their needs, and so did Denis Murphy. As the years passed and his family grew, slowly he healed.

Book Two

The

Sullivans

Of

Derrylea

County Mayo

Ireland

Chapter 1

Mayo

Ireland's western counties—Mayo, Clare, Galway and Kerry—were a time capsule in the 1800s. The farmers of western Ireland changed over to the new farming methods much later than counties in the east. Clachans still exited in the mountain glens of Mayo. Under the ancient rundale system of close communal quarters, the land constantly came under new tillers and grazers because of partible inheritance or death within the clachan. Therefore, when assessing the prospects of its young inhabitants, County Mayo always appeared at the very bottom of Ireland's counties. Beyond rundale, Mayo's remote location made it almost inaccessible even after the railroads arrived in the second half of the 1800s.[86]

Until after 1900, much of County Mayo sat in the hands of the 1st Viscount Dillon (Sir Theobald Dillon), an Irish military commander and adventurer. Viscount Dillon not only held extensive lands in Mayo, but also in the surrounding counties. During Oliver Cromwell's confiscations in the middle of the 1600s, Dillon lost some of his estate, but won it back over time. Derrylea sat in Dillon's Costello Barony—sometimes refered to as Costello-Gallin.[87]

When the Sullivans rented farms in Derrylea, they were dealing with Charles Henry Dillon, 14th Viscount Dillon, born in 1810. He died in 1865, leaving the family's estates to his brother Theobald Dominick Dillon, the 15th Viscount Dillon. Thanks to the Wyndham Land Purchase Act of 1903, Michael Sullivan—

with a loan from the British government—began the process of buying the fourteen-acre farm that his father Darby began renting before the Great Hunger. The land was wrested from Eric FitzGerald Dillon, 19th Viscount Dillon (1881–1946). Land purchase acts had been surfacing since 1870, but the early laws only compensated tenants for the improvements made while they leased the land. Later purchase laws, inordinately favored "strong farmers," those with more than 100 acres and the funds to purchase the land.[88]

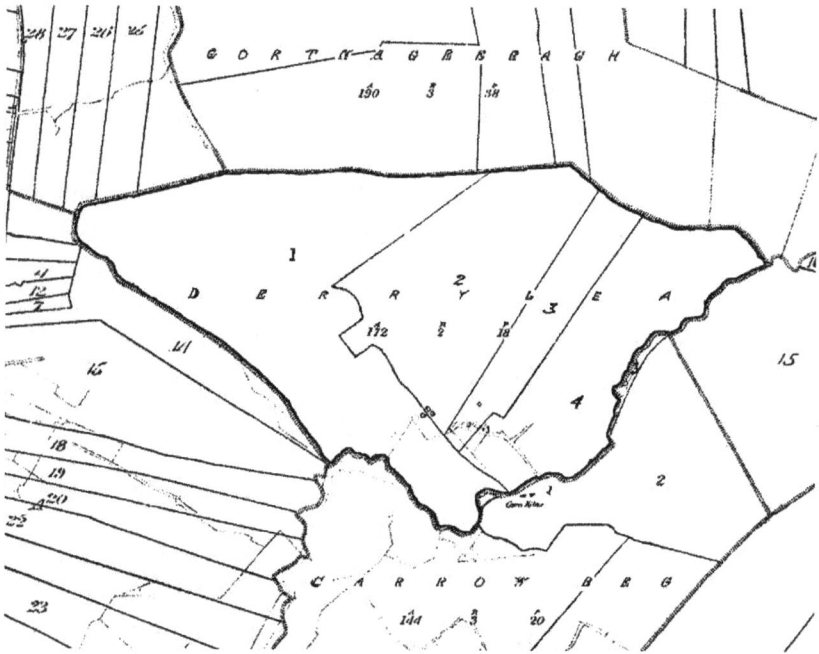

Map Of Derrylea, County Mayo

Michael Sullivan's farm is the bacon strip marked "3."

The Wyndham Act—the Land Purchase (Ireland) Act of 1903—featured a new non-compulsory sales agreement, attractive to landlords and tenants, based on the government paying the difference between the price offered by tenants and that demanded by landlords. It also featured a method of borrowing the cost from the government, with a nominal interest rate over forty years. By 1914, 75 percent of the tenants had bought out their landlords. By the end of the First World War, 85 percent of tenant farmers had already purchased their farms or were in the process of doing so.[89]

In 1903, Michael Sullivan turned sixty-one. Why would he buy his Mayo farm? Maybe because of the better-than-average soil? Perhaps because the dream of ownership was more than he could bear? And of course, Michael and Bridget Sullivan had nowhere else to go. It is well to remember that Irish Catholics lost their land eight centuries earlier. To the dispossessed, land was gold. After eight hundred years of war, rebellion, famine and struggle, they had finally won the right to reclaim Ireland. Could such an opportunity be ignored? Not hardly.

Taking Ireland as a whole, in the 1800s, only about 10 percent of its 20 million acres ever qualified as arable land. Of the thirty-two counties on the island, Mayo always came in last when calculating the amount of land under tillage.[90] Among other shortcomings, Mayo's climate wasn't helpful, with moist ocean air and from fifty to seventy inches of rainfall a year.

Even before the Great Hunger, times were bad enough that the English Parliament began building workhouses, as part of the Poor Law Act of 1838. These Poor Law Unions offered one more way to dice up Ireland on paper. County Mayo fell into eight Poor Law Unions (PLUs), and Derrylea sat in the easternmost part of the Claremorris PLU. In 1851, of the eight PLUs in County Mayo, Claremorris had more "area under crops" than any other PLU in Mayo. It also had more "area under grass"—pasture land—and the least amount of "area under waste." It stayed that way through the updates of 1876 and 1900. Too, the differences within Mayo were not slight. In 1851, the Claremorris PLU had five times as much "area under crops" as Belmullet PLU in far western Mayo.[91]

Ireland is ringed by mountains and contains vast areas of bog lands—particularly in Mayo. The northern part of Mayo consists largely of poor subsoils and is covered extensively with blanket bog. But in eastern Mayo, the land begins with a limestone base and then is capped with the gray-brown, loamy soils more often found in the eastern counties.

As the population of the Emerald Isle built toward the high water mark of 8.175 million in 1840, increasingly Mayo became pinched by hunger and overrun with evicted tenant farmers and laborers, driven from eastern counties. Partible inheritance had further subdivided properties within families. By the 1840s, County Mayo had been subdivided more than any other county in Ireland, with 73 percent of all farms between one and five acres.[92]

Regardless of the crowding in Mayo, land for lease still existed amid the mountainous land and blanket bogs of the west, as well as farms with fertile gray-brown soil in the east. Without question, the availability of land leases brought Thomas, and then later, Darby Sullivan to Derrylea from County Kerry and Cork—where 76 percent of the Sullivan households of Ireland sat in the mid-1800s. By contrast, in County Mayo during the same period, Sullivan households accounted for less than one-half of 1 percent of the total.[93]

As for government administration, County Mayo has 73 Civil Parishes created for record keeping and legal purposes. Annagh Civil Parish—on the far eastern side of County Mayo—has 76 townlands, ranging in size from 4 acres to over 5,000 acres. Derrylea is one of the smallest with only 172 acres.

Thomas Sullivan (the father), born about 1800, rented a seventy-eight-acre farm in Derrylea from Viscount Dillon. His wife Kate, born about 1823, had eleven children, but only one shows in the land records of Derrylea. Thomas (the son), born in 1836, married Catherine McGarry on February 21, 1867, when he was thirty-one. In 1866, the older Thomas Sullivan died, and his son Thomas—then age thirty—took over the farm.

Darby Sullivan, born about 1823, rented a fourteen-acre farm in Derrylea in 1841, about the same time as he married sixteen-year-old Bridget. (One of the defining feature of Mayo during this period was early marriage.) Little is known about Darby Sullivan except that he was probably the nephew of the elder Thomas Sullivan. When the Potato Famine hit in 1845, Darby was only twenty-two and his twenty-year-old wife Bridget had a four-year-old baby—Michael Sullivan. Undoubtedly the elder Thomas Sullivan—forty-five when the Great Hunger began—helped Darby, Bridget, and Michael get through the Famine.[94]

Derrylea's 172 acres held only four farms. The elder Thomas Sullivan and his wife Kate leased a seventy-eight acre farm, while Darby and Bridget settled for a fourteen-acre spread—the smallest of the four farms in Derrylea. It's obvious that the elder Thomas knew the family being evicted from the small farm and got word to his nephew Darby.[95] From the late 1830s until the 1870s, Mayo was a constant stream of evictions, with the farms going to "strong farmers," landlords or fortunate relatives like Darby Sullivan. Though fourteen acres wasn't much, Darby and Bridget Sullivan's situation wasn't dire.

Since a year's supply of potatoes for a family of four could be grown on a couple of acres, leaving the bulk of the land for cash crops to make the rent payment to the landlord, they could make a living. The cost of the rent—divided into two payments each year—and the taxes and forced tithing to the Protestant Church of Ireland would be impossible to calculate today. Rents varied so widely and were rarely in writing. As for the taxes and tithing, such records were lost years ago. About five years after Darby Sullivan's death, Griffith's Valuation of 1856 showed Bridget Sullivan's fourteen-acre farm valued at £2 11d ($12.39). (You could have the fastest horse in the county or Bridget Sullivan's farm—take your pick.)

Griffith's Valuation points out another interesting fact: Before the Potato Famine, there were only four families living in Derrylea. In 1856, when the Griffith's Valuation of County Mayo was completed, there were ten families living in Derrylea. The land was informally subdivided—so that other relatives might survive. The residents included Thomas and Kate Sullivan, Bridget Sullivan (Darby's widow), Bridget Kilfoyle (Michael Sullivan's cousin), and the families of Gilbert Judge, Walter Dowling, Patrick Coyne, Michael Feeny, Owen Doyle and Walter Jennings. During the Famine, Derrylea had become a microcosm for all of Ireland, as people crowded onto the arable land that could produce something besides potatoes. This overcrowding at length begs an important question: After the lion's share of the crops had been paid over to Viscount Dillon for rent, how many people could Derrylea support?

Griffith's Valuation shows that (1) Thomas Sullivan (the father) and his wife Kate still controlled seventy-eight acres from Viscount Dillon, although now there were three other families living on the land—Patrick Coyne, Owen Doyle, and Gilbert Judge (with his wife Mary). Only Patrick Coyne's family had a separate house and garden; (2) Michael Feeney still rented his original forty-two acre farm, which contained his family's home and outbuildings, plus an extra house and cottage. Bridget Kilfoyle lived in the spare house. A hired laborer probably used the cottage; (3) Darby Sullivan's widow, Bridget, still maintained the fourteen acre farm where she lived with her two children, Michael and Mary; (4) Walter Jennings continued at the same thirty-five acre farm, but now sublet some of the land to Mary Judge, William Connolly and Walter Dowling. A good guess is that the 172-acres of Derrylea supported almost fifty men, women and children—in addition to grinding out Viscount Dillon's rent money.

During the Famine, landlords resorted to evictions for failure to pay rents. These evictions were worst in the west—Counties Roscommon, Mayo and Sligo.[96] Landlords ran the spectrum from the humane to the depraved. Some landlords evicted tenants who could not keep up the rent payments; others rid themselves of tenants by paying their passage to Canada (the cheapest ticket to North America); and, some allowed tenants to keep enough of the crops to ward off starvation.

One descendant of a Famine survivor opined, "I must say the landlords were not all alike. My grandfather . . . went to pay . . . his rent to his landlord, a Bantryman. 'Feed your family first, then give me what you can afford when times get better,' he told him." Another said, "The fact that our people escaped . . . was owed to the landlord . . . Mr. Cronin Coltsman . . . When he saw the awful plight of his tenants, he caused a mill to be built . . . .When the mill was ready, the landlord bought Indian meal in Cork City and got his tenants to go with their horses and bring the meal . . . to the mill where . . . everyone who needed it got a measure or scoop of meal for each one in their family."[97]

Though there is no information one way or the other, it appears that Viscount Dillon behaved as an accommodative landlord, allowing the Sullivans and their relatives to stay on the land and survive.

As mentioned earlier, Darby Sullivan died sometime around 1851, at the tail end of the Potato Famine. His son, Michael, became the man of the family—at the age of nine. Leaving school—without learning to read or write—he worked the farm from that day forward. With a mother and infant sister to feed, he had to make decisions that usually settled on the shoulders of a much older man. In the process, he became something of an autocrat—not an easy label to pin on a blurry ancestor born 175 years ago. Nevertheless, accounts of the man differ little—he was an autocratic, stubborn Irishman.

On old maps, far more corn kilns can be seen in the eastern townlands of Annagh Civil Parish—up against the County Roscommon border—than anywhere else in the parish. This makes perfect sense because in the elevated section of northwestern Mayo—where the climate was colder and wetter—a thin layer of plant debris exists, providing the base for peaty bogs. However, in eastern Mayo—near County Roscommon—the soil was more like the gray-brown earth found in the midlands and the eastern counties of the island. Although fairly shallow, the soil was rich and, besides potatoes, it grows corn well.[98]

In addition to the potatoes and corn, Michael Sullivan also kept cows and pigs. After Michel Sullivan married in 1886—and the children began to fill his cottage—a fourteen-acre farm *might* not have been enough to keep a big family, pay the rent, taxes, and still have something left for St. Patrick's Church in Ballyhaunis, except for an interest Michael Sullivan had in a local peat bog. Ireland had been stripped of forestlands by the early 1700s, and the only heat source left was peat (turf). What could only be described as the crudest form of fuel in the world—peat was the only fuel available and the peat bog offered a stable, albeit meager, supplement to the Sullivans' field crops. At times, the peat represented the difference between making it and not.[99]

In some ways, County Mayo seemed like a separate country within Ireland. Besides the tiny amount of "land under crops," Mayo finished poorly in many other categories. For example, Counties Mayo and Kerry were the only two counties in Ireland where 60 percent of the housing was considered "the lowest class."[100] On the eve of the Famine, 85 percent of all the inhabitants of Mayo were illiterate. Farm laborers in Ireland were poorly paid, especially in Mayo. Where farm laborers were in active demand, the average wage was $2.60 a week compared with $2.10 in Mayo. (Just as a guide, a mechanic at a factory in any big American city was making $7.70 a week.) Not surprisingly, laborers couldn't support their families on this pittance.[101]

Michael Sullivan married Bridget Agnes Lyons from neighboring Clagnagh townland, in the Ballyhaunis Roman Catholic Church on Tuesday, April 13, 1886. (The church was St. Patrick's, but old records refer to it as the Ballyhaunis R.C. Church.) Michael Sullivan brought his bride to live with his mother, Bridget, in the small stone cottage in Derrylea. Two years earlier, Michael Sullivan's younger sister, Mary, married a farmer from Derrintogher, a nearby townland. Her spouse, Patrick Finegan and his father were also tenant farmers on Viscount Dillon's large estate.[102]

As laid out earlier, owing to the communal way of life, which the Irish embraced from ancient times, the Sullivan's living arrangements were not unusual. Perhaps because of the strong family ties of the clachan Irish, they were quick to name children after parents, aunts and uncles. The intent was far more important to them than the "hardship" of substituting pet names and the practice continued unabated. The name Dehlia, a nickname for Bridget, was taken by the younger of two Bridgets in the home. Along the same lines, the idea of an Irishman refusing to take care of his parents was rare under the old clachan communal system of rural Ireland.

The Sullivans lived in a small stone cottage with a dirt floor and a steep-pitched, thatched roof. (John Wayne and Maureen O'Hara's home, White O' Morning, in the movie *The Quiet Man* is a remarkably close look-alike, although no tenant farmer would bother to whitewash a stone cottage, and Michael Sullivan was no exception.) The first floor was divided into a living parlor and a kitchen. Upstairs the girls slept on one side of the staircase and the boys slept on the other. Privacy was nonexistent. Under such circumstances, the mind swirls to imagine how Michael and Bridget Sullivan continued producing children. Obviously they found a way.

On the sides of the cottage were stonewalled pens for pigs, and in back, a barn for the family's cow. Since the cottage lacked indoor plumbing, a privy sat in the backyard as well. For toilet paper, the Sullivans—like everyone else—used corncobs. Tenant farms all had cow barns inasmuch as buttermilk served as the most important extender for a potato diet, on which rural people depended. They also added bread, fish, and occasionally pork or chicken—pretty much whatever they had.

Incidentally, the stone cottage still stands to this day, though the thatched roof has been gone for some time. Under the tax laws of Ireland, once the roof is removed, no taxes need be paid on the structure. It sits forlornly in the backyard of a descendent of Mary Ann Sullivan's sister, Dehlia.

Like other couples, Michael and Bridget ("Dehlia") Sullivan started a family immediately. The first child, a girl named Mary, never enjoyed robust health and died within two years. Their second baby was also a girl and they named her Bridget after Michael's mother. Now there were three Bridgets under the same roof and the situation remained so until Michael Sullivan's mother died in 1895. Katherine (Katie) followed in 1890.[103]

Mary Ann Sullivan, now the third child of Michael and Dehlia Sullivan, was baptized after Sunday mass at St. Patrick's Church in Ballyhaunis on January 24, 1892. Birth records are something of a trial in Ireland. Discrepancies in dates between civil birth and baptismal records were quite common in the 1800s. Inclement weather, the fragility of an infant's health, or a host of similar reasons spring to mind, but one not-so-obvious dilemma was a fine imposed for an unrecorded birth. A couple, sensing that they might miss the deadline, altered the birth date to avoid the fine. Baptismal dates tend to be the only record remaining of many births. Among tenant farmers, cottiers and laborers, the civil birth record and the baptismal date can vary greatly. (Mary Ann Sullivan used the day of her baptism as her birth date all of her life, although she could have been born weeks before.)

To complicate the details of her birth further, the name Mary Ann represents an ongoing mystery and deserves some explanation. Although it has been misconstrued as such, Ann was never intended as a middle name. It was probably added because of superstitious reasons or merely to distinguish her from the first Mary, who died young. On any number of documents where the first name appeared, "Mary Ann" was recorded. The 1901 Census of Ireland, taken while Mary Ann Sullivan was nine, lists her name as "Mariann." Furthermore, on ship's manifests and other documents, both names are given as her first name. It should also be noted that, until the Sullivans' eighth and last child was born in

81

1902, none of Michael and Bridget Sullivan's children had middle names. Similarly, Michael Sullivan's cousin, Thomas and his wife, Catherine, had eleven children, all christened without middle names. It simply was not a common practice in rural, western Ireland.[104]

The middle name given to the last child, Michael Thomas (Uncle Mike), was obviously a tribute to Michael Sullivan's uncle Thomas, who helped the nine-year-old boy take care of his widowed mother, Bridget, and infant sister, Mary, in the destitute years following the Great Hunger and Darby Sullivan's death.

The aforementioned girls were joined by Norah in 1894, Patrick in 1896, Ellen (Helen), in 1898, and Michael Thomas in 1902. By the time their last child made an appearance, Michael and Dehlia Sullivan were sixty and forty-seven, respectively.

When Michael Sullivan first took over the farm, survival weighed on his mind, not marriage. He was only nine and he had a mother and a sister to worry about. Only after he learned to run the farm and provided adequately for them did he marry—at forty-four.

Michael Sullivan may have been contented with his lot on the farm and his interest in the peat bog down the road, but clearly he knew how limited his children's chances were in Ireland. He had seen too many crop failures and spent too much time under the thumb of Viscount Dillon to delude himself.

Besides, impartible inheritance would hand the farm to one son, leaving the rest of the children to fen for themselves. Sometimes dowries came into the picture, and soothed the pain of impartible inheritance for the disinherited children, but the Sullivans—and the rest of the farmers in Annagh Civil Parish—were of such meager estates that dowries were daydreams. Without their own farms, fewer and fewer of Mayo's young men were considered marriageable material. As for young girls striking out on their own, the practice was unknown in Ireland. Where would they live? What would they do for work?

Michael Sullivan had a plan though. While, it was true that he couldn't read or write, he had an excellent native intelligence. His solution? Early on, he made plans for all of his children to emigrate.

Michael and Bridget Sullivan were able to buy their fourteen-acre farm—with a loan from the British Government—but when one considers that they could not even afford to educate their children beyond the sixth grade, clearly there was no extra money lying about. As the Sullivan children grew to adulthood, it became harder and harder to feed them and still make ends meet. Beyond that, potatoes and corn in the fields require very little labor until harvest time, so a large family was of limited value for a small farmer like Michael Sullivan. He and his wife Bridget could—and did—run the place after their children had all settled in America. At length, all seven of Michael and Bridget Sullivan's surviving children emigrated.

During the Great Hunger, starving Irish subsistence farmers and laborers were forced to leave Ireland year round under conditions that gave a whole new meaning to the term *desperation*. Queenstown was not yet a port of call for steamships and the destitute Irish were forced to flee Ireland on 'coffin ships' from any port available. Some tried to sail directly to America. Others engaged smaller boats to take them across the Irish Sea where they could book passage from Liverpool. The trip across the Irish Sea was only a three-hour sail, so Liverpool did not seem out of reach.

By the early 1900s, emigration had changed markedly. The plans and machinations of the emigration process were infinitely more meticulous and humane, and Passenger Laws eliminated the abuses wrought by greedy ship owners during the worst years of the Famine.

Bridget (Dehlia) Sullivan, the oldest child, emigrated first. She left home about four months after her eighteenth birthday. Bridget, feisty and strong willed—irrespective of her status as the oldest—logically was the first to make the crossing. Employing the common sense dictum of safety in numbers, the local travel agency in Ballyhaunis brought together a total of ten young people from the surrounding townlands and booked them on the same Cunard liner.

Mary Fleming, the youngest at seventeen hoped to find work as a servant in Jersey City, New Jersey. Besides Bridget, there were two other eighteen-year-olds—May Mulligan, headed for Roxbury, and Ellen Moran, whose journey would end in

Dorchester. There were two nineteen-year-olds—Margaret Fitzmaurice, who listed her occupation as a servant and was headed for Fall River, and Mary Forde, who would come to journey's end in Roxbury. Most of these girls gave their occupations as "housework" as did twenty-year-old Sarah Neary, headed for Boston. Her sister, Ellen, gave her occupation as a "shirt stitcher," which, if true, would place her among the elite of all the young women who ever emigrated from Ireland. The oldest woman in the group, twenty-four-year-old Amelia Devine, would eventually do housework in Boston. Twenty-two-year-old Francis Roche—the only male of the bunch—gave his occupation as farmer-laborer, presumably hoping to get a job as one or the other when he got to Peabody.

Bridget alone hoped to wind up in Brockton where, according to the ship's passenger list, she had a bunk waiting in the home of her aunt, Mary Hunt, of 27 Skinner Street, Brockton. "Aunt Mary Hunt" is a puzzle. She was married to John Hunt Jr., an Irish laborer, but since there are no Hunts on the Sullivan family tree, one wonders if the "Aunt" was simply a ruse. Emigration authorities took steps to ensure that immigrants did not wind up on relief—or the girls in prostitution—by insisting they had some money in their pockets and a place to live. That would give them time to find work.

In any event, all ten of the young people from the townlands near Ballyhaunis took the train to Queenstown, boarded the *SS Ivernia* on Wednesday, April 17, 1907 and sailed into Boston Harbor eight days later. Dehlia's arrival in America in 1907—although unknown to her at the time—made her part of history because 1907 set the annual record for the largest number of immigrants entering the United States. In New York alone, one million men, women, and children washed up on the American shore, looking for a better life. That same year, about 200,000 entered the United States through Boston.

Once Dehlia had made the crossing and got a job in domestic service, she could help the others with money, and just as importantly, a place to stay while they sought work. By late winter, Dehlia made her way to Carl Mogren's cigar store on Main Street in Brockton—agent for Cunard lines—plunked down twenty-five dollars and bought a ticket for her younger sister,

Mary Ann, to emigrate in April 1908. A Royal Mail ship and the Irish postal service would see that the ticket got into the younger girl's hands in Derrylea. This transfer of funds from the US to Ireland was huge during the entire Irish emigration and paid for the overwhelming majority of the steamship tickets west. Humorously enough, correspondences from Irish immigrants back to Ireland, with no funds enclosed, were called "empty letters."

Immigrants of every ethnic class battled homesickness— sometimes with catastrophic results on their mental health. Therefore, it is reasonable to assume that Dehlia was anxious to see her sister after twelve months alone in a strange land.

In the natural emigration order, Mary Ann had hop scotched over Katie, but for good reason. Michael and Bridget Sullivan had a difficult decision to make. Katie was an extremely shy and uncommunicative girl, whose chances of success on such a strange odyssey seemed questionable. She would be almost eighteen by the time the ship left Queenstown the following April, but that didn't make much difference. What to do?

The flip side of Katie's reticent personality was the next in line, Mary Ann, who was by nature strong-willed and self-confident. Up to a point, that was fine, but she proved a problem of a different sort. She simply did not want to emigrate. Mary Ann had a very strong native intelligence, but more importantly, she had an iron will that brooked no compromises. Describing her own education more then sixty years later, she first summed it up by saying, "I went as far as sixth grade and I thought I was capably smart when I did." Later in the same conversation she spoke of her teacher in more guarded tones, "She was an old English teacher. We were controlled by the English government, which means that we did not have the better teachers . . . .We didn't have our choice of subjects . . . .We had to do just exactly as they said."[105]

In an effort to keep their native tongue alive, the older Irish paid tutors to come in at night and teach the young people the Irish language. Summing up that fiasco, Mary Ann Sullivan stated with just a touch of anger, "We had to have an evening class [for Irish], and pay for a teacher to come in evenings, and they [the British] even stopped that . . . .But we got along pretty good with it."[106]

Still later in the interview, she said, "I didn't even finish school. I should have gone further, but I didn't because my father and mother couldn't pay for it. The old teacher said, 'She's a good subject for a teacher if you want to pay for her teaching'. And the English government wouldn't pay you anything. So I says, 'Oh, the hell with them.'"[107]

The national schools sponsored by the English government were established around 1831. At the time, 80 percent of the Irish population could neither read nor write. The idea was to teach Irish children disdain of Ireland and everything Irish, and admiration for everything English. Even in Mayo where Irish speakers were abundant—and even more so the farther west one went—the children were taught that English not Irish was their native tongue.[108]

While Mary Ann seemed like the perfect candidate to take Katie's place, she so opposed emigration that Michael Sullivan was up against it. He had already told Mary Ann that the family could no longer afford to feed her, but she was unfazed. She even considered going to Liverpool and working as a barmaid, as so many other young Irish girls had done before her.

Father and daughter continued their sullen disagreement through the winter months of 1907-8, with their contretemps reaching fevered pitch at times. This classic tug-o-war between two strong-willed people often left Michael Sullivan holding the greasy end of the stick. He could shout and threaten if he chose, but short of marching her to Queenstown at gunpoint and forcing her onto a ship, he was stymied.

He did have one ace though—his cousin, Agnes Kilfoyle. Twenty-nine-year-old Agnes had been working in Southboro, Massachusetts, as a domestic servant for the better part of a decade. As luck would have it, this unmarried woman had returned to Ireland recently to visit her mother, Bridget Kilfoyle, in Derrylea. Michael Sullivan prevailed upon Agnes to speak with Mary Ann and help break the impasse. After a long heart to heart talk about what she could expect from each country, Agnes Kilfoyle said reassuringly, "You better come out with me." And, with that, the battle was over.

Many years later, Mary Ann Sullivan stated in a rather cryptic way that she had been mistreated in Derrylea, but the evidence extant points only to her epic battles with her father concerning emigration. That having been said, any sixteen-year-old girl, living in a dirt floor hut and sleeping on straw, may look back with a certain amount of bitterness, and indeed, this may be the poor treatment that Mary Ann alluded to. In any event, plans were made for her to leave on the first Cunard liner departing Queenstown in April 1908.

Mary Ann Sullivan did not have an "American wake" any more than the Murphy brothers of Killarney did. In the late 1800s and early 1900s, the older Irish speakers of County Mayo, and most of the west, preferred "the farewell supper." It is most likely that Mary Ann Sullivan and Agnes Kilfoyle enjoyed such a repast, though the matter has never been mentioned.

Ballyhaunis Railroad Depot

On the cool spring morning of Tuesday, April 7, 1908, Mary Ann Sullivan and Agnes Kilfoyle arrived at the Ballyhaunis Railroad Depot in their Sunday clothes, and each with a single, heavy-cloth satchel, to the smiling faces of their two traveling companions. Ellen Culkin, a seventeen-year-old, billed herself as a servant although, like every other female emigrant from a mud or stone hut in Ireland, she knew nothing about service work. The last member of the group was Thomas Ganley, a twenty-three-year-old laborer, who planned to meet his sister in Brookline. During these years in America, there were plenty of railroads, canals and aqueducts taking shape. Common laborers were in demand.

The young people from Ballyhaunis were a diverse collection of Irish domestics and laborers, but they had more going for them than they might have realized. Mary Ann Sullivan, for example, could read and write—unlike her parents—and she was young and strong, capable of hard work, something America treasured— even demanded. Beyond that, with the exception of Agnes Kilfoyle—and apart from their steamer tickets—they were each carrying more money than they had ever seen before.

Thomas Ganley had $30, not a trifling sum to a tenant farmer's son—especially when one remembers that Bridget Sullivan's property in Derrylea was valued at $12.39 in 1856—and Ireland's property values were still on the wane. Ellen Culkin had the least of anyone with only $7.50 to last her until she could find work. Mary Ann Sullivan had $10. The oldest, Agnes Kilfoyle had $15. Though they were headed in different directions when they finally disembarked in Boston, they would—like the Irish who arrived before them—see each other again at Irish club socials, dances and parades.

They waited on the platform for the Midland & Great Western train that would approach from the east. A fairly recent addition to the landscape of western Ireland, the MGWR line arrived in the early 1890s, when tracks were laid all the way to Killala—just west of Sligo Bay in the northernmost part of Mayo. (Perhaps as a direct result of the continuing emigration and the generally lethargic pace of life in western Ireland, the section of track that ran from Claremorris to Killala—a distance of about 35 miles— slipped into disuse by 1931. By then the line—along with two others—had fallen into the bailiwick of the Great Southern Railway.)

One can just imagine the world-wise and well-dressed Agnes Kilfoyle—along with her three skinny, starry-eyed companions— standing on the wooden platform of the Ballyhaunis Railroad Depot. As they talked excitedly, their breath filled the space between them with condensation. Then, hearing the rumble and whistle of the mammoth steam engine, they watched as the smoking, chugging hulk came to a stop at their feet. They held onto their hats as the train belched out excess steam from under its splashers, nearly deafening them in the process.

The trains of Ireland were painted in vivid colors in the early years of the new century. One guesses that this represented a transparent attempt on the part of the directors of the road to sell the rural Irish on the delirium of travel. Dull locomotives and carriages, matching the huts and outbuildings of the local farms, was no way to generate interest in travel. Bright colors were the ticket!

As the mammoth locomotive sat in front of them, it had lost the vagaries caused by the atmosphere in the distance and the form, shape and color of the machinery became vivid and exciting. By 1908, the locomotive's original royal blue color had been replaced by sap green with bright red pin striping. The same red lines were neatly edged around the chimney rim. Splashes of bright red covered the engine buffers and number plates as well. The crowning touch was brass beading around the splashers and a brass casing on the steam engine's top-mounted relief valve.

The railroad's initials were emblazoned on the coal tender in bright gold letters—"MGWR." The coach cars were a deep burgundy color, again with the tall gold letters of the railroad adorning the side panels below the windows. Mary Ann Sullivan had seen the train before on trips into Ballyhaunis, but the fact that this train was stopping for her changed everything.

The Midland Great Western train, as advertised, whisked them the ten miles to Claremorris—a slightly larger town due west of Ballyhaunis. At the Claremorris station, they boarded an even more substantial train, the Great Southern & Western Line, which took them south all the way to Queenstown. On this line, the engine and tender were dark gray, with red and white detail work. Devoid of any ownership markings, the eye was drawn immediately to the large brass number plate at the prow of the leviathan. The carriages were painted a deep claret color, highlighted with yellow and red pin-striping, and the tall gold initials of the line—GS and WR—were spaced on either side of the company crest, which incorporated the coats-of-arms of Dublin, Cork, Kilkenny and Limerick.

Claremorris lay 135 miles from Queenstown but, as the train inched south, it stopped at more than thirty-five townlands—

Galway, Gort, Ennis, Limerick, Mallow, Blarney and Cork—just to name the largest ones. At least a dozen of the stops had refreshment rooms and tea baskets were served on the train. But such an embarrassment of stops made progress slow and the sun dipped in the western sky by the time the group arrived at Queenstown.

When the great waves of emigration slowed to a trickle in the 1920s, the Great Southern & Western Line, the Midland Great Western and the Cork, Bandon & South Coast Railway were rolled into one road—the Great Southern Railway. About 1931, unable to earn its keep, the spur from Claremorris to Queenstown went belly up, forcing travelers to journey southeast to Portalington (near Kildare), from whence the main Dublin-Cork line could be accessed.

As the early April sun continued to drop, the train finally pulled into Queenstown station, located on the southwestern edge of an island in the middle of Cork's natural harbor. Behind the station, a tender ferried passengers out to the Cunard liner *SS Ivernia*.

So many Irish emigrants took a last look at Ireland from a ship departing Queenstown Harbor that it earned the melancholy sobriquet "Harbor of Tears." Originally, it was the Cove of Cork and one of the finest natural harbors in the world. The emigrants from Ireland ranged from those, like Mary Ann Sullivan, who did not want to leave all their childhood haunts, family and friends, to those who wanted desperately to leave. No matter what the circumstances or mindset of the emigrants though, saying goodbye, perhaps forever, to one's whole world wrenched everyone terribly.

Queenstown could never have been considered more than a glorified fishing village, with mostly two- and three-story Victorian structures built up a rocky hillside and covering a mere quarter-mile square. The tallest building was the neo-gothic St. Colman's Cathedral, its huge spire the first thing that visitors noticed—and the last thing that emigrants remembered of Ireland.

Mary Ann Sullivan and her traveling companions were escorted to a small boarding house—run under contract to Cunard Lines—and settled in for the evening. The need to board passengers provided another reason why Cunard was not originally anxious to enter the emigrant trade. Owing to the lack of money and travel experience, the Irish people were a high maintenance group. Built into the price of a £5 ($25) steerage ticket to America were meals and lodging before the voyage, meals during the crossing, and the possible cost of returning rejected passengers back to Ireland. Even with all those added costs, the emigrant trade still offered a better return on capital than any other passenger service in the steamship business.

The young people from Ballyhaunis were herded into the dining room for supper a short time later and excited conversation filled the remainder of the evening. They went to bed early because they were expected to make their final arrangements at the Cunard offices early the following day.

Just after sunup the next morning, a light breakfast was served and third-class passengers from all over the city descended on the Cunard office at quayside. In an earlier era, brigs and barks were able to tether to the shallow-water Cunard or White Star wharfs, which were only a few hundred feet from one another. The advent of the iron-hulled, 14,000-ton steamships changed all that. Now tenders steamed back and forth to the 600-foot leviathans—with deep-water drafts—in the middle of the harbor.

Passing through the first floor of a squat building, the women answered questions designed to weed out the sick, the daft and the penniless. Judging by the questions and answers on the ship's manifest, the conversation between the clerk and Mary Ann Sullivan went like this:

"Name?" asked the boarding representative.

"Mary Ann Sullivan."

"How old are you?"

"Seventeen." A nervous mistake. She has just turned sixteen and certainly knew her own age. At any rate, she must have recognized the blunder and corrected her mistake, for the recorder crossed out the "17" and wrote "16" slightly above the original entry.

"Who paid for your passage?"

"My sister."

"What is your destination in America—street address and town?"

"203 West Elm Street. Boston." Again, a small mistake, since she was clearly going to stay with her sister, Dehlia, in Brockton.

"No, I meant Brockton." Once again, the clerk dutifully crossed out "Boston" and wrote "Brockton" above it.

"Besides your ticket, how much money are you carrying?"

"Ten Dollars."

"Your height?"

"Five foot-seven."

"Complexion?" Eyeing her closely, he wrote "Fair."

"Hair color?" Again, he eyed her naturally wavy blonde hair and entered the word "Fair."

"Color of your eyes?" Looking up, he hesitated because the color was a pale color that could be gray, hazel or blue.

"Blue," she offered.

"And where were you born?"

"Ireland." She perhaps thought the question foolish, since she had never lived anywhere except the little stone cottage that had been, at this point, leased by her family and her ancestors for about three-quarters of a century.

"Father's name?"

"Michael Sullivan," she blurted.

And where was your last residence?

"Derrylea, Ballyhaunis."

With the questioning concluded, Mary Ann Sullivan boarded the steam tender that would deliver her—and her friends—to the steel stairs hanging alongside one of Cunard's most luxurious liners, the *SS Ivernia*. The ship had embarked passengers at Liverpool the day before, April 7, and Queenstown figured as the ship's last embarkation point before sailing to America. When all of the passengers were boarded, the chain windlass in the forecastle deck raised the anchor and the *Ivernia* slipped out of Queenstown Harbor.

The *Ivernia* got underway on Wednesday, April 8, 1908 and, for the first few days, the weather seemed "very seasonable, changeable, and cool but, on the whole, fair."[109] The passengers milled about the decks and the sun swung through the middle of its arc, as many on board said good-bye to the land of their birth— to family, to school chums and all that was familiar to them— forever. Mary Ann Sullivan did not return to Ireland for more than sixty years, and then for only a short visit. She never saw her parents again.

Mary Ann Sullivan's £5 ticket bought a far nicer passage on the *Ivernia* than would ordinarily have been the case for an emigrant. As a natural response to the crushing competition for steerage passengers between the largest steamship companies, great opportunities were created for the traveling public.

SS Ivernia

Accommodations in steerage were vastly improved. Launched in 1900, the *Ivernia* and her sister ship, the *Saxonia,* were 14,000-ton steel-hulled, twin-screw leviathans. An even cushier design detail was that cabins were incorporated into third-class for more then 70 percent of the steerage passengers. All this was thought to be possible by reducing the size of the engines, thus slowing the speed of the vessels by five knots. A consequence of this tinkering—considered monumental at the time—was that the ships would burn 30 percent less coal. Unfortunately, the price of coal spiked up wildly and the anticipated savings never materialized. Any competitive edge, real or perceived, was lost even before the ships came down the ways. Adding insult to injury, competition heated up as emigration reached its zenith and all supposed advantages amounted to naught.

The subject of speed on the North Atlantic is worthy of mention because it points out some rather surprising truths. From the earliest days of steamships, the desire for speed ruled supreme for two reasons. To begin, as with all methods of transport, the excitement derived from excessive speed presented an overpowering temptation as well as a heart-pounding thrill. Furthermore, a belief abounded that the lion's share of the emigrant trade would accrue to the line that could cross the Atlantic in the least amount of time. Curiously, this proved not to be the case.

In the late 1800s and early 1900s, passengers cared far more about a carrier's reputation for good accommodations than they did for the speed of the vessel. This was coupled by the obvious need of emigrants, at least when they could (like in the early 1860s), to chose the liner offering the cheapest fare. This last statement has some obvious caveats in that even steerage passengers were swayed by a carrier's reputation for safety and its general treatment of passengers.

The *Ivernia* was an impressive ship, having been built by C. S. Swan & Hunter in Newcastle (northeastern England). Measuring 582 feet long and 65 feet at the beam, the ship corresponded precisely with the classic 9 to 1 ratio, which the most conservative of shipbuilders adhered to like an eleventh commandment.[110]

Cunard had been dragged kicking and screaming into the emigrant trade, but when it finally accepted the challenge, financially it set records that its competitors envied. With the launching of the *Ivernia* and the *Saxonia*, Cunard embarked on an upgraded—and unmatched—level of steerage comfort. Besides the aforementioned cabins for third class passengers, there was still a large open area in the fore-steerage for unmarried men and some double-decker berths arranged dormitory style for young women in the aft-steerage. Unfortunately, this "third class cabin" innovation proved costly, with less than the hoped for return on investment, and Cunard later dropped the design.[111]

While the passage to America had taken up to a month in the days of the wooden square riggers—the 'coffin ships'—Mary Ann Sullivan's trip across the North Atlantic would be a slow eight days, steaming along at sixteen knots. To fill the hours, there was little. "Eat and sleep; that's all we did," was her assessment. On Sunday, April 12, the *Ivernia* ran into the edge of a rare North

Atlantic hurricane. At a spot that Mary Ann Sullivan estimated to be "the middle of the Atlantic Ocean," the ship encountered such a fierce storm that the captain idled the engines and dropped a sea anchor—to keep the ship pointing into the wind—while everyone suffered the bad weather. It grew into an eighteen-hour wait.[112]

The *Boston Globe* reported later, "Terrific gales and zero weather made the passage . . . one of the most disagreeable of the winter. It was the coldest trip for this season of the year that any of her officers ever experienced." The paper continued, "On Monday, when the gale was at its height, the wireless apparatus of the ship was put out of commission by the gale breaking some of the connections aloft."[113]

Many years later, Mary Ann Sullivan confessed that she had been "scared to death" by the storm. To the English captains and the mixed bag of less-than-savory seamen, the sight of Irish peasants saying the rosary was unnerving to behold. The mysticism of the beads and the crucifix did not translate well. It smacked of preternatural superstition, inspiring immense fear instead of comfort.[114]

Barring such storms, the length of the North Atlantic crossing had been whittled down nicely over the years. Nonetheless, for most of the liners plying the frigid waters—including the *Ivernia*—the crossing still took twice as much time as ships like the *Mauritania*, whose top speed was 27.4 knots.

The manner of processing "aliens"—as the officials of Boston were wont to call immigrants—had achieved an acceptable level of ennui by the time Mary Ann Sullivan crossed the North Atlantic. Owing to the American public's long history of unbridled fear of infectious disease, it wasn't always that way. The indelicacies of the immigration process were, regardless of the port of entry, time-consuming, nerve-wracking and tiring for the passengers, who wanted simply to get on with their new lives. While considerably streamlined by 1908, the immigration process still took significant time and immigrants endured it to get from just beyond the limits of Boston Harbor into the city proper. Although she did not know it, Mary Ann Sullivan had it much easier than the millions of emigrants who arrived before her.

Since 1600, more than 60 million people have immigrated to the United States, the bulk of these people arriving in the 1700s and 1800s. New York became America's largest seaport after the Black Ball Line first inaugurated scheduled sailing times in 1818. Naturally enough, New York opened the first immigration depot.

New York's whole immigration processes operated differently from that of Boston, and with good reason. Between 1892 and 1924, the peak years of emigration, 12 million people passed through Ellis Island, or on average, 375,000 per year. During the same period, Boston processed about 75,000 annually—only 20 percent as many.

Originally, New York's Port Physician examined immigrants on their vessels in New York Harbor. After the routine checks and paperwork, tugs towed the ship to South Street Seaport on the East River, where passengers disembarked.

In 1855, Castle Garden—a fortress converted into a concert venue—underwent the remodeling necessary to become New York's first emigration facility. It sat on a rocky outcropping off the southwestern tip of Manhattan and connected to the mainland by a long wooden causeway. Much later, after years of "land filling," the fortress became firmly connected to Manhattan. (Today, Castle Garden is a New York State historical site in Battery Park.)

After an onboard inspection, emigrants disembarked at Castle Garden. While all the baggage went to nearby warehouses, the immigration process began. Customhouse officers and immigration agents huddled in the center of the building, listening to immigrants' personal histories. Immigrants could stay at Castle Garden while they looked for housing and work. Settlement societies aided the new arrivals in every way possible.

Between 1855 and 1892—when Ellis Island opened—Castle Garden processed more than 8 million immigrants. Soon enough, processing centers were established at all other U. S. ports of entry. After Ellis Island began operations in January 1892, the number of immigrants swelled to the point where simply processing them was nothing short of miraculous.

Owing to the smaller number of immigrants passing through its harbor, Boston never experienced the kind of pressure that existed in New York to maintain highly-efficient, centralized facilities like Castle Garden or Ellis Island.

In the late 1600s, a ship lying at anchor near Nantasket experienced an outbreak of smallpox. Visitors to the vessel inadvertently contracted the disease and brought it ashore, leaving a thousand Bostonians dead.

Boston's General Court should have acted with dispatch, but did not. It wasn't until 1717 that Boston bought Spectacle Island from Samuel and Sarah Bill, with plans for a quarantine hospital. Unfortunately, many Bostonians felt that the hospital on Spectacle Island was too close to the city. Beyond that, other occupied islands almost completely surrounded it. Perhaps most irksome of all was the poor anchorage offered for detained vessels. Rocky shoals surrounded all thirty-six of the harbors islands—some with wonderfully descriptive names like Nix's Mate and The Graves. In any case, only a few of the larger islands offered good anchorage, a subset that did not include Spectacle Island.[115]

The matter came to a head in 1736, when another committee settled on Rainsford Island for a new quarantine hospital. By 1737, the name was unofficially changed to Quarantine Island and ill passengers relied on the new hospital facility there.

Almost a hundred years later, in 1832, a steam-powered quarantine boat ferried doctors from Rainsford Island to ships lying at anchor outside Boston Harbor. This arrangement worked satisfactorily until 1847, the worst year of the Irish Potato Famine. The dilapidated 'coffin ships,' loaded with desperate refugees, were also laden with passengers suffering from ship's fever (typhus). The position of Port Physician was created and Dr. John M. Moriarty took the job for $1200 annually (plus board). He was charged with inspecting the passengers aboard any vessel coming from a list of "quarantinable ports." (These ports were the usual suspects when it came to disease.)

Ships flew flags to request inspections. The quarantine boat would slip alongside a ship and the Port Physician inspected all of the passengers on board the vessel, sometimes five hundred or more at a time. Those who were sick were helped onto the quarantine boat and whisked away to Rainsford Island.

Soon Boston abandoned the small hospital on Rainsford Island, in favor of a new quarantine hospital and poorhouse—the House of Industry—on Deer Island. There, fifty doctors, nurses and support staff manned the hospital wards. Despite this well-equipped facility and its huge staff, the flow of immigrants overwhelmed the system.

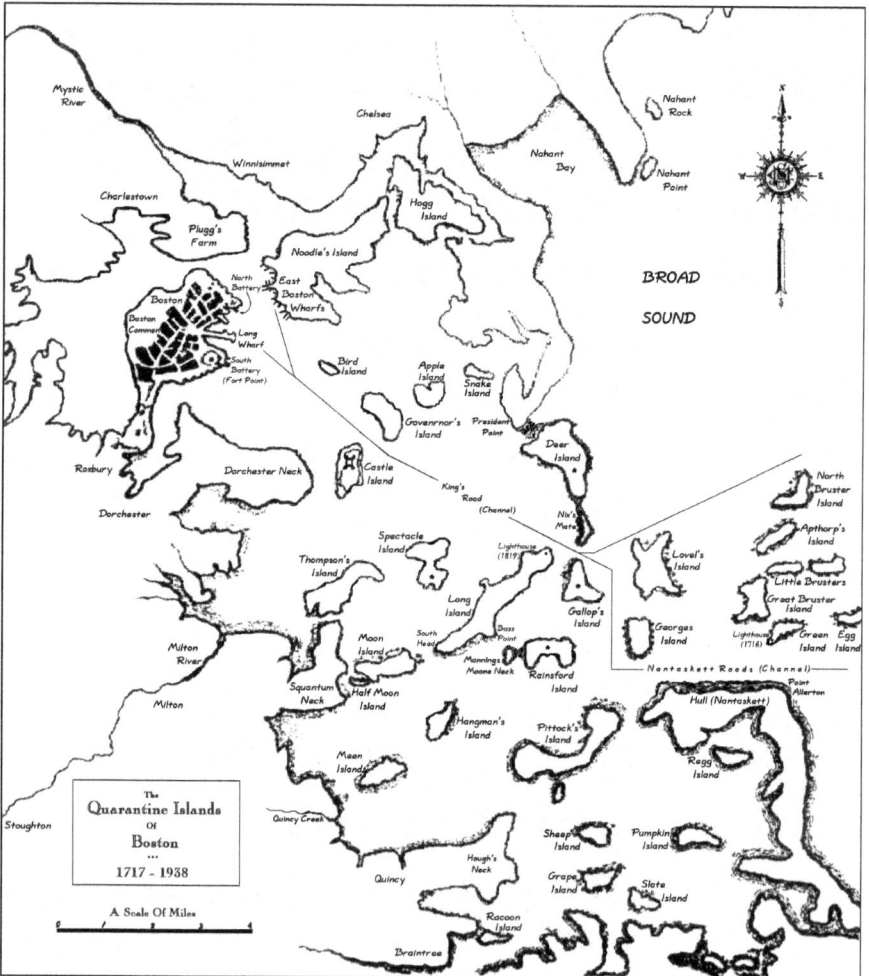

Desperate to contain a dire situation, Boston purchased Gallop's Island in 1860. A few years later, the first patients were removed to a new hospital there. The island remained a U.S.

Public Health Service quarantine station until 1938 when the U.S. Coast Guard commandeered it. Thereafter, the flow of immigrants plummeted and local hospitals cared for sick passengers on a contract basis.

After the Port Physician examined the passengers on the steamships in—and just outside—Boston Harbor, the vessels proceeded to the disparate wharfs on Noodle's Island in East Boston. In 1904—after numerous complaints about rats eating records—immigration officials at Boston rented a building from one of the steamship companies in an effort to upgrade the Port of Boston Emigration Facility on Marginal Street.

Noodle's Island, one of the largest islands of East Boston, covered an area of about 200 acres, and much of Boston's maritime activity centered on it. Samuel Cunard's steamships—as well as those of his many competitors—embarked from the docks of Noodle's Island. Beyond that, Noodle's Island housed some of Boston's biggest manufacturers and gave the city electric lamps and machinery.

In 1908, about 85,000 aliens arrived at Boston. In 1913, the Port of Boston processed 101,700 immigrants, but the number began a protracted tailspin thereafter. By 1915, the number of immigrants arriving at Boston had dwindled to 11,250, and never bested that number again.

***

After nine days at sea, the *Ivernia* sat southwest of Deer Island, just inside Boston Harbor, waiting for the Port Physician to inspect her passengers. Around 9 o'clock in the morning on April 16, 1908, a launch carrying the doctor and his medical staff from Gallop's Island bumped alongside the *Ivernia*. As with every passenger ship entering Boston Harbor, the third-class passengers lined up for inspection. The doctor would eyeball these immigrants and separate anyone he deemed unhealthy. The singled out passengers—along with those in sickbay—were transferred to the doctor's steam launch and brought to the hospital on Gallop's Island. The rest of the ship's passengers continued on their way. Incidentally, first and second-class passengers were deemed healthy without a glance from the doctor.

Most of the steamships entering Boston Harbor used the northern channel, King's Road, because it offered a straighter shot—and a deeper channel—than Nantasket Roads on the south. The *Ivernia* steamed slowly along King's Road until it got near Long Wharf, where tugs took control of the ship and eased it into one of the Cunard berths on Noodle's Island.

Since the girls would be shuttling through Boston on subways—starting near the docks of East Boston—the deck of the *Ivernia* gave them the best view of Boston they would ever have. While they took in the sights, tugs pushed and pulled the giant steamer into port. The passengers could see the old waterfront, where Long Wharf had captured the interest of so many since it was completed in 1810, and where Boston's maritime trade flourished since the earliest days of the Massachusetts Bay Colony. All over the waterfront were commercial warehouses built to further that trade. Countless small craft filled the waters of the harbor as fishermen, cargo handlers, and passenger ships competed for the available dock space.

Behind the waterfront, tall buildings were everywhere, some as high as ten stories. The streets were an eclectic mix of dirt lanes, granite and cobblestone roads, and even asphalt-paved streets. Though asphalt had been in use for more than a decade, the city fathers were reluctant to change the historic nature of the city by paving everything in sight.

The first- and second-class passengers were allowed to disembark immediately, while the third-class passengers were paraded into the Port of Boston Immigration Facility on Marginal Street. As has been mentioned before, the authorities at the immigration ports were wary of young girls entering America unescorted. Contrarily, Mary Ann Sullivan and her traveling companions had firm destinations and relatives to house them until they could find work, so they were not detained.

As the *Ivernia* crawled toward one of the Cunard berths on Noodle's Island, Dehlia Sullivan was traveling up from Brockton to meet her younger sister at the immigration building. Once Mary Ann Sullivan and her friends were successfully processed, Dehlia joined them and the whole group walked two blocks to Maverick Square, where they caught the subway under the harbor to Court Street Station in downtown Boston. From Court Street Station, the young people took the new Tremont Street Subway to South Station, where Dehlia and Mary Ann Sullivan jumped on the southbound Old Colony Street Railroad.

Port of Boston Immigration Facility c. 1904

Boston—and for that matter all the cities of eastern Massachusetts—were full of oddities in the early 1900s. Traveling opera companies performed only a couple of weeks each year at Mechanics Hall in Boston because the new Opera House on Huntington Street wasn't completed until 1909.

People walked about Boston in the early 1900s routinely carrying a Boston Bag, a leather satchel about one foot square with a flat bottom and two handles. The top of this bag closed using a leather strap, and men and women, boys and girls, young and old alike, carried it everywhere.

In the older parts of the city, one could still hear the cries of organ grinders, rag pickers, and venders. The soapgrease man trundled about the city in his grimy cart, collecting grease and selling soap. Fish peddlers and fruit venders cried out loudly, while the iceman quietly delivered forty-pound blocks of ice. These strident street sounds were mixed with the sound of bells ringing from the horse wagons. The bells dangled from horses' harnesses or from the wagons' pulling shafts.

By the time May Ann Sullivan arrived in America, Boston had become a woman's city. More so than in other American city, women went to the theater and to restaurants unescorted. Boston women were singularly independent, with so many of them employed in stores and offices that even the sight of respectable women alone on the streets at night didn't hint of indiscretion.

Women carried heavy travel bags and all sort of other items. They dressed in the finest clothing although they were far more likely to ignore the fashion of the day in favor of last year's well-tailored outfits. Millinery shops regularly hung signs that read "No Admission For Men." In addition to the unusual freedom that the city's women enjoyed, there were many fashionable women's clubs. Without a care, single women listed their full names in the city directories.

As previously mentioned, the young people from County Mayo traveling south, caught the Old Colony Line at South Station. In 1893, the New Haven Line had purchased the Old Colony Railroad. With the stroke of a pen, J. P. Morgan's New York, New Haven & Hartford Line became the largest railroad in southern New England. In the late 1890s, Boston's city fathers decided to consolidate the railroad depots, so they built Boston Terminal Station (South Station) at the intersection of Summer Street and Atlantic Avenue. South Station sat just minutes from downtown and the first train left the depot on January 1, 1899. Soon, South Station was the largest railroad depot in the world.

In 1908, the Old Colony Street Railroad steamed through Mattapan, Quincy, Braintree, Holbrook-Randolph, Montello, Brockton, Campello and Bridgewater on its way to Fall River. The South Station—Mattapan—Brockton part of the journey was a 75¢ ride.

When she was eighty-two, Mary Ann (Sullivan) Murphy toyed with listeners, "I packed my bag and came out to the United States of America, because I thought I could meet a nice, rich man, who could take care of me for the rest of my life. . . ."[116]

Her life in Brockton turned out differently. Sometimes, it was beyond a young girl's dreams, and at other junctures, it was an absolute nightmare. The good with the bad—as all lives are.

Chapter 2

J.J. & Ellen Cahill

When Mary Ann Sullivan finally settled in with her sister Dehlia, they had much catching up to do. The great tidal wave of information moved from Dehlia to Mary Ann because so little had changed back in Ireland. In Brockton, things were clamorous and exciting. For the younger of the two girls, there was so much to learn.

Except for Boston, Mary Ann Sullivan had never seen a city before. She hadn't visited Dublin and had never even seen a crowd of more than a couple hundred people. Queenstown, bloated by the constant movement of emigrants, always seemed larger than life. It actually had fewer than 10,000 residents. The population of Ballyhaunis in 1908 was only 1,000. When the Sullivan girls were first reunited in Brockton, the city had a population of 50,000. What must Mary Ann Sullivan have thought?

Brockton was like an exposed nerve in 1908. Granite blocks paved Main Street and double trolley tracks ran up and down the center of the principal streets, as overhanging wires delivered electricity to the juddering steel cars. The city had recently been declared the largest producer of men's shoes in the world and the population had grown apace. There was constant movement in the shoe and boot businesses as new workers—mostly immigrants—arrived daily to run the McKay sewing machines and the Goodyear welters. Brockton pulsed with raw energy, its shoe factories belching out steam and coal soot with the work of an army of skilled and unskilled workers, cutting, stitching, lasting, welting, sewing, marking, grading, polishing and boxing millions of pairs of shoes annually.

Shoes, shoes, shoes. Everything was shoes in the churning, grinding, whirling dervish that was Brockton. The 100 shoe factories—while the single most important part of the city's success—were only one sector of the shoe and boot manufacturing industry. Equally important were the 100 firms that supplied everything from rock maple wooden lasts (shoe forms) and steel shanks to eyelets, laces, polish, and dozens of other items. There were another 51 shops engaged in custom shoemaking and still another 28 retail shoe stores. For all practical purposes, these companies fueled Brockton's incredible growth. The success of every other business in the city depended on the health and well being of the shoe and boot industry.

The monstrous W.L. Douglas Shoe factory in Montello and the equally gargantuan complex of George E. Keith in Campello were the two bookends of the business. In between were wedged all of the other players. Some of these factories were well-established firms and worthy competitors—like M.A. Packard and Stacy, Adams—always nipping at the heels of the two giants. Others were small, upstarts with a yearly production of only a small fraction of what the top shoemakers produced.

For the visiting salesmen and purchasing agents, eleven substantial hotels offered lodging at Centerville—the old name for the area around the crossroads at Main and Center Streets. For the resident population, there were another seventy-one establishments that fell into the category of hotel-apartments. Catering mostly to the needs of the business class, the city boasted more than thirty-five restaurants.

There were already more than 11,000 residential properties in Brockton and home ownership had skyrocketed to more than 50 percent of the population—well above the national average of 42 percent. Furthermore, 80 percent of the homes in the city were owned by people directly or indirectly involved in the shoes industry. Ice and coal companies ensured a level of comfort in homes unknown in the less developed areas of the state. Skilled shoe workers—at least in 1908—were oblivious to the enticements used to lure shoe factories to distant locales because a skilled shoe worker could always find work.

In many ways, Brockton was a city in transition. There were already 236 automobiles crawling and backfiring along the wide boulevards, signaling the slow move away from horse-drawn buggies. Even so, there were still more than 700 residents who owned horses and 16 blacksmiths, all somehow convinced that the motorcar was just a passing fad. Most factory workers owned neither though, relying instead on electric streetcars that, for a nickel, would transport them anywhere in the city. Also, the Old Colony Street Railroad ran the length of Brockton, with stations at Montello (in the north), Centerville (downtown) and Campello (in the south).

On any given day, the downtown-shopping district bustled with people, who descended on Centerville for every consumer good under the sun. There were women—or alternatively, their domestic servants—shopping for produce and meats at the Brockton Public Market or any of the other 32 retail markets dealing in household provisions. This did not even include the 172 small corner groceries sprinkled throughout the city or the 36 purveyors of fresh fruit. For patrons who insisted on fresh bread and fancy confections of a more delectable nature, there were 17 bakeries, each catering to one of the city's major ethnic minorities—Irish, Swedish, Italian, Greek, Czechoslovakian and a dozen smaller groups.

Downtown in Centerville, a person might make a mortgage payment at any of the 7 banks, settle a bill at the Edison Electric Illuminating Company or the Southern Massachusetts Telephone & Telegraph Company, which boasted "direct connection could be made with all of the primary towns and cities of the Northeast and states east of the Mississippi River."[117] Telephones in homes were not exactly ubiquitous, but pay phones were abundant, with more than a 100 wired up in markets, stores and hotels. (In the first decade and a half of the 1900s, long distance phone calls were still a shouting match until vacuum tube amplification was invented in 1915.)

Befitting such a large slice of humanity, 31 medical doctors and 34 dentists met the health needs of the city's residents, and there were also a smattering of osteopaths and homeopaths. Filling the prescriptions of these professional healers were the pharmacists at 21 drugstores.

For the well-dressed woman, the great department stores and smaller specialty shops—fanning north and south from the corner of Center and Main—were a thief's Eden of fashion. Edgar's was the largest and most exclusive department store with Frazer's Dry Goods, B. E. Jones & Company, J. T. McWeeney and H. W. Robinson enjoying an impressive following as well. The most modern hairstyles could be had at any of 60 hairdressing shops, while 114 dressmakers and 35 milliners enjoyed a cushy living from the revenues provided by their own specialties.

Firms fought for the lucrative business of moving hordes of shoppers and businessmen around Brockton. About this time, a rogue group of jitneymen swarmed into the city intent on making a killing. In defense, the Eastern Massachusetts Street Railway informed Brockton officials that it would cease operating its trolley cars if the jitneys were allowed to continue their ill-conceived efforts. Without the trolleys, business would suffer, so the board of aldermen and the mayor quickly revoked the licenses of all service automobiles operating in Brockton.[118]

The newly formed McCue & Cahill theatrical firm brought the first nickelodeon to Brockton in 1906 and only three years later, 10 theaters flooded the town with silent movies. These early movies featured no stars, assigning credit to directors like D.W. Griffith, who produced his first movie, *The Adventures of Dollie,* for the Biograph Film Studio. Offerings by the other theaters in Brockton were almost interchangeable—and jumpy—melodramas. Those who resisted these amusements could play billiards at any of the 20 pool halls in town or pick among 3 bowling palaces.

Golf was relatively new to American shores, but Brockton embraced the sport whole-heartedly. The first nine-hole course in town was the Brockton Country Club, located in Campello. By 1908, the Thorny Lea Golf Club—in the western part of the city—offered an eighteen-hole layout.

The tremendous commercialization that Brockton enjoyed was not without its hardships. Steam power, produced by enormous steam boilers, made extraordinary levels of shoe and boot production possible. Generally, these massive boilers were dependable but, in the wrong hands, they could be deadly.

Occasional boiler explosions killed dozens of workers and injured hundreds of others.

Georgietta Reed, the widow of John Reed, a shoe worker, employed Dehlia Sullivan as a domestic. Mrs. Reed lived just off Main Street at 203 West Elm Street. The Irish were good at helping their own. Mary Ann Sullivan could stay with Dehlia as long as needed. Just as in the shoe industry, employers wanted to vet new workers in person. Therefore, until Mary Ann Sullivan got to Brockton, she couldn't line up a job. Thanks to Agnes Kilfoyle, she understood the game and began a job search immediately after she was settled.

Traditionally there were almost always more Irish women emigrating than men. In the early 1900s, there were about 36 percent more females than males. By the 1920s, there were twice as many young women as men.

As impartible inheritance took hold in Ireland, the chances of marriage grew slimmer. The farm went to only one son, and the rest were reduced to laborers or forced to emigrate. Either way, young Irish women didn't consider these men marriageable. In the interregnum between the Great Hunger and the First World War, the number of Irish marriages dropped by half. Not surprisingly, women married later—if at all.

However, the vast number of Irish girls flooding into America created problems because so few were educated or skilled. In the mid-1800's, almost 75 percent of these girls became servants. By 1900, Irish girls comprised about 54 percent of the domestics in New England and another 7 percent of the laundresses. In the year that Mary Ann Sullivan first set foot on American soil, Irish-American children in Fall River—just thirty miles south of Brockton—produced 45 percent of their families' incomes, largely through labor in local textile mills. The situation was not much different in Brockton where whole departments of shoe factories—for example, the last room where the wooden lasts were pulled from great bins for use and later restocked—were the domains of young boys.

In 1908, 18 percent of all the households in America had domestic servants. Maybe because of this staggering competition, Mary Ann Sullivan's first job interview was at Brockton Hospital, where she hoped to learn nursing. Sadly, sixteen was too young and she was dismissively told to try again the following year. Well and good, but in the meantime she had to make a living. Reassessing domestic service, she eventually landed a job for a couple in their mid-thirties—J.J. and Ellen Cahill.[119]

Although she didn't know it at the time, she had hit the jackpot. Firstly, the Cahills were as Irish as Paddy's pig except that they had arrived in America one generation earlier than Mary Ann Sullivan. This gave them a certain connection not found in the "old North Bridgewater Yankees," more recently dubbed the "Brockton Four Hundred." Secondly, unlike so many Protestant women, who expected their domestics to work from six in the morning until late in the evening, the Cahills were infinitely less demanding. Lastly, the Cahills were lovable people who treated her more like a daughter than a servant. Over the next twelve years, Mary Ann Sullivan worked for J.J. and Ellen Cahill and found a level of kindness that few immigrants experienced.

The Cahills remain something of an enigma in the story of Mary Ann Sullivan, her husband Denis Murphy, and their three sons, because they popped in and out of the Murphys' lives with such astounding regularity. This is particularly true of J.J. Cahill. As Mary Ann Sullivan's story unfolds, we will see some truly uncanny coincidences that, in a fast-moving, crowded city like Brockton, are downright stupefying.

John Joseph Cahill and Katherine (Ellen) Clark were both from Wisconsin, but from altogether different backgrounds. J.J. Cahill's Irish immigrant father, Patrick, was a day laborer, while his mother, Mary, kept house in Fond du Lac—located about half way between Milwaukee and Green Bay. Patrick Cahill, with a wife and five children, was tangled in the machinations of relocating his eighty-four-year-old mother, Kate, and his brother's family from Ireland to Wisconsin. Michael Cahill (the brother) and his wife, Ellen, had five children and this crushing mass of humanity eventually shoehorned its way into Patrick Cahill's tiny house on Cedar Street in Fond du Lac. John Joseph was six-years-old during what might be termed the "Cahill family's stockyard period." J.J. wasn't particularly put off by the close quarters, but the circumstances must surely have oppressed the adults.

Conversely, Katherine Cahill's father, John J. Clark, was an Irish immigrant who sailed to America in 1841. A born hustler,

J.J. Clark quickly opened his own dry goods store and built up an impressive estate. J.J. and his wife, Margaret Ellen, had four daughters—May, Katherine, Camille and Estelle. By the turn of the century, J.J. Clark had matured into a "capitalist" and added two servants to the family's lavish home at 615 East Avenue, Waukesha (just east of Milwaukee). The four Clark girls were showered with the finest clothes that Waukesha dressmakers could produce, they dined in style, and stayed single—and in the bosom of luxury—right through their twenties.[120]

J.J. Clark may have been born in Ireland, but Margaret Ellen (Haster) Clark was born in New York and her people were from Germany. They weren't Prussian nobility, but what little is known about Margaret Haster suggests that she was to the manner born.

Katherine "Ellen" Clark eventually gravitated toward a place more exciting than Waukesha, Wisconsin. In fact, she relocated to New York. In the early 1900s, she met another energetic, self-possessed J.J. from Wisconsin—J.J. Cahill. In New York, the two enjoyed an on-again, off-again relationship for the next half-dozen years.

After graduating from high school in Fond du Lac, J.J. Cahill lit out for New York to study music and receive vocal training. After two years of this specialized schooling, he partnered with another Irishman, John W. McCue, and took to the stage. McCue & Cahill worked vaudeville's Keith Circuit.

Benjamin Franklin Keith created the vaudeville circuit, opening a number of theaters for performing artists beginning in 1882. The "King of Vaudeville," opened a theater just outside New York City and over the next forty years, this single vaudeville house would evolve into the nation's largest single theater chain—the Keith-Albee-Orpheum Circuit.

J.J. Cahill was a round-faced, bigger-than-life Irishman, who might have continued on the gritty Keith-Albee-Orpheum vaudeville circuit, but while he was in New York, he saw his first Kinetoscope. These flickering "shorts" changed everyone's life in a small way, but they changed J.J. Cahill's life in socko-boffo fashion. Sensing correctly that his future a singer was limited—and that vaudeville was about to undergo a sea change—he heard the sweet *lieder* of Lorelei and seized the opportunity of a lifetime.

The earliest "movies" burst on the American scene after Thomas Edison invented the Kinetoscope in 1891. The earliest promoters chose to debut these movies in New York because of its huge audiences. From the get-go, the business was a declasse affair. Slowly, movie houses evolved from grimy, back alley joints to slick, upscale theaters. The Kinescopes flickered away for under a minute, featuring shorts, films and documentaries. The public couldn't get enough of them. Predictably, vaudeville and the new movie houses locked in a fight to the death. In just a few years, the nickel theaters—nickelodeons—replaced vaudeville shows. In the nickelodeon houses, the films were taken from a dreary pile of dramas, comedies, and documentaries. Between films, an energetic piano player worked up a sweat in an attempt to keep patrons in their seats.

Fortunately, Edison sensed that the public would tire of the Kinetoscope and followed with the Vitascope projector. The new projectors overtook Kinescopes and eventually movies got longer. Holding on for dear life in the sub-basement of the new movie business, the Kinescope houses where—now for a penny—offering viewers sixty-seconds of time-wasting nonsense.

Meanwhile, new film studios—Vitagraph, Biograph, Selig and Lubin—began to crank out feature films. By 1917, there were 500 projectors in America. During the age of the silent films, studios paid actors a mere $5 a day. This petty wage held until moviegoers fell in love with Mary Pickford. This opened a Pandora's box of fan clubs, perks, escalating salaries—you name it. Theater owners were up against it.

In Haverhill, Massachusetts—the largest slipper-producing city in the world—Louis B. Mayer kept his little theater immaculate, sweeping the floors and cleaning the seats every night after the main show. Still, nickelodeons were only a segue between vaudeville and movie palaces.

The nascent film companies graduated to feature-length productions, and suddenly the palatial movie house blossomed. Starting with New York's Strand, movie houses began to outdo the splendor of the opera houses of a bygone era. As theaters became more ornate and lively, the nickelodeon houses died.

In 1906, J.J. Cahill saw the nickelodeon and never looked back. Convinced that the movie business was an idea whose time had come, he talked John McCue into joining him in a nickelodeon house. Understanding J.J.'s astute business sense, John McCue readily agreed. In New York, however, there was a nickelodeon house on every street corner. Where would they set up?

As McCue & Cahill searched for a home, Louis B. Mayer's operation in Haverhill, Massachusetts came into focus. J.J. Cahill knew that Mayer was on the right track, but J.J. also knew that he didn't want to compete with Mayer. J.J. Cahill's elusive dream city had to have a moneyed population—with an overarching desire to spend. The shoe manufacturing cities of Massachusetts were naturals. The Boot and Shoe Union guaranteed good wages and also ensured that workers only worked forty hours a week. But what shoe city would it be? Haverhill meant Louis B. Mayer and Lynn was too close to downtown Boston. Among the really big shoe cities, that left Brockton. Since John McCue was born in Brockton, it was an easy reach for J.J. Cahill.

Brockton was indeed the logical place. In 1906, the city had a population of 45,000 and the shoe industry appeared still on the rise, with 100 factories running at peak production. With all those workers bringing home an average of $18.75 a week, and plenty of free time to spend it, how could McCue & Cahill lose?

Wonder of wonders though, there was only three theaters in Brockton. The first was the old Opera House on Main and East Elm Streets. Built in 1884, it was a glitzy place with twin balconies and perhaps two-dozen private loges on the sidewalls. The place was dripping with ornate plaster moldings and *trompe l'oeil* accoutrements. Despite the panache, it was too cavernous for movies. The second playhouse was the relatively new City Theater on Main Street, which offered a revolving collection of tiresome stage dramas. Both theaters offered seats from 25¢ up to $1.50. Sheedy's Theater, the last outpost of entertainment in the city, was a small wooden vaudeville house tucked between much larger buildings—for all intents and purposes on all four sides. Patrons used entrances and egresses that fed to alleys between the other structures. Sheedy's only charged 10¢ a show and was lucky to get that. Could Brockton accommodate a nickelodeon, where a shoe worker could have some fun for 5¢?

Packing their bags, the two entrepreneurs headed for Massachusetts, rented the first floor of the Ancient Order of Hibernians Hall at 52 Ward Street, installed their nickelodeon machines, and attached a large McCue & Cahill sign to the front of the building. As the first movies in Brockton, they were a huge hit. Without exaggerating, the nickelodeons were like one-arm bandits. For 5¢ a patron could see either a moving picture or a talking book. As an added attraction—and so the partners would not have to pay a piano player—audiences got to hear John McCue and J.J. Cahill sing along with the illustrated pictures. Not long after their debut, the crush of business forced the pair to open an annex across the street. The two amusement venues proved a license to print money.

McCue & Cahill moved into Brockton at just the right time— ahead of the competition by a single year. By 1907, there were two more nickelodeons—Bullock & Davis and the Nickel Theater. The following year, the Hathaway Theater joined the fray. Each year, another movie theater set up shop in Brockton. Still and all, for a time the nickelodeon business was fine and the partners slowly graduated to legitimate movie houses.

When he first arrived in Brockton, J.J. Cahill boarded in different locations around the city, including but not limited to, 10 Central Square and 148 Lyman Street. His last rent was in a triple-decker at 48 Warren Avenue. In early 1909, thirty-seven-year-old J.J. Cahill finally married Katherine "Ellen" Clark, who was a year younger. Nine months later, baby Margaret arrived. Given Ellen Cahill's cushy background, an infant meant household help— simple as that. Before baby Margaret even made her appearance, Mary Ann Sullivan hired on as the Cahill's new cleaning lady, diaper changer, governess, food shopper, and cook.

Meanwhile, John McCue met a Brockton girl, Grace Kennedy, and the two were married in 1908. Grace's father was Canadian— her mother was born in Massachusetts—but the family was still in Canada when Grace was born in 1875. By and by, the family drifted down to Brockton so James Kennedy could get a high-paying shoe factory job.

Based solely on talent, John McCue would have died a painful death on stage, but instead became wealthy in the theater business. With money pouring in, he bought an interest in the Brockton

New England baseball team. Local baseball teams are irresistible temptations for those who love the game, but they are also monumentally bad investments. John McCue learned this lesson the hard way.

McCue & Cahill Amusements Company took over the management of Hathaway's Theater in 1912. As their movie business expanded into ever-grander theaters, J.J Cahill swam with the flow. Continuing his natural proclivity to lead the pack, J.J. Cahill became manager of the most prestigious movie house in Brockton, City Theater, only a couple of blocks away from his nickelodeon house. J.J.'s early entry into the nickelodeon business taught him management skills that were rare and the rewards never stopped flowing his way.

In 1915, the partners converted their nickelodeon house on Ward Street to a legitimate theater, hoping to recapture the business that they were losing to the other nine theaters now operating in Brockton.

Times were booming. In 1916, J.J. Cahill concentrated on managing other theaters while John McCue held down the fort on Ward Street. As J.J. Cahill managed the Hathaway and the City theaters, he began to manage a third theater—the Strand Theatre on School Street, which he ran until 1925. The Strand was a new theater although it occupied the same site where Sheedy's vaudeville theater once did business. After Sheedy's folded, the Empire Playhouse used the site until a fire of mysterious origin destroyed the place. Showing enormous talent, J.J. managed the Strand, the Hathaway and the City theaters at the same time. In business, J.J. Cahill mimicked a perpetual motion machine.

The Hathaway Theatre was small compared to the new houses opening in downtown Brockton and, as a result, had difficulty turning a profit. This coincided with the public's slackening interest in McCue & Cahill's little theater on Ward Street. Apparently, the theater-going public never truly accepted it as the real thing and the partners had no choice but to close it down. The public's antipathy toward the Ward Street operation matched John McCue's flagging interest in the movie business. In 1919, the Hathaway Theater—never really able to compete with the larger theaters in the city—was sold for the land, and hoping for greener pastures, John W. McCue and his wife, Grace, moved to Boston.

J.J. Cahill never missed a beat. Managing the City and the Strand theaters, he kept his ear to the ground for opportunities.

By the mid-twenties, the owners of the City Theatre decided to build another movie palace, and the sky was the limit. Nothing short of the finest theater in Brockton would do. The twenties were the years of the grand spectacle theater—spacious lobbies swathed in lush, gaudy carpeting, mirrors everywhere, and huge multiple balconies. The twenties saw keen competition too, as a dozen theaters now slugged it out in the shoe city. To ensure success—and premium ticket prices—the company had secured a fabulous location at 184 Main Street (near Crescent Street), right in the heart of the entertainment district. However, managing the new Brockton Theater would be a full time job, leaving no time for J.J. Cahill to run the City and the Strand theaters. To assuage J.J., the Brockton Theatre consortium gave him an even larger stake in the new theater. J.J. Cahill managed the Brockton Theatre for the rest of his life.

The Cahills had an aversion when it came to proper names and settled on comfortable nicknames instead. John Joseph was universally called J.J., and his wife Katherine, who was baptized Catherine, preferred the name Ellen—her mother's middle name. (It's possible that John J. Clark called his wife Ellen and that's why Katherine Cahill liked the name so much, but this is just speculation.) Whatever the circumstances, she was always called Ellen.

Starting in 1910, there were some changes in the Cahill household. To begin, the family moved to an ark of a house at 51 Highland Terrace, on the more fashionable west side of town. Roughly coinciding with this move, Ellen Cahill gave birth to her second child, Mary. Finally, three years afterward, she had a son, John Clark, named after the boy's father and maternal grandfather. He went by the name Clark to avoid confusion. All the while, the Cahills continued to live in the lap of luxury, as J.J Cahill managed the Brockton Theatre and his stock in the company rose quite nicely through the years.

He and his wife, Ellen, had Mary Ann to mind the house and a chauffeur to drive J.J. on his rounds during his busy workdays and nights. The job of theater manager was no soft sinecure. His business activities ran seven days a week and required J.J. to work

114

until midnight almost every day of the year. Lest anyone shed a tear for J.J Cahill, the money he made more than compensated for the hours. For instance, at the tail end of the Great Depression— when factory workers could barely get nine months work and brought home about $700 a year—J.J. Cahill made more than $5000 annually.[121]

Mary Ann Sullivan never took out naturalization papers during the twelve years that she worked for the Cahills. The laws regarding naturalization were an odd mix in 1908—and, for that matter, still are. Before 1906, an alien could become a citizen by merely taking an oath, but after that time, federal laws required a candidate to appear before a court, prove some level of dexterity with the English language, and answer questions on American history and the Constitution. With this small change, the naturalization process usually took five years.

The first step for an alien, who had resided in the U. S. at least two years, was to file a Declaration of Intent with a court. Three years later, the alien could file a form, Petition for Naturalization, with the same court. Assuming the requisite facility with the English language and a passing knowledge of American history, the immigrant won a Certificate of Naturalization. Under these conditions, many immigrants postponed citizenship indefinitely.

Mary Ann Sullivan never became a naturalized citizen in her own right for several reasons. To start, if she were to marry— which was her hope—she would automatically become a citizen if her spouse were one. From 1790-1922, wives of naturalized men automatically became citizens, and women who married naturalized men automatically became citizens too. (Curiously enough, American women who married aliens automatically became aliens, even if they remained in the U.S.) Mary Ann Sullivan's children would automatically become citizens if she married a naturalized citizen. From 1790-1940, children under age twenty-one automatically became naturalized citizens upon the naturalization of their father, which is how her future husband, Denis P. Murphy, became a citizen.

Along a different line, if she tired of America and decided to return to Ireland, any efforts to obtain a naturalized U.S. citizenship would have been a waste of time. Finally, inasmuch as the government allowed aliens to stay as long as they liked without obtaining citizenship, there was obviously no reason for her to rush a decision in the matter.

Chapter 3

More Sullivans Emigrate

Other Sullivans followed Dehlia and Mary Ann to America, as Michael Sullivan of Derrylea forwarded his plan. Words like love, family, home, hearth, security—that are tossed about so freely in wealthy countries—were obviously missing from the lives of those left to cope with an abandoned Ireland. From a land of plenty, it's perhaps difficult to understand what a golden opportunity Michael Sullivan forced upon his children.

On April 21, 1909, the *Ivernia* once again left Queenstown Harbor for Boston. It had begun its voyage at Liverpool the day before and left the harbor in mid-afternoon. On board was Mary Ann Sullivan's older sister, Katherine, known to everyone as Katie. The ship's manifest even wrote her name officially as Katie Sullivan and recorded her age as 18. Her sister, Dehlia, paid for her ticket, and she had only $5 in her pocket. She stood smaller than the other Sullivan girls, just five-foot-four, but had the same fair complexion, fair hair and blue eyes.

Katie Sullivan was a "servant" and could read and write English, although her spoken words were thick with an Irish accent. Katie was withdrawn compared to her siblings and barely said a word to anyone.

She planned to travel with her cousin, Thomas Lyons, also of a townland near Ballyhaunis, but for some inexplicable reason he did not board the ship. His name was crossed off the passenger list, with no reason given for his change in plan. Katie recorded that she expected to stay at the home of Dehlia Sullivan at 203

West Elm Street, where Dehlia still worked as a domestic for the widow, Georgietta Reed.

Katie worked as a domestic servant for a time, and then on Saturday, October 12, 1929, she married a Brockton native, John J. Ennis, at Saint Patrick's Church. Katherine was thirty-nine, the same age as her betrothed. John Ennis began his work life as a leather sorter in a shoe factory. He later drove a truck for an oil company and then a coal firm in Brockton. A few years later, the couple moved to Hillside Circle in Somerville, Massachusetts, where John Ennis was a foreman for a sewage company. Financially, he never did very well. For example, in the late 1930s, when a teacher's annual salary was $1400, John Ennis made $730.

Later, when Mary Ann Sullivan was married and had children, her youngest child, Ed, roomed with John and Katie Ennis while he was an undergrad at Tufts College. Although he adored Katie, he did not get on well with John Ennis, whom he considered a "narrowback." (Irish immigrants built many of America's aqueducts, canals, railroads, and bridges; they were especially prized for their broad backs, so it was an insult of the highest order to call an Irish-American a "narrowback.")

John and Katie never had children, and after John died in late 1953, Katie went back to Brockton to live with her younger sister, Mary Ann, at 551 Warren Avenue. She stayed for almost six years, at which time Mary Ann sold the Warren Avenue property to a Greek couple named Deftos. Katie then purchased her own home on Green Street (behind the Central Fire House). She lived there until her death in 1964 at seventy-four and was buried in St. Patrick's Cemetery.

The next of the Sullivans to emigrate was Norah who was born in September 1894 and made the crossing in 1912. She was seventeen at the time of the voyage and embarked from Queenstown Harbor on a different Cunard Liner, the *RMS Laconia*. (It was around this time that Cunard Lines reassigned the *SS Ivernia* to their Hungarian-American routes.) The *Laconia* was another steel-hulled, twin-screw steamer, launched the previous year. It was slightly longer than the *Ivernia* at 600 feet. The only significant differences between the ships were that the *Laconia* weighed 30 percent more and required 35 percent more horsepower to achieve the same lackluster speed. In truth, the

Laconia was a typical Cunarder, utterly dependable as it plowed through the North Atlantic at an underwhelming sixteen knots.

Norah's father paid for her ticket, although the funds probably came from Dehlia, Mary Ann, and Katie in America. Norah was of nobler estate than her sisters when they emigrated. She had $20 in her pocket. Other than that, she resembled her sisters. Norah was taller though at five-eight-and-a-half, but had the same Sullivan blue eyes. One distinguishing feature though was her hair—just as light as blonde hair could get. The clerk at the embarkation station even went to the trouble of recording her hair color as "Ivory." Of the 300 passengers in the hold of the *Laconia*, she was the only one whose hair garnered such a *beau mot* from the registration agent.

The passage to America had become routine by now, and with her confidence boosted by letters from America, Norah needed no traveling companions from Derrylea or the surrounding townlands. To a person, those who knew her remember Norah as a confident, strong-willed young woman. This may be the reason Michael Sullivan let her ship out alone. If the *Laconia* had left Queenstown even a day later, a shocking bit of news concerning another ship might have made Norah's voyage a little bit more worrisome.

On April 14, 1912 while Norah Sullivan walked up the gangplank of the *Laconia*, another drama was about to unfold in the posh cabins and elaborate dining saloons of a different steamship plying the waters of the North Atlantic—the White Star Line's new *RMS Titanic*.[122]

On her maiden voyage, the *Titanic*—the most luxurious addition to the White Star fleet—had left Southampton, England on April 10, 1912 at noon. The ship reached Cherbourg, France at 6:30 P.M. and embarked more passengers. At 8:10 P.M., it left for Queenstown, Ireland. On the morning of April 11, it embarked more travelers—mostly Irish emigrants—who brought the total number in third-class to 709. (At 1317 total passengers, the *RMS Titanic* was only half booked because of scheduling changes brought on by a coal strike in the U.K.) The ship left Queenstown on April 11 at 1:30 in the afternoon.

As Norah Sullivan made herself comfortable in the aft-steerage women's dormitory of the *Laconia*, the well-heeled passengers of the White Star Line's mightiest Goliath were about to enjoy a sumptuous lunch. At the time, the *Titanic* was clipping along at 22 knots and was about 100 miles southeast of the Grand Banks off Newfoundland.

After a bland supper in the third-class compartment, Norah Sullivan kibitzed with the other passengers and slowly quieted down after the most exciting day of her young life. Eventually, she climbed into a cheerless bunk and nodded off to sleep. While Norah slept, the *Titanic* hit an iceberg at 11:40 P.M. on April 14. People scrambled for the few lifeboats available, but just a third of the passengers could be saved. (Only a quarter of the third-class passengers survived.)

About two and a half hours later, at 2:20 A.M. on April 15, the White Star Line's "unsinkable" *Titanic* dipped beneath the waves en route to the bottom of the ocean. Six and a half days after the disaster, the *Laconia* passed within miles of the spot where 1514 passengers and crew lost their lives in a steamship disaster that has become synonymous with unimaginable catastrophes of all sorts. Among the wealthy passengers to die when the *Titanic* went down were American millionaires John Jacob Astor, Benjamin Guggenheim, and Isidor Straus.

Timing is everything. Had Norah Sullivan arrived at Queenstown three days ahead of schedule, she could have exchanged tickets and sailed on the *Titanic*. Or Michael Sullivan could have chosen the newer, faster and more luxurious *RMS Titanic* for Norah instead of the *RMS Laconia*. As of this writing, there is an untold number of Irish-Americans who owe their lives to a fractious Irish farmer, Michael Sullivan, who for his own hardheaded reasons, stuck with Cunard and its enviable safety record, rather than switch to the White Star Line's posh *Titanic*.

On April 22, 1912—eight days after leaving Queenstown— Norah Sullivan, walked buoyantly down the *Laconia's* gangplank to a new life in America. She landed a job doing housework and lived at 888 Montello Street. In 1917, after five years in domestic service, she married Cleveland McGee, who was born in Augusta, Maine, but now hailed from Rockland, Massachusetts. The ceremony took place on September 26, 1917 in the rectory of St. Edward's Church on East Main Street in Brockton. Cleveland and Nora (Sullivan) McGee had six children.[123]

During the First World War, Cleveland McGee registered for the draft on June 5, 1917 and was described as "short, with a medium build, brown eyes, and brown hair." The draft registration records indicate that he was working as a chauffeur. By the time he married Norah in September, he was a "bridgeman." In 1920, he had become a "meat cutter" in a butcher shop. Obviously, Cleveland McGee was born under a wandering star.[124]

Norah & Cleveland McGee

Sadly, Cleveland McGee's marriage to Norah Sullivan did not last. In the mid-1930s, Cleveland McGee abandoned Norah and their six children. Norah and the children lived on the razor's edge of starvation after that. For example, in 1939, Norah had no work and didn't earn a dime the whole year. She did however, "receive money other than wages or salary." Whether or not this means that Cleveland McGee contributed to the family's upkeep is not known. A stronger possibility is that money came from the

Murphys and Sullivans. (The clachan Irish would heap scorn on one who refused to care for his own!)[125]

After the Great Depression, there isn't much known about Cleveland McGee. One story is that an older man in Rockland, Massachusetts once asked the young Cleveland McGee, Jr. if he would like to meet his father. Nodding his head yes, the older man said, "He's standing right next to you!"[126] The few records that exist suggest that Cleveland McGee completely dropped off the radar until his death on November 1, 1969 in Falmouth, Massachusetts. He was seventy-six.

Mary Ann Sullivan's remaining siblings—Patrick, Helen and Michael—came to America when they were in their late teens or early twenties. Patrick arrived in 1926 and stayed for part of 1927. Denis and Mary Ann (Sullivan) Murphy put him up at their home on Forest Avenue. Although he stayed in America for more than a year, he returned to Ireland and married May Doyle soon thereafter. They had three sons.[127]

Helen Sullivan, the seventh child of Michael and Bridget Sullivan, sailed to America and arrived in Brockton a little while after her brother Patrick. Helen thought America was fine, but didn't like Brockton. It's possible that she didn't like her siblings much either. On the other hand, maybe the cold weather was more than she could bear. For whatever reason, she went alone to California where she worked a number of different jobs, including on an assembly line in an airplane factory during the Second World War. She never married and returned to New England for her last few years. She stayed with Ed and Kate Murphy in Windsor, Connecticut, and later entered a convalescent home in Wethersfield, Connecticut, where she died on September 10, 1994. She was ninety-six.

The last of Michael and Bridget Sullivan's children was Michael who sailed for America about 1925. There have always been rumors to the effect that Michael Sullivan was forced to emigrate because of his activities with the Irish Republican Army (IRA). These stories claim that Michael was particularly active against the Black and Tans—British soldiers who were brought into Ireland after 1918 to augment the Royal Irish Constabulary (RIC)—during the Irish War of Independence (Jan 1919-July 1921). Supposedly, Michael was forced to sleep in the fields at night as his activities escalated. Michael was between the ages of seventeen and nineteen during the war, and certainly could have been involved. But Michael Sullivan—just like his favorite nephew Ed Murphy—preferred to keep his mouth closed regarding these rumors.

The Irish War of Independence was a guerilla war and there were ambushes and killings all over Ireland. In 1920, the East Mayo Brigade of the I. R. A. fought the Black and Tans regularly. Whether or not Michael Sullivan was involved, we will never know.

In America, Michael ("Uncle Mike") always boarded in Boston. In 1940, it was on Massachusetts Avenue. With only a sixth grade education, Michael worked as a freight handler at a railroad depot and probably considered himself lucky to get that position. He never married, and during 1939—as the Great Depression slowly wound down—he was only able to get thirty-five weeks of work and was paid $700. This annual salary sits at the lower end of the national pay scale and Uncle Mike never did much better. For a full 52 weeks, a laborer at the Post Office made $1600 and a machinist in a shipyard earned $2100. Uncle Mike's classification as a naturalized citizen—and his registration for the draft on October 8, 1942—were probably the highpoints of his early life in America. Then again, maybe not.

Bob Murphy once said that Uncle Mike was drafted when he was about forty and "the government couldn't do a damn thing with him." Apparently, they just sent him home. The Irish who applied themselves in America had a low opinion of those who did not. Bob Murphy once made a pejorative comparison between "those who got serious in America and those, like Uncle Mike, who didn't." Michael Sullivan died in Boston on February 22, 1978 at seventy-six.[128]

Dehlia Sullivan, the oldest child of Michael and Bridget Sullivan, and the sister who welcomed Mary Ann Sullivan when she first arrived in Brockton, only stayed in America a short time. She returned to Ireland and married an Irishman, Pat Moran. Together they had four children.[129]

Pat and Dehlia Moran eventually inherited the family farm in Derrylea and built a modern house in front of the old stone hut where the Sullivan children were reared. (Author's note: By using the maps in this book as a guide, Google Earth-Street View will show the reader the new house and the old stone cottage on the fourteen-acre strip of land in Derrylea that Michael and Bridget Sullivan rented—and ultimately purchased—from Viscount Dillon. Readers can also view the Derrylea School at the far west side of Derrylea townland.)

The tensions in Europe—as World War I became a foregone conclusion—changed the fortunes for Cunard and its competitors on the North Atlantic routes. No longer would those mighty carriers ply the frigid water unfettered by anything more than rough seas and bad weather. As the different liners were pressed into service as troopships and cargo ships, German U-boats hunted them down like wounded animals, determined to bring the allies to their knees. The once comfortable *Ivernia* which had ferried three of the Sullivan girls to America, brought her last load of emigrants to the new world in March 1912. For more than two years, the ship was reassigned to the company's Hungarian-American routes connecting New York with Funchal, Naples, Palermo, Messina, Trieste and Fiume.

The *Ivernia* was requisitioned by the English government as a troop ship in September 1914 and later served as a prison ship (along with the *Saxonia, Andania* and *Ascania*) in 1915. Still later in the war, the ship was employed as a transport ship to India and the Mediterranean. The once tastefully appointed, steel-hulled ship was sunk by the German submarine U-47, fifty-eight miles off Cape Mattapan, Greece, on New Year's Day 1917, with the loss of 200 lives. Commanding the *Ivernia* was Captain William T. Turner, who was at the helm of the *Lusitania* when it was sunk off the Old Head of Kinsale, Ireland in May 1915. (Author's note: Capt. Turner was saved, along with 700 of the 2000 passengers when the *Lusitania* was sunk in 1915, and also survived the sinking of the *Ivernia* in 1917. He died in June 1933.)

Chapter 4

Early Days in Brockton

Mary Ann Sullivan was just one of hundreds of thousands of unskilled Irish women who traveled to America in search of work as domestic servants and housekeepers. Few of these Irish emigrants had enough education to qualify as schoolteachers, nurses, typists, bookkeepers or secretaries. Further dogging the efforts of these women, was the enormous cultural divide between their mother's kitchens and parlors in stone or mud cottages in the poorest parts of Ireland and the more affluent households where they hoped to find employment in America. Potential employers knew that the young women would have to be trained from scratch and their wages reflected their lack of skills. It should be noted, however, that domestic servants received room and board, and the money earned annually was more than they had ever seen before.

Still, the pay was less than they could have earned in industry. For this reason, in Brockton, women worked in great numbers in the shoe factories, doing work that was more suited to them than to men. They were particularly good at the demanding detail work of the stitching room, and they could grade and box shoes as well as the men; the jobs of secretaries and bookkeepers were, of course, a natural fit for women as well.

Perhaps put off by the comments of Agnes Kilfoyle or her sister Dehlia, Mary Ann Sullivan had no interest at all in working in the shoe factories. This is not so shocking when one considers the number of men and women who found the work hard, monotonous and even depressing. As if the work itself wasn't difficult enough, there were periods of the year when business slowed to the point where layoffs were necessary. The first such time was in the spring, but the month of July was the worst, with layoffs of three to eight weeks a constant concern. This held especially true of the smaller shoe shops. The larger factories— with the ability to offer discounts and rewards on early purchases—were able to book large enough orders to carry their workers through the slow times. Still, the uncertainty of the work augured for a high turnover rate accompanied by the alcoholism that is so typical of blue-collar factory towns.

Unskilled Irish workers benefited mightily from preexisting Irish-American secret organizations, such as the Ancient Order of Hibernians and the Massachusetts Catholic Order of Foresters. Perhaps even more important were the tight-knit Irish neighborhoods, which harkened back to the clachan Irish by placing enormous importance on family ties. These support groups were wide-ranging in their ability to meet the needs of the transplanted Irish. They were involved in the economic, political, educational needs of the Irish people and were centered usually on the local Roman Catholic Church. Attendant to these other functions were those of the church's charitable arm, which provided a safety net for the less fortunate or the families of the victims of industrial accidents—of which there were many.

In Brockton, Mary Ann Sullivan, in a way, found refuge in the Foster Street Gang, because her employers, J.J. and Ellen Cahill, lived originally at 48 Warren Avenue, only a few blocks north of the families from western Ireland, particularly Counties Mayo and Kerry. Such a neighborhood eased her transition into the clamorous industrial city where the screaming factory whistles signaled the cadence for the average family. The Cahill's triple-decker apartment sat comfortably on the northern fringes of the Foster Hill Gang, settled comfortably in and around the small streets just west of Centerville, and all of the homes and factories within a quarter mile radius of City Hall.

This neighborhood spared many Irish emigrants what some perceived as the biggest change of all—a complete break with a communal life that valued relationships among kin. Often, the concern for neighbors, so rich in the customs and traditions of western Ireland, accounted for little in a society that valued money so much. While emigrants generally went out of their way to help those who remained back in Ireland with money and help in emigration matters, even this longstanding practice vitiated after a few years in America. The hardworking domestic or shoe worker, caught up in the struggle to survive in an alien world, lost interest in those back home in Ireland.

The Irish who settled near Boston had one last support—their own Irish newspaper, *The Pilot*, published since 1829. Originally run by laymen like Patrick Donohoe, the paper's founder; later, Catholic priests took control. Besides its obvious function of keeping the Irish-Americans informed, *The Pilot* served as an agent in the transfer of funds back to Ireland. Initially an area of fraud, money movement became less risky in 1871 when the British and American governments agreed on a system of postal money orders.

Originally, Mary Ann Sullivan's duties were only of a housekeeping nature, but eventually she acted as a governess for the Cahill's three children, born in 1909, 1911 and 1914. For this she got room and board plus $2 a week. She claimed later, with a defiant pride, that, "They couldn't keep me at home. I'd go out every chance I got." Then with an amused glint in her eye, she added, ". . . looking for a man."[130]

With only $2 a week to buy essentials, domestics like Mary Ann Sullivan didn't excite the owners of the most luxurious shops on Main Street. Brockton's quarter-mile shopping district was a crowded, noisy cross-section of life, with streetcars, automobiles and horse-drawn carriages delivering men and women of every station into the retail section of town. Women of means purchased custom-made dresses, suits and millinery tailored of the finest imported cottons, wools and silks. The prices made young newcomers take notice. Women's dress suits at any of the upscale shops started at $25.

The housewives and single women, of ordinary means, bought personal items at less-exclusive stores whose counters, racks and shelves overflowed with ready to wear hosiery, gloves, corsets, overcoats and hats. The prices were still overwhelming. Cotton hose was almost $.50, kid gloves were $1.50 and hats were $5.

127

Even shoe stores, disposing of seconds and bankrupt stock, were charging $1.50 for a pair of women's kid oxfords.

The price of the larger household items went beyond the pale. The cheapest cast iron coal cooking stove retailed for $23; the deluxe model commanded the lordly price of $65. Refrigerator stores let their economy model wooden iceboxes go for $8, but charged up to $25 for the refrigerator (icebox) with corrugated tin shelves.

Other shoppers in Centerville were housekeepers and domestics who sought to stock the wooden iceboxes of their employers with fresh produce, meats, poultry, fish, butter, eggs, and milk. California oranges were 17 cents a dozen, a good rib roast sold for 12 cents a pound and eggs were 16 cents a dozen.

If Mary Ann Sullivan found the prices in Brockton staggering, she would not have been the first immigrant to feel that way. The high cost of living in America filled the pages of letters to family and friends back in Ireland. Nevertheless, in spite of such high prices and the paltry pay of domestic servants, young women were still able to dress better than they ever had before and some even managed to send money back to Ireland. Though the amount of money sent back to Ireland can never be much more than an educated guess, the historian Arnold Schrier made the most definitive study of this money transfer and concluded that during the second half of the 1800s, more than $260 million was sent to those who remained behind in Ireland.[131]

A look at Brockton's use of cash indicates a city of less educated workers. In a study of the use of checks in industrial cities of the Northeast, it was found that when it came to deposits of paychecks in national banks, Brockton was only 46 percent of the workforce compared to 80 percent in Fall River. Nationwide, payrolls made up with checks were $24 million while those made up with cash were $86 million. Cash was still king in manufacturing centers.[132]

Domestic servants' tales of fun and frivolity were limited to activities that took place from Saturday night until late on Sunday. Mary Ann Sullivan went to the dances at the Hibernian Hall and even collected money at the door. She summed up her involvement succinctly, "When the Hibernians were running it, I was secretary there for a while." For some odd reason, a few of the men who remembered the dances at the Hibernian Hall, also remember that she was called "Molly" Sullivan, although this may have been a generic nickname, used as flippantly as the Boston police used the expression "another pregnant Bridget."[133]

The dances at the Ancient Order of Hibernians Hall were socials where revelers could dance and there would be ice cream, cake and soft drinks. Unnoticed, older partygoers would slip into the barroom of the old hall and pay 5¢ for a glass of beer. Also, a middle-aged Irishman, Bill Maher, played the fiddle while the young people—in their teens and early twenties—moved about doing square dances and an occasional waltz. To break things up, there would even be an Irish jig once in a while. Curiously, whether because the young people now thought of themselves as Americans or because they had little exposure to Irish dance back in Ireland, the jigs were not of much interest to them.

On other occasions, Mary Ann would catch a ride with Connor Burke—Gerry Burke's grandfather—to Onset Beach. It wasn't a date; they were just friends. At other times, she caught rides to the beach with some of the wealthier boys. Onset Beach was the most popular destination for the working class Irish of Brockton. It was a ninety-minute ride, over forty miles of dirt and cinder roads, but a welcome break from the stale factory air of Brockton. The Cape was thought of as wilderness before 1920 and Onset Beach—on Massachusetts's South Shore—was where the wealthy maintained summer cottages.

Although the literacy rates of all Irish immigrants of the early 1900s had never been higher, they were ill prepared for a complex place like Brockton. Letters to family in Ireland ran the gambit from well-adjusted domestics like Mary Ann Sullivan to ill-treated servants who warned siblings and friends to avoid domestic service at all cost.

Book Three

Denis & Mary

Murphy

Of

Brockton

Massachusetts

Chapter 1

Denis & Mary Wed

For Mary Ann Sullivan, her first twelve years as a domestic went by in a flash. The Cahills were the best employers she could possibly have found, and despite her claims of exhaustive and uninterrupted husband hunting, the new experience of money jingling in her pockets and the fresh feeling of independence probably proved an impediment to marriage. Also, since her own mother, Bridget Lyons Sullivan, didn't marry until she was thirty—and late marriage or none at all, was a fact of life in western Ireland—initially she *might* not have given the matter much thought.

This changed in 1918 when she met Denis P. Murphy, a good-looking, twenty-nine year old fireman, originally from Killarney in County Kerry. Denis was a shy man, but a good dresser. Standing about five-foot-seven, he had brown eyes, brown hair, and arrived in America in 1894, when he was only five years old. The Irish-born people distrusted state schools—undoubtedly because of the restrictive curriculum of the British National Schools (N.S.) in Ireland—so at six years old, his parents enrolled him in the "old" Saint Patrick's Parochial School (corner of Perkins and Lawrence Streets). Fifteen Sisters of Charity of Nazareth taught 550 students—almost forty to a class.[134]

Denis Murphy attended St. Patrick's from the first through the eighth grades, and graduated in 1903. He finished his education with four years at Brockton High School, and then went to work at M.A. Packard Shoe Company on Warren Avenue. M.A. Packard was convenient for Denis, just up Warren Avenue a single block, on the corner of Foster Street. Different members of the Packard family built a number of shoe factories in Brockton, but M.A. Packard was the last of them.

In city directories, shoe workers made it a point to list their exact specialty within the intricate shoe world for several good reasons. To begin, there was simple pride. If a man learned a certain skill and consequently rose to an estimable position within the vast shoe network of Brockton, this was a way to advertise that fact. Additionally, since the Irish were fairly repetitious with given names, it proved a way to differentiate men of the same name from one another. Looking for a Patrick McCarthy, in the city register wasn't much trouble when he listed himself as a "sole edger." In this way, he differentiated himself from the Patrick McCarthys who were "skivers," "cutters" or "lasters." The directory publishers helped. Keeping in mind that telephones had been around since the late 1870s, even as late as the 1940s, an asterisk was placed in city directories next to the names of the families who owned phones!

Furthermore, in a city where the factories and the workforce were in constant motion—not unlike a real-life game of musical chairs—men advertised their particular skill in the hopes that better job offers might come their way from other shoe companies. To a man, the factory owners belonged to the National Boot and Shoe Manufacturers Association of the United States, headquartered in Boston, and had unwritten, gentlemanly rules barring the outright theft of talent from one another. That said, these strictures were just window dressing. In short, they enabled shoe manufacturers to meet on the golf course without brandishing firearms.

The reality of life in a large, highly industrialized city like Brockton was as Darwinian as a plane crash in the Andes. If Knapp Brothers's best hand cutter died during the night, where would the company get another one? How about from the W. L. Douglas plant in Montello or George E. Keith's firm in Campello? Better still, maybe they could hire one from a smaller shoe plant like Stacy, Adams or Kelly-Buckley. Either way, the city directory made the search easier.

Denis Murphy stayed at M.A. Packard Shoes for eleven years. During that time, he worked his way up to the best paying job in the place—hand cutter. In spite of—or perhaps because of his production—he could rise no further. The job of foreman in the cutting room might open up—cutters and foremen moved around more than any other men in the shoe factories—but the shoe business was losing its hold on Denis Murphy. Perhaps, after watching his own father, Dan Murphy, work away his life as a hand sewer, he saw the limitations of the factories. With so many family members in the industry, maybe someone figured out that Brockton's shoe business was on the wane. How many years did it have left? And how much competition among shoe workers would there be as firms relocated or went belly up?

Denis Murphy knew that if he could find something better, he would be smart to take it. Shoemaking wasn't for everyone. For every man who tried to keep his children out of the shoe factories, there were plenty of others who encouraged such a move.

At length, Denis Murphy saw the Brockton Fire Department as his ticket out of the factories. The Great Depression had wreaked havoc with pay scales, particularly in the shoe business. Annually, few men could get more than thirty-five weeks of work. Based on fifty-two weeks work, a hand sewer made $1500; a skiver, $1350; a trimmer, $1150; and a stitcher, 1100. Many of these shoe workers—because of the shortened schedules—could make about the same pay working as a laborer for the government. A W.P.A. laborer in 1939 brought home $700 a year.

While private business suffered, a Brockton policeman made the same as a fireman—$1800 annually. Believe it or not, a meter reader for the Gas Company got the same $1800! Aberrations abounded as welders in shipyards brought home $2100, and a few secretaries-office managers in leather companies made even more.

Denis P. Murphy was appointed to the fire department on November 18, 1918, when he was 29 years old. After his initial training, hoseman Murphy was assigned to Engine No. 5 on March 19, 1919 and later reassigned to Engine No. 1 on February 23, 1920. Since the Murphys didn't have a car, the purchase of 551 Warren Avenue in June 1929 was a blessing because Denis could easily walk to the Central Fire House—Engine No. 1—on Pleasant Street.

Central Fire House - 1941

Sadly, the wage difference between a shoe shop and the Brockton Fire Department didn't tell the whole story. The Boot and Shoe Workers Union—the Boot and Shoe, for short—had won for workers the right to a straight forty-hour week (in good times). Most firefighters belonged to the Massachusetts Permanent Firemen's Benefit Fund—more of a life insurance fund than anything else—and they also belonged to the Fire Fighters Union #144, but the nature of the job dictated the hours, not the union. The 84-hour week that the fireman worked was a tough trade off. Granted, much of that time was idle time, spent waiting for alarms that never materialized, or sleeping through the night, but it was still a long time for a man to be away from his family. A fireman's days and hours went this way: 10, 10, 24, X, 10, 10, 24, X, 10, 10, 24, X, and so forth. (This looks like 88 hours a week, but averages 84 hours over a whole year—including a two-week vacation.) The men rotated so that the stations were never unmanned. Still, to be "on call" 84 hours a week was punishing.

Not surprisingly, in 2013, the U.S. Fire Administration called firefighting "one of the most dangerous career paths." Typically, firefighters work long shifts, which contributed to physical fatigue and weighed heavily on family life and emotional well being. For 2013, firefighting was considered the third most stressful job in America.[135] In his book *Working*, Studs Terkel records the words of a New York fireman. "A fireman's life is nine years shorter than the average working man because of the beating they take on the lungs and heart . . . I never heard a fireman living to sixty-five . . . There's more firemen get killed then cops; five to one . . . They have a saying in the firehouse: 'Tonight could be the night.' . . . But nobody thinks of dying. You can't take it seriously . . . Everybody dies. . . ."[136]

The key for Denis Murphy was security. Tax breaks and other lures were constantly dangled under the noses of the shoe factory owners to relocate, and at a fairly regular clip, they took them. There were also layoffs. Someone once joked that when there was a layoff, the shoe workers got between three and five hours notice! On the other hand, the Brockton Fire Department demanded long hours, but there were never any layoffs.

As far as the courtship of Mary Sullivan and Denis Murphy, they met at a Hibernian Hall dance, and "She liked the look of Denis." To hear her tell it, she did the pursuing. Their courtship was unrecognizable by modedern standards. Since Denis Murphy had no car—in fact, did not drive—often he called on her at J.J. and Ellen Cahill's house and they played cards for the evening. Other times, they would "take a walk to Highland Park or someplace else." Again she confirmed that, "He was shy, but I 'pushed him a little bit, sometimes asking him to dance.'" Later just to set the record perfectly straight, she added, "He had enough to say at times."[137]

After a courtship of about two years, he finally gave her a diamond ring and they decided to marry on October 20, 1920. The timing seems unusual unless one considers that money was tight and October was off-season, perhaps keeping the whole affair affordable. On a weekly basis, Mary was now up to $2.50 and

Denis brought home $25, before he kicked in for room and board at his father's place. Cost was definitely a concern.[138]

As plans for the wedding began to take shape, J.J. and Ellen Cahill took charge, making sure that their girl had a first-class wedding. Ellen brought Mary to her personal dressmaker, Sadie Cohen, who together with her husband, Nathan, ran a small boutique, Sadie Cohen's Fifth Avenue Shop, on Main Street. Sadie ran an enormously successful business, as women of means considered her the most exclusive ladies' tailoress in Brockton.

Reflecting back over those exciting months, Mary—as she was now referred to—recalled that, "Mrs. Cahill picked out the dress . . . a beautiful tannish-brown (faun-colored) dress with lace about the décolletage . . . and she picked out my superficials . . . a very expensive suit, with a sable fur collar . . . the hat was made at Harris's, the most expensive store in Brockton." Reflecting later, she called it "The most expensive thing that I ever had." During these reminisces, she was asked if she still had the hat and she said dismissively, "Noooooo. Glad to be rid of it."[139]

When Wednesday evening, October 20, 1920, rolled around, Mary's sister Katie acted as her maid of honor, while Maurice Murphy acted as Denis's best man. Maurice was Dinny and Ellen Murphy's firstborn son, now a Brockton attorney in the firm of Thorndike & Murphy. Maurice received an appointment as a special justice on the District Court of Brockton in 1933 and held that position for the rest of his working life.

Common practice dictated that smaller, weekday weddings—during the colder months—were held in the rectory, instead of St. Patrick's Church. To stoke up the furnace and heat the cavernous building for a small wedding didn't make sense. The assistant pastor, Father Charles Blanchard—who had only arrived at St. Patrick's in July—performed the ceremony. At the time, Denis P. Murphy was living with his father and sisters at 172 Forest Avenue and he was 31 years old; Mary Sullivan was still working for the Cahills at 51 Highland Terrace and she was 28.

As maid of honor, Katie Sullivan received a nice bracelet as a gift from the bride. Denis Murphy gave his best man a Knights of Columbus amulet and, for his bride, he offered a pearl necklace.

In a gesture of largesse, J.J. Cahill lent Denis and Mary his automobile and chauffeur for the occasion. The Murphys were driven to the rectory for the ceremony, and then a wedding supper

Denis & Mary Murphy
with their son T.J. (Joe)

at a Boston hotel. Afterwards, the chauffeur drove the couple to the Cahills' summer home at Onset Beach, where they spent their honeymoon. Unforeseen by most observers, the chauffeur had a busy week since Mary Murphy insisted that Lena, Nonie, and others, visit her at Onset Beach. Some even came for a visit of several days in a row! Presumably, the chauffeur whisked them back to Brockton before bedtime.[140]

In those days Onset Beach—near the southern entrance to the Cape Cod Canal—was a far more desirable location than the Cape because the Bourne and Sagamore Bridges were not built until the 1930s. Therefore, entrance to the Cape lay with the slow moving, rotating cantilevered bridges. After a week's time, the chauffeur collected the newlyweds and delivered them to a monstrous triple-decker at 208 Winthrop Street in Brockton. Mary continued to work for the Cahills during the day, until she was almost ready to deliver her first child in September 1921.

Mr. And Mrs. Denis P. Murphy began their married life in a rented five-room apartment on Winthrop Street. The house was very typical of all of the houses of the Foster Street Gang. It had a foundation of large irregular stones, three apartments stacked on top of one another and a gently rising hip roof. Each unit had a porch half way across the front of the unit with a rounded bay window filling the remainder of the front elevation. At that time— and especially in a blue collar factory town—it was also customary for a newly married couple to rent an apartment only a few blocks from their parents, assuming that their parents had come to America. In this case, Denis and Mary Murphy behaved like the clachan Irish, for the Winthrop Street apartment was only four blocks north of Daniel Murphy's rented flat at 172 Forest Avenue.

Mary Murphy was pregnant soon enough. Brockton Hospital was the preference for most women in town, but Mary called Dr. Droan too soon and he told her to go back to work. Mildly chastened, Mary decided to have the baby at home and a nurse came to stay with her. Between two and four o'clock in the morning on September 27, 1921, Thomas Joseph Murphy—named after Denis Murphy's older brother, Father Thomas Murphy—was born. (There were still a number of Thomas Murphys in the family, so the baby was nicknamed Joe.)

Dr. Droan was a well-respected obstetrician, and thoughtful too. He got $3 for an office visit and $16 for a home delivery, but he always arrived with a box of chocolate for the mother.

September of 1921 was glorious time to start a family. The First World War and the Spanish Influenza had finished their nasty business three years earlier. The war's increased need for military shoes and boots allowed for wage increases in Brockton. So said, the production of shoes rose rapidly during the war and into the early-1920s. Beyond that, the country was on the verge of the Roaring Twenties, perhaps the most carefree and enjoyable time in America since the late 1880s. In Brockton, the shoe industry had slipped to 75 factories again, but the city ranked first in the shoe industry with 86 percent of its manufactories in shoes. Strangely enough, in 1921, the population of Brockton was over 60,000 and poised for an explosive run to almost 100,000 in 2010—a time when every last shoe factory was gone.[141]

Denis and Mary Murphy had two other children, both boys. On March 30, 1923, Robert Daniel entered the world, and four years later, on April 9, 1927, Edward Francis rounded out the family. Denis Murphy had strong opinions on acculturation. He wanted his sons to be thoroughly *Americanized* so he insisted that they be given names that would help them in life. He did not want them saddled with names that would mark them as immigrants. After all, his sons were Americans by birth.

Though Mary Murphy may have wanted her sons to go to work after Brockton High School, they did not take the commercial, academic, or industrial arts courses in secondary school as did 90 percent of the student body. They took the college course. An educated guess is that Denis Murphy insisted on it. There would be no harm done if they took the college course and then settled in a career that didn't require a college degree.

Denis Murphy may have carried the concept of acculturation to an extreme because he added an extra "n" to his first name for the same reason that he gave his sons American names. At St. Mary's Cathedral in Killarney, he was baptized Denis—with one "n." On his 1917-1918 Draft Registration card for the First World War, he signed his name Dennis P. Murphy—with two "n's." (Because Denis claimed "Part Support" for his father, he declared an "exemption from the draft.")[142]

141

Dennis P. Murphy

Signature

In 1924, Denis and Mary Murphy bought a triple-decker house at 242 Forest Avenue, where they stayed for three years. When their third son, Edward, was born on April 9, 1927, they needed something bigger. In 1929, the two oldest boys were in grade school, Ed was two, and Denis and Mary Murphy were house hunting.[143]

Chapter 2

551 Warren Avenue

Everyone in the eastern United States knew that triple-deckers were a way to get financially ahead. The rents from the two upper apartments took care of the bank payment, taxes, utilities, insurance, and maintenance. Mary Murphy was notoriously close with a dollar—to the point where the other Irish women in Brockton found her off-putting. All her life, Mary Murphy had few women friends. For a while, she was close to Dehlia Hunt, but how long that friendship lasted is not known. Mary Murphy wasn't the type to care about friendship. Throwing her opened palm downward, she would say, "Oh. Too bad about them." She had her husband and her three boys, and that's all she cared about.

In time, a triple-decker at 551 Warren Avenue hit the market. At a whopping $9000, ordinarily Mary Murphy wouldn't even look at the place, but this property had possibilities (as we shall see later).[144]

On June 20, 1929, they purchased the place for $8950 with a loan from the Campello Cooperative Savings Fund & Loan Association—Campello Bank at 1106 Main Street, on the corner of East Chestnut—for $5000. The loan was to be paid off at a rate of $50 a month. The going rate was 6%, so the final payment would be in 100 months (8.3 years). After only 37 months (3.08 years), on July 31, 1932—at the very bottom of the Great Depression—the loan was paid in full. Mary Murphy couldn't make money sing and dance like Hetty Green, but she was *very* good with it. A further clarification: Since the going rate was 6%, each $50 payment contained about $3 interest. As originally penned, the Murphys' loan would have netted the Campello Bank approximately $300 in interest. By making triple payments whenever possible—and paying the loan off early—Denis and Mary Murphy paid interest of a little over $100.

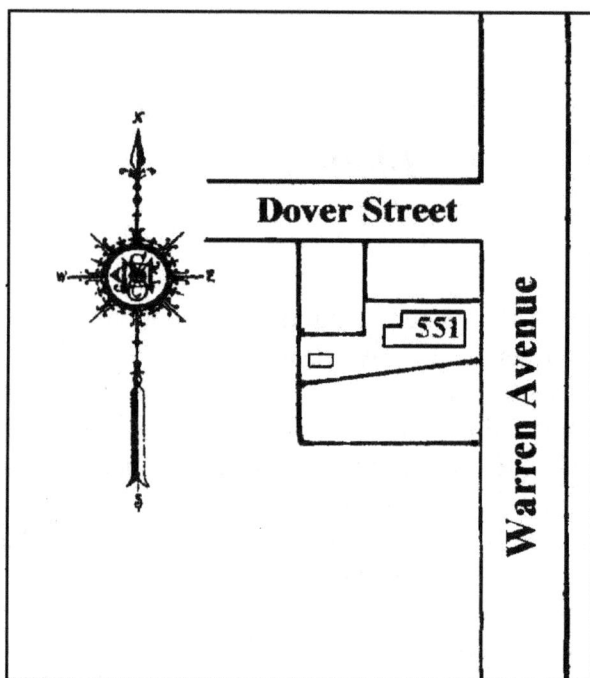

The triple-decker at 551 Warren Avenue was painted a mustard color with brown window trim, doors and rake boards. The steep gable end of the roof faced the street. It featured a six-room apartment on each floor. The lot was small, only 57 feet of frontage on Warren Avenue and extending back roughly 160 feet. At the extreme southwestern corner of the property was a rickety one-car garage. At the front, the apartments were narrow, allowing only the living room to overlook the street.

Brockton's zoning laws—at least in the Centerville section of town—were almost non-existent. Shoe factories, food stores, service stations and houses were all mixed together, a throwback to simpler times. Directly across from 551 Warren Avenue was

O'Neil's Garage, where Bob O'Neil sold Texaco gasoline and repaired cars. One could sit in Mary Murphy's front parlor all day long and watch as Bob O'Neil filled up the cars and washed the windshields of a good cross-section of Brocktonians.

Denis and Mary Murphy always lived on the first floor, while Denis's two maiden sisters, Mary and Nonie, lived on the third. The second floor was let until 1938 to a shoe worker, Robert Taylor, and his wife Winifred. Thereafter, another shoemaker, Patrick "Parky" Kelleher and his wife, Theresa, rented the second floor. Sometimes, Parky ran the lawnmower and he always had a cigar hanging out of his mouth. Eventually he died from cancer of the mouth and throat.

As Denis Murphy tended the flowerbeds under the living room windows, he used to take a break to chat with passersby, including the young girls who had their eyes on his sons. Muriel and Madeleine McCarthy of Blaine Street remember talking to Denis Murphy whenever he was working in front of the house.

Besides giving his sons American names, Denis Murphy insisted that his boys attend public schools. For first through sixth grade, the boys walked around the corner to James Edgar Elementary School on the corner of Harvard and Fuller Streets. The school was named for James Edgar, the department store magnate. The brick school building had a huge schoolyard on the south side and James Edgar Park abutting it to the west. For the seventh and eighth grade, the boys attended the Goddard School on Union Street (east of Main Street).

The oldest boy, Joe, came home from school each day and taught his brother Bob what he had learned. By the time the younger boy got to school, he was so far ahead of his classmates that he skipped second grade. (This is rarely done nowadays, except in the case of child prodigies, but was more common in the late 1920s.) At any rate, it didn't affect Bob in any way. In truth, he was president and class orator of the Brockton High School Class of 1940.

One interesting classmate of Bob Murphy at Edgar Elementary School was Rocco Francis Marchegiano, better known as the heavyweight boxer Rocky Marciano. His father, Pierino Marchegiano, worked as a "laster" at Stacy, Adams Shoes on Dover Street (corner of Warren Avenue).[145] Pierino and

Pasqualina Marchegiano lived at 80 Brook Street (now Marciano Way) next to James Edgar Park. Young Rocky worked as a sweeper in a shoe factory and a chute man for Brockton Ice & Coal Company. Then his father got him a job as a "last puller." By alternating hands, the arduous work built up his biceps and pectoral muscles on both sides of his body. The Ancient Order of Hibernians Hall on Ward Street hosted his first boxing match and offered a purse of $30.

One of Rocky's unusual strength-building techniques was to use the swimming pool at the YMCA to throw punches underwater. The resistance of the water built up his strength markedly. Another story—perhaps apocryphal—has the young fighter using the punching bag on the third floor of the Central Fire House to work on his punch.

Rocky Marciano wore the belt as Heavyweight Champion of the World from 1952 to 1956, defending his title six times against such greats as Jersey Joe Walcott, Ezzard Charles and Archie Moore. After the financial problems of the Great Depression, Rocky Marciano never trusted banks. He used cash for everything and hid wads of it hidden all around his home on Main Street in Hanson, Massachusetts. In 1969, Rocky Marciano died in a small plane crash near Des Moines, Iowa, on the eve of his forty-sixth birthday.

Leaving Ireland at the age of five, Denis Murphy was accustomed to hearing the accents of his mother and father. But through his association with American kids in the Brockton school system, he left all that behind. Mary was a tougher case because she had sixteen years to build up a powerful County Mayo brogue, but she too lost her accent and her boys grew up without a trace of it. Denis took the boys to the library at least once a week and the movies when he could. He was a good father in every way.

Denis Murphy drank very little and sometimes smoked a pipe, but his vices were few. Owing to his 84-hour week at the firehouse, he had precious little time for sports and hobbies.

During the summer vacation, Denis borrowed a pop-up tent camper from his tenants Robert and Winifred Young, and the Murphys parked the camper in a state park on the Cape—perhaps Nickerson—and everyone had a wonderful time for two weeks. This was during the Great Depression and two weeks at the Cape was far more than most folks could expect. Denis's job seemed secure, but during the dark days of the Depression, nothing was cut in stone.

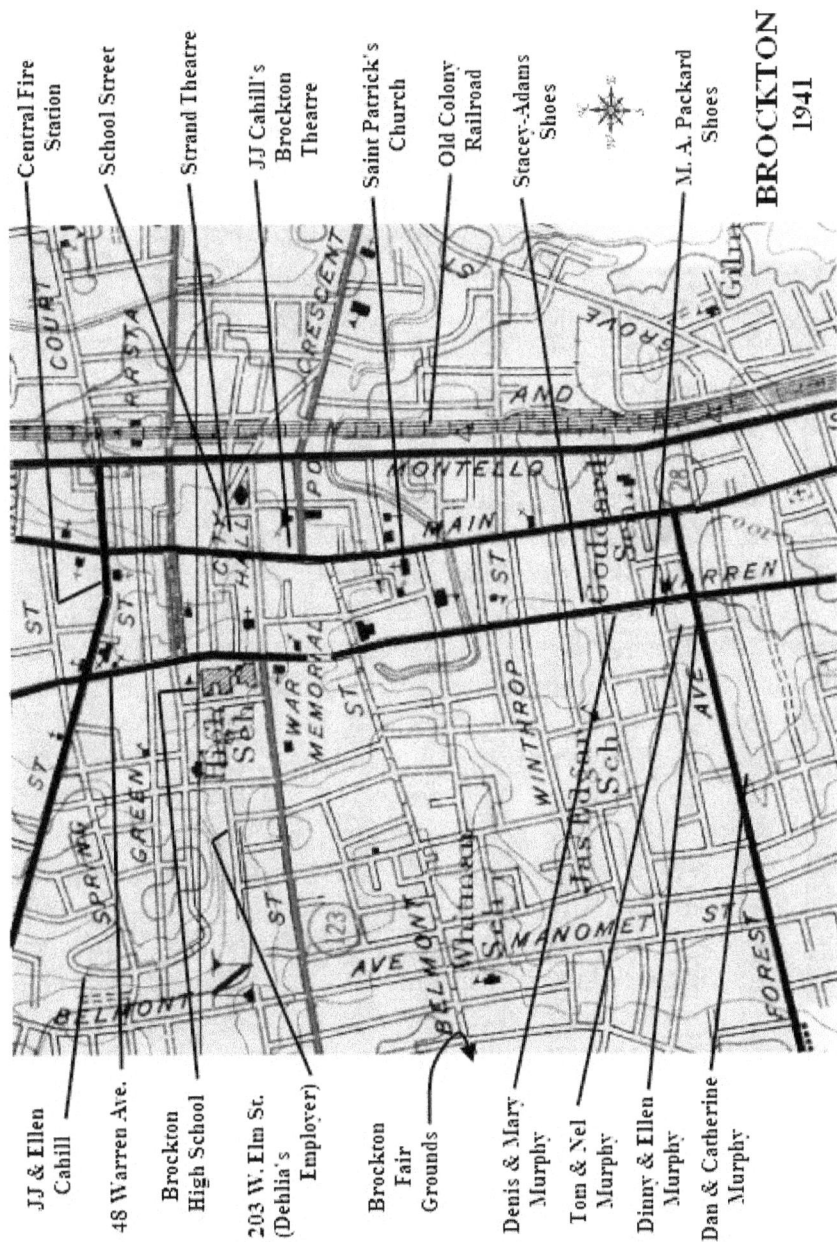

BROCKTON
1941

Central Fire Station

School Street

Strand Theatre

JJ Cahill's Brockton Theatre

Saint Patrick's Church

Old Colony Railroad

Stacey-Adams Shoes

M. A. Packard Shoes

JJ & Ellen Cahill

48 Warren Ave.

Brockton High School

203 W. Elm St. (Dehlia's Employer)

Brockton Fair Grounds

Denis & Mary Murphy

Tom & Nel Murphy

Dinny & Ellen Murphy

Dan & Catherine Murphy

During the prohibition years, from 1920 to 1932, the average American felt that the law was wrong and loved to exploit its loopholes. In 1924, the *Boston Globe* did a study of arrests for public drunkenness in twenty industrial towns of Eastern Massachusetts—including Brockton—and they found that, "The total for 1923 was 62,755, nearly double that of 1920, the first year of prohibition."[146] Flouting the law was a harmless pastime for everyone—including Denis Murphy. The law didn't forbid the production of alcohol; it only outlawed the sale of spirits.

The way that Denis and Mary Murphy's property sat on Warren Avenue, their backyard touched that of an Italian family at 64 Dover Street. The patriarch of the family, Erminio Campanini, drove a truck for Superior Baking Company. He was also a great wine lover. As the two men got to know each other, Erminio talked Denis into a winemaking partnership. The ideal situation would have been to grow the grapes up the south side of the Murphy's wobbly one-car garage.

Erminio, of course, claimed he knew all about winemaking. No matter. The vines did well in soil that hadn't been farmed for a century or more. Despite good intentions, a better batch of vinegar never came from the sandy soils of Brockton. Denis Murphy was no vintner. In an Irishman this flaw could be overlooked, but for the only Italian in Brockton who didn't know how to make wine, the shame was palpable.

While the Murphy boys grew up, they caddied at Thorny Lea Country Club where the "A" caddies got $0.75 a round, the "B" caddies got $0.65, and the "C" caddies got $0.55. Caddies could play golf at Thorny Lea on Mondays, but they preferred to play at D. W. Field Golf Course, where they could play an unlimited number of holes on Mondays for $0.65. Also the Murphys ushered at J.J. Cahill's Brockton Theatre for $0.25 an hour. All through the Great Depression, while the shoe factories laid off workers in a pathetic march toward oblivion, the Brockton Theatre held its own. This is one of the ironies of the Depression—the economy was bad, but Americans still spent money on entertainment. When theaters across the country should have been closing up like other businesses, somehow they made good money.

Mary Murphy had some interesting ideas about instilling a sense of responsibility in her sons. According to the terms of their note with the Campello Cooperative Bank, Denis and Mary Murphy, beginning in June of 1929, had to pay $50 a month until their $5000 loan was retired in October of 1937. By making extra payments along the way, they actually paid the loan off in its entirety by July 1932. Astounding really, when one considers that 1932 was the very bottom of the Great Depression and shoe workers throughout the city were working only thirty-five weeks a year or being laid off. As a city fireman, Denis Murphy job was secure, and together with the careful ways of his wife Mary, they pulled off this minor miracle.

It should be noted that Campello had become the Swedish section of Brockton known for tough bar-fighting, block-headed Swedes. Still, Mary Murphy insisted that her two older boys—Joe, 10 and Bob, 9—walk the mile to the Campello Bank and make the monthly mortgage payment. After 1929, families were especially fond of cash and that's all Mary Murphy trusted. She would put $50 in an envelope and explain to the boys that if for any reason they weren't able to make the payment, the family would lose the house.

Obviously, since Mary Murphy was making triple payments, she had already made two of the three payments while the boys were at school. The house was secure no matter what. As nervous as two kids tied to the Old Colony railroad tracks, Joe and Bob Murphy walked to Campello Bank and made the mortgage payment. Month after month, they saved the house!

Decades later, the author explained to Dr. Robert Murphy about Mary Murphy's little "responsibility builder." Bob Murphy refused to believe it! The documents were shown to him, and he still claimed it was rubbish!

Of course, people believe what they want to believe, and in this case, Bob Murphy grew up believing that he and his brother Joe had saved the family in the depths of the Great Depression. It was part of his belief system—like blue eyes. Nothing was going to change facts like that!

Incidentally, Mary Murphy was enormously successful with her little games. She knew just how far she could push; never to offer encouragement; never to say a kind word; never to say "well done." In the hands of a lesser person, the results could have been disastrous.

Joe Murphy said once he was convinced that his mother never wanted her sons to go to college or medical school. Instead, she wanted them to go into the shoe factories and bring home some money. She had little patience with an education regimen that meant the forfeiture of ten years income, while others were earning a good week's pay. The long Depression undoubtedly contributed to her sense of uncertainty about such a long academic road. Adding insult to injury, Joe had vivid memories of his medical school discussions with his brother, at the close of which Mary Murphy would enter the room and say, "Who would pay to see you two as doctors?" (The ghosts of the clachan Irish undoubtedly smiled down on Mary Murphy as she ridiculed her sons' dreams.)

One can never truly understand the dynamics of Mary Murphy's taunts. Did she ridicule them because she knew it would goad them into working harder, or did she really want to reduce them to the next generation of hide cutters at M. A. Packard Shoes? Another trick she adored was to play one against the other, the same as she did with her grandchildren many years later. But this can be a dangerous game. In the hands of a master, the results could be fantastic; in the hands of a fool, the results could be disastrous.

When Joe Murphy was courting Muriel McCarthy, Mary Murphy used to lock the doors so he couldn't get back into the house after his date. Muriel and her sister Madeleine were fine young women from an excellent family, but perhaps Mary Murphy thought Muriel dressed a little too nicely. Or maybe she thought Muriel had an unreasonably high opinion of herself. The real reason is lost to history; nevertheless, she did everything in her power to keep Joe and Muriel apart. In a diary that Joe Murphy kept at the time, he wrote, "How can a woman who claims to love me, treat me this way?"[147]

Chapter 3

Brockton Fair

America has been holding agricultural affairs since the early 1800s. These fairs showcased the fruits, vegetables, and livestock grown on the farms of the area. Therefore, it's ironic that the Brockton Fair wasn't organized until 1874, as the town transitioned from an agricultural hamlet into an industrial city focused on the production of shoes and boots.

The First Annual Exhibition of the Brockton Agricultural Society came together on October 7, 8, and 9, 1874. The more established businessmen of old North Bridgewater, organized the fair. They felt that it was "for the encouraging and promoting of material prosperity of the community in every form of productive industry, in the cultivation of the soil, in the rearing and improving a domestic animals, in the mechanical arts, and in whatever pertains to these." The most noteworthy exhibitions were a "Show of Fowls," a baseball game between two local teams, and on the final day, a "Firemen's Trial," pitting various fire departments against one another. The fair included fowl, pigs, heifers, and other farm animals. Farmers brought wagonloads of produce, and women brought brightly colored afghans, quilts, fancy work, and baskets of pears and apples. Starting an exciting tradition, hot-air balloons became a feature of the fair. Popcorn sales were from open carts, and various vendors passed through the crowd pushing their treats. There were amusement rides and cotton candy galore.

On October 7, 1909, the year after Mary (Sullivan) Murphy arrived in America, the Brockton Fair attracted 75,000 people.[148] But the Brockton Fair enjoyed ups and downs, mostly due to the weather. When the days were clear the fair did well, but when it rained, all was lost. The real heyday of the Brockton fare was in the 1920s, when good times were treated in America as a birthright. On the 78-acre fairgrounds on Belmont Street, crowds came from far and wide and sometimes approached 100,000.

From the very beginning, horse races with trotters and pacers were a highlight for the adults. Gambling was not originally allowed, but it enjoyed free reign. (The Brockton City Council finally allowed pari-mutuel betting in 1941.) The horses raced every day and provided never-ending thrills and the 296-foot grandstand of 1876 had to be expanded to 540 feet in 1890. The fairgrounds eventually featured a poultry building, an agricultural building, and paddocks and stalls for the horses. Meanwhile, the ever-growing grandstand continued to expand.

The huge grandstand fronted the "quarter stretch" of the horse track, a natural place for folks to sit as they eyed the finish line. For this reason, the quarter stretch also featured a never ending parade of the best-dressed women from miles around. Even high school girls donned their finest dresses and paraded along the quarter stretch. Beyond that, a fashion show drew the young ladies to the Cow Palace (agricultural building). Under the grandstand rested a huge ballroom where dancing went on until all hours.

In addition to the horse racing and gambling, they were horse shows for purists. There existed an uneasy peace between the gambling crowd—who followed the trotters and pacers—and the folks who preferred Class A horse shows. For this reason the horse shows were discontinued from 1933 to 1939. The horse shows started up again, but in 1959, breeders showed up with their horses and reservations only to find racehorses in their stalls. The tension between the gamblers and the "horse show people" killed horse shows at the Brockton Fair.

New attractions were added annually, and in 1896 it was the horseless carriage. By 1916, automobile shows were all the rage. A beautiful collection of new cars and accessories were displayed in commodious buildings adjoining the auto campus. By 1931, the fair had been expanded to five days in late September and auto races were added. Daredevils exploded out of cannons, high divers dropped 100 feet and splashed into six feet of water, and men parachuted from balloons. These were just a few of the many events that captured the imaginations of the young.

Night shows were begun in 1919 and that year the greatest fireworks display ever seen in this country took place. The fireworks have continued ever since. Like any fair, there was a spit 'n sawdust midway area that young people loved, but it attracted a low-class crowd. On these midways, the shell and pea games vied with the World of Myth for fair-goers' money. The promoters of the fair always promised to replace the midway's bad element and build an industrial showcase for Brockton's accomplishments, but these were just soothing platitudes. As long as the crowds enjoyed the midway, it stayed.

People came from everywhere. The New York, New Haven and Hartford railroad brought 400 carloads of people to the fair in 1907. Throughout the fair, little open trolley cars shuttled people between the railroad station and the fair grounds. In the same year, there were more than 3,000 automobiles parked at the fair.

For everyone in town, the Brockton Fair was the highpoint of the year. The first day of the fair was Children's Day, and kids got in free. The school kids packed lunches and ate them in "the grove."[149] Older kids never tired of jumping over the fence to avoid the admission fee. A never-ending procession of show people—including Martha Raye, Paul Whiteman and his Orchestra, Eddie Duchin, and Pat Boone—entertained fair goers.

In the fall of 1912, when William Howard Taft was running for reelection as president, he and his wife, Helen, visited the Brockton Fair. Taft pontificated, "It is impossible not to feel real interest and pleasure in an exhibition of such magnitude, charm, and diversity as the Brockton Fair. It seems to me truly wonderful that you assemble 80,000 people for such a fall carnival and maintain such perfect order. I shall always remember this visit with great pleasure."

But the massive wooden grandstands proved troublesome. At two o'clock in the morning of June 16, 1936, the grandstand caught fire. The conflagration quickly became a general alarm, and the grandstand burned until just a pail of ashes remained. A damaged gas line fueled the spectacle as timbers crashed down. At the time, it was believed that homeless men, who slept in various buildings on the fairgrounds, set fire to the grandstand where dignitaries sat to watch the fair.

Muriel and Madeline McCarthy couldn't be kept from the Brockton Fair. They loved the pageantry and the chance to wear their best clothes somewhere besides St. Patrick's Church on Sundays. The McCarthy girls were the closest watchers of the Murphy boys, but they never once saw them at the Brockton Fair. A good guess is that Mary Murphy didn't want her sons using their savings—their college money—to play sucker's games on the midway.

The Brockton Fair did well until the close of the 1920s. The New York stock market reached a peak of 381.17 on September 3, 1929, but a series of crashes followed: Black Thursday, October 24; Black Monday, October 28; and, Black Tuesday, October 29. However, the cogent point is that the stock market continued to fall slowly, but relentlessly, until July 8, 1932, when it bottomed at 41.22. In less than three years, stocks had lost 90 percent of their value! Moreover, the market would not reach the lofty 1929 high for twenty-five years.

The Brockton Fair languished as the Great Depression deepened. Shoe sales plummeted nationwide and more of Brockton's shoe manufacturers closed or moved to places with cheaper labor costs. Upon request from manufacturers, the Massachusetts Board of Arbitration decreased wages by more than 25 percent.

There were a great many men out of work. For the first time in memory, manufacturers were searching desperately for a way to spur sales by lowering the cost of their shoes. That, of course, meant cuts in shoe workers' wages. Growing numbers of unemployed workers kept the existing workforce on their toes.

Especially during the Depression years, faraway towns clobbered by the economic downturn, offered unbeatable tax breaks for shoe manufacturers to relocate. The belt tightening spread throughout the city.

As he watched the downturn in the shoe industry, Denis Murphy must have thanked his lucky stars that he jumped from M. A. Packard to the Brockton Fire Department in 1918. These days, his biggest concern was the education of his boys. Unlike his wife, Denis Murphy wanted badly to help his sons pay for their educational expenses. He even told Bob Murphy that if he (Bob) could just get himself through Tufts undergrad, then he (Denis) would pay for medical school. This wasn't terribly realistic, but a nice offer all the same. Far more likely, scholarships, grants, government programs, and part time jobs were the path to medical school for the sons of Denis and Mary Murphy. Denis's youngest boy, Ed was thirteen and a freshman in high school when Joe, then Bob, left for college. Ed professed to have no interest in the lofty goals of his two older brothers. He would rather be a lawyer, but in the end, Ed followed his brothers into medicine.

When Bob Murphy went off to college in the fall of 1940, his father Denis offered only one pearl of wisdom. He said to always remember that there wasn't one single person at Tufts—among the teachers, advisors, administrators, or his fellow classmates—who cared whether or not he made it. It was up to him to steer his own ship and, if he made it, the result would be because of his own hard work and nothing else. In the fall of 1940 when Bob Murphy left for the Tufts College campus in Medford, he was seventeen years old.

While the bad times in Brockton are difficult to describe evenly, some historic numbers speak volumes. Around 1900, there were 431 factories of all types in Brockton. Almost 100 of them made shoes and boots. By the end of the Roaring Twenties, the total number of factories had slid to 244—a drop of 43 percent. Almost immediately after the stock market crash of 1929, manufacturing in Brockton began a death spiral. As shoe workers lost their jobs and were forced to accept relief, Brockton's welfare commissioners "felt that the efforts to help people in economic difficulty had 'tended to make the receiving of something for nothing so eminently respectable that one wonders if wishbones will take the place of backbones in the future.'"[150]

From 1929-1932, overall shoe production in Brockton dropped 38 percent. During the same three-year period, sales at W. L. Douglas fell from $9.5 million to $4.4 million—a drop of 54 percent at a factory that specialized in inexpensive shoes. While others catered to buyers willing to spend $5 for a pair of men's shoes, W. L. Douglas specialized in the $3.00 and $3.50 models. A lot of good it did him.

There were of course signs of real desperation in Brockton. By 1932-33—and apart from the obvious slump in production numbers, sales figures, and employment data—relations between owners and workers hit a nadir. The owners of the shoe factories demanded wage concessions. The workers resisted. Tensions got so high that the National Labor Relations Board had to step in to referee the dispute. In September and October 1933, about 7,000 shoe workers went out on strike because of a spat between the Brockton Shoe Manufacturers Association and the Boot and Shoe Union. Among other issues, the Boot and Shoe was getting a little heavy-handed in the collection of dues. Ultimately, shoe workers left the Boot and Shoe in favor of the Brotherhood of Shoe and Allied Craftsmen. By the end of 1933, the "Brotherhood" represented almost all of the shoe workers.[151]

As late as 1939, the shoe business was still unsettled. One newspaper noted, "An 85 percent rise in orders for Massachusetts textile industries in September is maintaining payrolls in cotton and woolen industries at the high levels previously reached. . . . Laggard in this area now is the shoe industry. Dipping definitely under last year's output in October, expectations are for a 10 percent to 15 percent decline from 1938 in the next two months. Brockton, Haverhill and Lynn may have increased relief rolls soon."[152]

Throughout the city, people were struglling and also looking for income. That included Mary Murphy. While her home at 551 Warren Avenue was zoned as a three-apartment structure—the number of families in it when she purchased the home—she began to take in extra boarders. By 1937, Mary Murphy's family occupied the first floor, longtime tenants Robert and Winifred Young rented the third floor, and the recently widowed Abbie Cook leased the second. Well and good, but scattered around the building were Mabel Kelley, a housekeeper; Chester Miller, a decorator; and another housekeeper, Martha Powers. One wonders where they all slept.

Mary Murphy's enterprising spirit must have caught the eye of the zoning department of the City of Brockton, but she met their entreaties by leaving the Murphy family out of the city directory for a few years. Presumably, this allowed her to claim that her family wasn't living there.

Chapter 4

Central Fire House

Daniel Murphy's son, Denis, stepped off the *SS Cephalonia* onto Marginal Street in East Boston at the beginning of October 1894 and was in St. Patrick's Parochial School within a year. (There was no kindergarten in those days.)

Brockton was a cauldron of immigrants—mostly Swedes, Poles, Lithuanians, Italians and Irishmen—so there was no problem fitting in because no one fit in. It was a blue-collar working city built by North Bridgewater Yankees, who laterally expected immigrants to make them rich. The only true insiders were the owners of the shoe factories, who lived in opulent style, mostly on the west side of the city. In the coming decades, they would become outsiders as they moved with their factories to wherever they could rack up the most benefits. By 1950, they would almost all be Southerners or Midwesterners. Ironically enough, they became the ultimate outsiders.

Irish immigrants have always considered public schools suspect and Daniel and Catherine Murphy were no exception. Consequently, Denis—along with all of his siblings—went to St. Patrick's Parochial School on the corner of Perkins and Lawrence Streets. After Brockton High School and eleven years at M.A. Packard, Denis wanted a job with the Brockton Fire Department. It paid better, was more interesting, and offered greater security.

Brockton's town fathers began using a single cylinder pumping engine as early as 1825, but turned over all fire fighting to a private company two years later. Then the town bought two Hand-Tub pumpers—"Protector" was kept at Center Village and "Enterprise" at Campello. Each cost $750. By 1846, there were three firehouses. Throughout the Gilded Age, Brockton added to its fire equipment regularly.

In 1909, Brockton awarded a contract to Pope Manufacturing Company in Hartford, Connecticut, for a special chemical and emergency truck for the Brockton Fire Department. The motive power was the 40-horsepower Pope-Hartford stock engine that would propel the machine over the road at a maximum of thirty-five miles an hour. "Squad A, Fire Dep't" was painted on either side of the hood.[153] By 1918, when Denis Murphy got his appointment to the Brockton Fire Department, there were six fire stations, three of them built since 1900.

During Denis Murphy's years with the Brockton Fire Department, the place to be was the Central Fire House. Located at 40 Pleasant Street—right in the center of downtown Brockton—it saw more action than any other station. In an occupation where the weeks were 84-hour monsters and the work boring—sometimes bordering on sheer tedium—action was the elixir that kept the men sharp.

Denis Murphy had been lucky. After a short training period and a brief hitch at Engine Company No. 5, he was reassigned to Engine No. 1 at the Central Fire House. That glorious day was Monday, February 23, 1920. Within the Central Fire House, there were three units—Squad A, Engine No. 1 and Ladder No. 1. About ten years later—in a minor shuffle of talent—he was reassigned to Squad A. Beyond the fire fighting equipment at the Central Fire House, there was a bay on the east side of the building where Chief Dickinson's car was kept and also that of Deputy Chief Lynch. They chose their drivers from among the available firemen, and when the alarm went off, these cars were driven at breakneck speed to the brass's homes to ferry them to the fires. This folderol with the cars and the drivers wasn't necessarily the most efficient use of firemen, cars or top executives, but had evolved over a long period of time and was something of a sacred cow.

The Central Fire House was built in 1884 and conformed to the French Second Empire school of architecture. The building stood three stories tall and had four separate bays. Unlike modern buildings that present a flat facade to the world, the station was designed so that the two end bays were stepped back about four feet, giving the two center bays greater play. The first two floors were jacketed in red brick white cut granite lintels, while a mansard roof of dark gray Pennsylvania slate enclosed the third floor. Two elaborate brick chimneys stood guard on each end of the fancy edifice. At the back of the structure—and centered—a ten foot square tower shot seventy feet into the sky, crowned with an open belfry and dizzying spire. The sidewalls of the tower were covered with beautifully scalloped wooden shingles and the roof was a match for the slate that covered the mansard roof of the third floor. Inside hung an outsized bronze bell, which in the days of horse-drawn pumpers, was the main alarm for the city.

The second floor had three single windows over each of the two bays in the center of the first floor and only one window over each of the recessed side bays.

The windows on the third floor showed a scholar's attention to detail. High above the center section of the building, three units were framed neatly into the mansard roof with the center unit composed of two windows mulled together. Above the side bays were mounted only one window on each side.

Clearly an afterthought, a tall white flagpole poked into the sky from a bracket mounted in the center of the mulled window unit. The steel bracket supporting this flagpole was an architect's nightmare as additional supports swept wildly from both sides of the window trim.

When the Central Fire House was first built in the mid-1880s, it was the first fire station in the United States to be wired for electricity. When Thomas Edison did the work at the Central Fire House, he used asbestos covered wires and wooden cleats to keep the lines away from the beams and joists on the inside of the building. Unfortunately, Edison was a firm believer in direct current (which could not maintain voltage over long distances) and the original wiring had to be removed in 1927 and replaced with the familiar knob-and-tube wiring of the time—along with electricity of the alternating current variety.

By 1920, when Denis Murphy was reassigned to the Central Fire House, the horse stalls at the back of the easternmost bay had been floored over and the twenty-five by forty-foot area was converted to locker and dorm space for firefighters. On the street side of the second floor, there were another four bedrooms and behind them were more locker rooms, shower and toilet facilities. In each of the bedrooms was a three-foot diameter hole in the floor—next to the wall—which was lanced by a 2 ½" diameter brass pole running from the ceiling of the bedroom to the concrete floor of the bay below.

In Edison's first wiring of the firehouse, a number of ingenious devices were incorporated. For example, when the alarm went off, three things happened in unison: Every light bulb in the whole building came on, bathing the place in the an ocean of light; the horses in the stable area—in back of the easternmost bay—were released from their stalls; and, the twin flaps at the brass poles in the second floor bedrooms popped open, readying the way for the now-wide-awake firemen to reach the engines below. Though seemingly of the Rube Goldberg school, everything worked well.

Next to these poles in each bedroom were four similar brass poles that delivered men from the third floor down to the second. With just the minimum of dexterity, a man could descend from the third floor to the bedroom level, catch the next pole to the ground floor, and be on one of the trucks in less than fifteen seconds.

At the back of the second floor was a large lounge where Denis Murphy—and the other firemen pulling the twenty-four hour shift—could listen to the radio, read newspapers or play cards. Most of the walls of the living area were covered up to a height of four feet with vertical pine wainscoting and a wide, beaded chair rail. The floors were four-inch wide yellow pine throughout and the ceilings were stamped tin.

Easily the most important part of this rabbit's warren of rooms was the kitchen, located at the back of the building and to the east of the hose-drying tower. It was the biggest room on the second floor, with a separate pantry full of mismatched china plates, cups, and saucers. In the top drawers of the lower cabinets sat an equally mismatched collection of knives, fork, spoon and other essential kitchen utensils. Unlike the rest of the building's yellow pine flooring, the kitchen had linoleum and the walls were covered with tile up to a height of five feet.

The third floor was one giant cavernous room. It had a sixteen-foot high ceiling, broken up only by a couple of trusses composed of huge timbers and 2" steel rods. These architectural members allowed for the great open spans on the first floor where the trucks where garaged. On the west side were some pool and ping pong tables, and a room with tools and a sewing machine, where the men worked on their equipment. Functionally though, the most important item on the third floor was the entrance to the hose-drying tower. Usually a younger member of the company scurried up the shaky ladder and waited for the end of the fifty-foot hoses to be delivered to him, using a hundred foot piece of manila rope looped over a pulley just below the belfry. As the ropes delivered the ends of the 50-foot hoses, they would be attached to a metal clip and then hung from a horizontal steel bar. After all the wet hoses were hanging like strands of pasta, the fireman would descend the ladder, not to return until the hoses were dry. The business end of the manila rope was weighted and would drop back to the first floor, ready to raise more wet hoses or retrieve the dry ones.

The importance of the kitchen arises from the strange work schedules of firemen. Not to put too fine a point on it, but Denis Murphy actually worked in excess of eighty-four hours a week because it was customary for each shift to show up fifteen minutes early. That way, if an alarm came in at precisely eight o'clock, the new shift would have already completed roll call and could respond immediately.

Balanced against this extra time, he slept eight hours of the shift. Nevertheless, Denis Murphy was required to have his "night hitch" (a combination of calf-length rubber boots, bunker pants and suspenders) bunched up next to his bed so that he could spin on the edge of the bed and slide his feet directly into the boots. Standing up, with one quick motion, he could then pull up the bunker pants and snap the suspenders onto his shoulders. Under such conditions, it takes almost no imagination to recognize that the quality of Denis Murphy's sleep at the firehouse was restless. While no statistics are available—with regard to disrupted sleep because of alarms—it is obvious that during the winter months, when furnaces, stoves and fireplaces were blasting away all over Brockton, that his sleep was, at best, fitful. Denis may have been under the covers with his eyes closed but, even under the best of circumstances, it was never the sleep of the innocent.

On the first day of his schedule, Denis Murphy worked from eight in the morning until six at night. The second day was a repeat of the first. The third day was the stump puller, for he showed up at the usual time, but did not go home until eight the following morning. After a day off, the cycle began all over again. By breaking each company into three units, and staggering the days when each unit worked its long day, there was always a crew at the firehouse overnight.

Still, the workings of the Brockton Fire Department were complicated by a few oddities within its design. Firstly, when an alarm sounded, every firefighter went into action. This left personal gear behind and the front doors wide open. Naturally, there were issues with theft. Secondly, with vacations, illnesses and other emergencies, men were moved around to fill gaps in the schedule. Though clearly unavoidable, this caused some men to pull more than their share of twenty-four hour hitches. Finally, at the Central Fire House, there were three separate companies— Squad A, Engine No. 1 and Ladder No. 1—each with some overlapping capabilities. To a lesser degree, this held true at the other five firehouses as well. Depending on the size and location of a fire, a duplication of capabilities was unavoidable. Besides the age-old dilemma of whether or not to send firemen into vacant buildings, there were simpler dilemmas. At a big conflagration, what chief hasn't asked, "Do I have all of the equipment in the right place—where it will do the most good?" Questions like this really strike home when engines are double-parked at congested fire scenes—as we shall see later.

During the short days, Denis Murphy's life could be as normal as any other man, but the twenty-four hour hitches were difficult. Unfortunately, they were also necessary. The Brockton Fire Department could never maintain a rapid response time without a crew at the fire station around the clock.

Denis Murphy's duties ran the gamut from the barely tolerable to the pleasantly mundane. He left with Squad A, of course, to extinguish fires wherever and whenever they arose. Between these alarms, he cleaned and shined the equipment. He also had a long list of duties, which were of a more ancillary nature. For example,

164

he took his turn doing inspections throughout the business district and spent a certain amount of time mending, cleaning and fixing his boots, jacket, helmet and other gear. In addition to the important work of keeping things in shape at the firehouse, the firemen gave each other haircuts and then brought in their children for buzz cuts. The firemen at the Central Fire House considered it unthinkable "to pay some greenhorn down in Campello to cut their hair" or that of their children. This little chore they could manage on their own.[154]

Denis Murphy had strong feelings about America and his family's place in it. He believed fully that he was no longer an Irishmen, but an American. For Denis himself though, there were some minor concessions with regard to his master plan of acculturation. Irish cuisine was (and still is) almost an oxymoron in that it has always been limited to the single dish of corned beef and cabbage. Indeed, with a history of deprivation, the Irish had little need for fancy recipes. All the same, they had become accustomed to a few indigenous foods like soda bread and yeast cake. Denis Murphy, for all his quiet regard for the manners and customs of America had no intention of giving up these simple pleasures. Hobbled mildly for life by the habits of his youth, there was one other weakness that he indulged in with abandon—the Irish card game of Forty Fives. (Forty Fives is a descendant of the Irish game Spoil Five. In America, it started in the Irish communities of Northeastern Massachusetts near Lawrence. It was also played in Haverhill, Methuen and the surrounding towns.)

Gambling was strictly forbidden at the fire station. The bad blood—the handmaiden of gambling—was inimical to the needs of an efficient, well-run fire department. These men held each other's lives in their hands and could not be hamstrung by the festering feuds that gambling debts would inevitably create. Nevertheless, during the long evenings of their 24-hour shifts, the men played Forty Fives endlessly while they listened to radio shows in the upstairs lounge. As early as 1922, the original cast of the Broadway musical *Shuffle Along* was performed live on station WNAC in Boston. By the mid-twenties, the firehouse had its own radio in the upstairs lounge. Over the years, the firefighters graduated from the earliest serials, like *Sam & Henry,* to the familiar favorites *Amos & Andy*, *Lum & Abner*, *Fibber McGee & Molly*, *Gangbusters* and *Edgar Bergen & Charlie McCarthy*.

There was little time for cards or radio during the day though. Each time the cotton-jacketed hoses got wet, they had to be strung up in the drying tower, and there was an endless parade of busy work between alarms. When the long list of chores was completed, the hours dragged by endlessly.

In 1941, there were more than 62,000 people living in Brockton. The fire department held at six fire stations, which were spaced to cover the whole 21.5 square miles of the city. Even in far western Brockton, a fire alarm brought a quick response.

On payday, Wednesday, April 20, 1932, Brockton's firefighters were forced to take a 5 percent cut in pay, enabling the city to reduce taxes. The following day, Brockton's Finance Committee voted to request all city employees to accept a 10 percent reduction in pay to further lower resident's tax bills. The city's finances were in tatters; its administrators couldn't even negotiate a short-term loan. The next payday, Wednesday, April 27, the firemen went unpaid, beginning a drought that lasted a month. After agreeing to the 10 percent pay cut, the firemen finally received a paycheck on May 17. However, once the city government got a taste of employee givebacks, they couldn't control themselves. At a meeting of the city council in early December 1932, Mayor Baker unveiled a plan to impose a 15 percent cut in the salaries of all city workers.

The city workers balked. The policemen and firemen took the matter to court. Considering the joblessness and harsh times that were gripping Brockton, the outcome seemed inevitable. The court ultimately dismissed the petition of the police and fire departments. Because of the U.S. entry into World War II in December 1941, the consumer economy never had a chance to get better. Production in the shoe factories picked up as the military needed more shoes and boots, but wartime rationing crippled consumer spending. The pre-1932 municipal wage scale did not return until the late 1930s.

For Denis Murphy, each passing year nevertheless offered confirmation that he had chosen wisely when he left the shoe factories for the Brockton Fire Department. If a foreman in a shoe factory could get fifty weeks pay, he could earn $20 to $25 a week, while even a rookie at the fire department started at $28. By 1939, a veteran like Denis Murphy was making $34.62 a week. True, he worked longer hours in a far more dangerous job, but it seemed like the best work a man could get with only a high school education. The American dream wasn't some hackneyed slogan; it was real. Denis's father, Daniel, had few choices when he arrived in America. A hand sewer at Brockton Ideal Shoe, and then Kelly-Buckley Shoe, was the top of the ladder for him. Not only did his children have more choices because they had more education, but the barriers for the Irish (and for that matter all immigrants) fell a bit more each year.

Even though Denis Murphy had stepped off the *Cephalonia* in 1894, he had never seen a "No Irish Need Apply" sign. With wagonloads of Irish customers, a merchant would have been a fool to put such a sign in his front window.

At any rate, as immigrants' children acquired more education, and became more thoroughly assimilated, they were able to scramble over the backs of those who came before them and grab an even meatier chunk of the American dream.

Those like his uncle, Tom Murphy, who had helped his father, Dan, and his uncle, Dinny, get to America and find work as shoemakers, never earned the kind of money or enjoyed the security that Denis had at the fire department. Still the unions—first the Boot and Shoe and later the Brotherhood of Shoe and Leather Craftsmen—kept the work week strictly at forty hours. For a time, the shoemakers enjoyed more free time, but they paid a terrible price for those leisurely hours. By 1940, Brockton had only 50 shoe factories, employing fewer than 8,000 people.

Denis Murphy was living through some turbulent times, but he was married to a good woman—headstrong and domineering though she was—and two of his three sons were off at Tufts College. His youngest boy would finish eighth grade at Goddard School in June and start Brockton High in the fall. Denis Murphy may not have known that less than 10 percent of young men received bachelor's degrees from colleges in 1941, but he was smart enough to realize that his boys were destined to have better lives than most. Early on, he sensed that they were extremely intelligent. It was a fact that completely baffled him, for he was an average man in every sense of the word. His wife, Mary, on the other hand, was a quick study. He marveled sometimes at how a girl who never got past sixth grade could grasp the import of situations with such facility. She clearly had an innate intelligence that now thankfully had been passed onto their sons.

Denis's intellectual shortcomings confronted him in a most embarrassing fashion when he decided to take the test for lieutenant. In those years, the Brockton Fire Department was akin to a beehive in that it had few bosses but legions of workers. Under such circumstances, there was very little chance for advancement unless one of the bosses died or retired, either of which were once in a lifetime events. Still, in the late 1930s, a retirement freed up a lieutenant's job and Denis decided to take the test. Unfortunately, the rarity of the event brought fierce competition to an otherwise routine promotion. Moreover, since all of the applicants had a good, practical knowledge of the workings of pumpers, ladders and hoses, the way to slip past the irksome bottleneck was to ace the written test. Unhappily, this was a giant red flag for the easy-going Denis Murphy, who never showed particularly well on paper.

This lieutenant's test was a cruel refinement of the torture, keying on math problems and other conundrums that were handled automatically with the turn of a knob on the control panel of new pumpers. In order to pass the written test, a candidate had to have a genuine facility with numbers. But the lieutenant's exam went deeper than the mundane math skills that all firemen learned early on. More specifically, it measured an applicant's mental agility with the most intricate problems associated with the speed, pressure, and volume of water flowing through hoses and nozzles under a wide variety of conditions.

Bernoulli's Principle—named after the Swiss mathematician and physicist who first enumerated the law—states that the total energy in a steadily flowing fluid system is constant along the flow path. Therefore, an increase in the fluid's speed must be matched by a decrease in its pressure. In short, the speed and pressure of water in a hose, for example, are inversely related. The principle is particularly relevant to the nozzles of fire hoses, whereby flow decelerates and pressure rises as the nozzle size is reduced. The principles employed in the Venturi Fire Pump Flow Meter were enumerated in Arnold H. Gibson's 1912 *Hydraulics*

And Its Applications. Therefore the need to calculate flows rates wasn't really necessary, but a part of the written test for lieutenant all the same.

Denis Murphy was in trouble. Just as with his late brother, Thomas, math had never been his strong suit, and he even left all of the simple household bill paying to his wife, Mary, who was a ciphering wizard. His grades in math at St. Patrick's Elementary School and Brockton High had always been the lowest ones on his report cards and now this old nemesis had returned to undermine his future. His two oldest boys tried to help. Night after night, Denis sat at the dining room table with Joe and Bob, working with sample test questions. First, they walked him through the simplest examples and later graduated to problems that were more complex. Try as they did though, they simply couldn't reach him. Right up to the day of the lieutenant's exam, he labored tirelessly on the sample questions and the variables of the formula. The harder he tried, the less he retained. He was completely flummoxed.

The morning of the exam, he pushed his eggs around on the plate, but just could get anything down. At the time, he was making $28 a week, and knowing that the few extra dollars in his pay envelope each week might mean something to his sons' educations, he left the house in a dither. With all of the familial variables flip-flopping around with the numbers inside his head, he was thrust again into the role of the little child so anxious to please the people who loved him.

Despite a mountain of resolve and the requisite hours of practice and study, Denis Murphy developed no dexterity at all with Bernoulli's Principle. It was a foreign language to the otherwise capable hoseman of Squad A. His performance on the test was a pencil-breaking, flop-sweating, ocean-going disaster. Until the department saw fit to simplify the exam by eliminating the questions dealing with Bernoulli's Principle, it was hopeless. Denis Murphy never became a lieutenant and, in truth, never even took the test again. Out of respect for their father, his three sons never mentioned the matter.

Indeed, he knew that his sons hadn't gotten their brains from him. The Sullivan side of the family was where the brains resided. Of that he was sure. Perhaps they had gotten their good-natured personalities from him? Denis Murphy might not have been introspective enough to chase this line of thought. We'll never know. He did however have enough innate pride to feel that he was a good breadwinner and a good fireman. When it came to fighting fires, he had the right instincts and the *cajones* to walk into burning buildings and get the job done. Not many men could do that.

On any given night, there would be seventeen firemen sleeping over at the firehouse—five from Squad A, five from Engine Co. 1, five from Ladder Co. 1, and Axel Larsen, the driver for Deputy Fire Chief Lawrence Lynch and also Clarence Hamilton, the driver for Fire Chief Dickinson. Undoubtedly, there was plenty of snoring and farting, but the men slept the best they could.

During their short days, these men brought a lunch to work with them or had a sandwich delivered by one of their children. Another option was to shoot across the street to the Rex Home Lunch for a bite to eat. Alternatively, the men sent out for sandwiches or fixings at one of the three markets closest to the firehouse. There was the Mihos Brothers Market diagonally across from the firehouse on the corner of Beacon Street (now Hereford St.), Pleasant Market on the west side of the Central Alarm Building, which abutted the firehouse, and the Mohegan Market around the corner on Main Street. Brockton Public Market—four blocks to the south—was a further choice, but usually not worth the walk. On the 24-hour days though, Denis Murphy brought a lunch or depended on one of his sons to bring him something to eat at noontime.

Suppertime was special for the firemen—a smorgasbord in an almshouse. Men who could cook were treasured in the fire department and the best cooks always found their way to the Central Fire House. The fact that the Chief and his Deputy worked from this building—and very often took their meals there—was purely coincidental. In March 1941, the best cook on the Brockton Fire Department was William E. "Eddie" Hogan.

One of the most fascinating facts in Eddie Hogan's background was that his Irish emigrant father, Thomas, was born at sea, off the coast of Gibraltar. Eddie's grandparents were among the Irish who figured that a quick trip to the sun-drenched

Mediterranean beat a long and dangerous journey across the North Atlantic to America. They booked passage accordingly. Since they eventually settled in the United States, their earlier plans were obviously flawed.

Brockton was a good fit for Thomas Hogan, but the jury was still out on Eddie. He barely got past the eighth grade and by 1915 was working as a shipper in a shoe factory. On the flip side, when he got to eighteen-years-old, he was of medium height, with a slender build, and a winning disposition. Add some blonde hair and a pair of deep blue eyes, and the young girls of Brockton were entranced.[155]

Predictably, Eddie began dating a cute-as-a-button, sixteen-year-old sales clerk, Marion Wills, who got pregnant in record time—or at least she convinced Eddie that she was. Either way, since Eddie was the only one making deposits, he began to sweat. While everyone else in Brockton prepared for the birth of the Savior, Eddie and Marion started laying the groundwork for the appearance of another Hogan.[156]

Marion's mother, Viola Belle Wills, had married her husband, Willard Wills, at sixteen and the results were disastrous. Still, a pregnant sixteen-year-old wasn't uncharted territory in the Wills's household. Naturally, the Hogan and Wills families tried to put the best light on the situation that they could. Marion's birth certificate conveniently disappeared, and the marriage license became a work of fiction. Suddenly Marion was eighteen, and living at Eddie's place (1068 Montello Street). Since everything on the marriage certificate technically passed muster, Rev. Alexander Hamilton of St. Margaret's Roman Catholic Church on Main Street agreed to marry the lovely couple in the rectory. On Christmas Eve 1915, in a furtive little ceremony, the young lovers were joined in holy matrimony. The nuptials went smoothly and William and Marion Hogan were joined "for better or for worse."

Within the first year of marriage, "for worse" got the upper hand. For some inexplicable reason, Marion never produced a baby. Presumably she had a miscarriage—real or imagined. Meanwhile Eddie discovered that marriage didn't even remotely resemble one of the thrilling rides at the Brockton Fair; lo and behold, it was hard work.

As this little charade played out on Montello Street, the First World War raged in Europe. In the 1916 presidential election, Woodrow Wilson ran on the slogan, "He Kept Us Out of War," allowing Americans to breathe a sigh of relief as they pulled the Democratic lever on the new voting machines.[157] A month after taking office—dishonest politician that he was—Woodrow Wilson talked Congress into declaring war on Germany and he signed the measure on April 6, 1917. A national military draft ensued.

By the time Eddie Hogan registered for the draft in mid-summer 1918, his marriage was over. He was working for the Bay State Street Railroad Company and moved back in with his parents at 1110 Montello Street. Uncle Sam quickly inducted Eddie and taught him to cook. The United States's official involvement in World War I comprised eighteen months and ended on November 11, 1918, the day the fighting ended. (It took another eight months to settle the terms of surrender and war reparations, pushing the Treaty of Versailles to June 28, 1919.) That said, the Army needed cooks until every last soldier returned home, so Eddie's hitch was a bit longer than that of his fellow doughboys.

When Eddie finally got back to Brockton, his life lay scattered on the ground in little pieces. He was out of the railroad business and spent his days attaching heels to shoes; Marion's parents, Willard and Viola Belle Wills divorced in 1916; that same year, Willard Wills married a new woman, Blanche, and had an infant son, Beverley; and Eddie's ex-wife Marion, was nowhere to be found. As a final crescendo to this symphony of human wreckage, the world was left to wonder whether or not a baby ever existed.[158]

Wary of connubial bliss, Eddie Hogan did not remarry until 1924, when he exchanged vows with a young Swedish girl, Lilly, and they quickly filled their home on Copeland Street with four little children.

One hair-thin, silver lining surfaced for Eddie Hogan. Traditionally, veterans are given their pick of city jobs when they return from war and Eddie was no exception. Even though he first went back to the shoe factories, he later improved his life markedly by taking a position on the Brockton Fire Department. Without question, the fact that he had been a cook in the army, greased the skids.

In 1941, Eddie Hogan was forty-four. Between the military and the fire department, he had been cooking for twenty-six years and was good at it. In truth, Eddie could easily have cooked in a fancy restaurant if he ever got tired of putting out fires, but that was the stuff of dreams. Eddie Hogan—erstwhile shoe heeler— was a fireman at heart and spent the rest of his working life at the Brockton Fire Department.

At the other fire stations, the chow was sometimes so bad that the men's wives sent their children scurrying to the firehouse with a wholesome meal at suppertime. While some of the men at other stations were eating fish chowder and pea soup as main courses, Eddie Hogan laid out baked hams dappled with peppercorns, twenty-five pound turkeys with small baked potatoes and three different vegetables. In a pinch, he made shepherd's pie. He capped these sumptuous meals with deep-dish pies and homemade puddings. His knowledge of food was profound. Eddie Hogan's meticulous preparation knew no bounds, as he shopped at three different markets for just one meal. Mihos Brothers had the best turkeys, but for good beef, he insisted on Pleasant Market. Vegetables were another story. The Brockton Public Market was the place for fresh beans, carrots, spinach, lettuce and tomatoes. All of Brockton's forty food stores bought their bread from the same twenty local bakeries and Eddie knew the pedigree of each loaf. He made his purchases accordingly. After cooking a fabulous meal, Eddie simply added up the receipts and divided by the number of people present. Each man paid about 20¢ for one of the best meals of his life.

This clever system worked flawlessly but for one exception. Stores weren't open on Sundays in 1941 and Eddie hated canned food. For him, eating canned foods was like kissing your sister. Eddie Hogan, however, was a resourceful person and found a way to, at least partially, blunt the impact of Massachusetts's harsh blue laws. On Sundays, he made spaghetti and meatballs. The spaghetti and tomato sauce came from boxes and cans, but with a few spices and his educated palate, Eddie managed to put some kick into the dull sauce. The ground beef, salad fixings and bread he purchased the night before and brought to work with him on Sunday morning. With a little planning, Eddie could still deliver a

173

delicious meal despite a few hardships, like the inability to buy fresh ingredients.

Hoseman Eddie Hogan was a remarkable study, in that he was a slow-moving, sturdy—and later portly—man, standing five-foot-eight, and about as garrulous as any Irishman ever got. Yet, in the kitchen, he was transformed into a blur of deft motions and quick commands to his helpers. He rarely ate more than one plate of food at a sitting, but he was a serious artist when it came to preparing food. Others firemen tried to relax on the long shifts, but not Eddie. When the markets were open, he shopped diligently and slavishly passed the afternoons in the kitchen coaxing the flavor from a pork loin or a rump roast. Aside from the pleasure of enjoying a good meal, his only other reward was that he did not have to clean the dishes. As with the finest restaurants of the world, that chore fell to a special crew. (Still another bunch set the table.)

On the dot of six, Eddie would emerge from the kitchen with the main course on a platter. Some of the smiling faces around the table nodded their approval; still others ribbed Eddie about the number of pots and pans he used or some other meaningless banter.

Suppertime was extraordinary for more than just the seventeen firemen stuck at the firehouse. Eddie Hogan's reputation was a hard thing to keep under wraps and in no time the secret leaked out like water through a colander. Soon, the cops on the beat—along with a colorful collection of "sparkies"—began to take their meals at the Central Fire House. These sparkies were fire enthusiasts who, for whatever reason, never managed to become firefighters. These shortcomings notwithstanding, they hung out at the firehouse for the vicarious thrill of rubbing shoulders with real firemen. With enough cops and sparkies, the number of diners could get almost out of hand. But Eddie Hogan never complained and just allowed for a little more shopping and preparation time. The firemen of the Central Fire House lived in close quarters and their work demanded dependence on one another. A hothead didn't last long in firefighting. Though Eddie may have had a temper in the kitchen, as a firefighter he was cut from the same bolt as the other men.

On Sunday, March 9, 1941, Denis Murphy was scheduled to work one of his long shifts. The day began like all such Sundays with 6:30 A.M. mass at St. Patrick's Church. The early mass would allow him plenty of time to get to the Central Fire House by 7:45 A.M. Walking quickly back to Warren Avenue after the service, he grabbed his lunch, kissed Mary good-bye, and shuffled off to the firehouse. It was a short walk of less than three-quarters of a mile and he had come to enjoy it. As he walked diagonally across Warren Avenue, heading north, Stacy, Adams Shoes was the first building he passed. The huge place was eerily quiet this Sunday morning and buttoned up tight. On his days off, he watched the men coming and going from Stacy, Adams and the M.A. Packard Shoe Company at the south end of the block where he lived—a constant reminder of his time spent in the shoe industry and the road not taken.

The temperatures in the first couple of weeks of March 1941 hovered just above freezing during the day and there were still small piles of snow here and there around the city. While he walked, Denis Murphy thought about what everyone else in Americas was thinking about in early 1941—the war in Europe. Many of the firemen, like him, had sons who would be sent to the seat of war immediately if the United States became involved in the fighting. With Austria, Czechoslovakia, Poland, Denmark, Norway, Holland, Luxembourg and France under German control, it seemed unlikely that the United States could remain neutral much longer. Franklin Roosevelt's lend-lease pact with England practically guaranteed that America would enter the war.

Denis Murphy was not worried about his youngest boy, Ed, but he was concerned about his two older boys. If the United States entered the war, what were the chances that the government would allow two pre-med students to finish college? If the country got into the war, the Allies would need doctors by the bushel basket, but counting time for internship, the earliest that his two sons would be available for service was a decade into the future. How would Uncle Sam treat his pre-med sons? Would the government be willing to let them continue their educations? All of this presupposed that enough money could be scrapped together to somehow get them through medical school. There was plenty to worry about.

Squad A Ladder Truck

Completely lost in these foreboding thoughts, Denis marched to the firehouse in a few minutes and stood in the bay where the Squad A truck was usually parked. While Denis Murphy was attending mass at St. Patrick's, Squad A responded to a call at a house with a chimney fire near the corner of Belmont and Clinton Streets. They also went to a cellar fire at the Capital Market on Main, just around the corner from the firehouse. The earlier shift hadn't returned from the market yet, but would be back shortly.

The other crew would have no time to wipe down the fire truck and hang the hoses to dry, so Denis Murphy's shift would start with those chores. The work was welcome; it would break up the long hours and the comaraderie of a shared task was enoyable. The twenty-four-hour shift could be hours of endless boredom or it could be one emergency after another. There was no way to predict the outcome. It took a special kind of person to endure the endless hours of boredom and still present a cheerful face to the world. With twenty-two years on the job, Denis Murphy had learned to cope with the vicissitudes of a firefighter's life.

He greeted the other members of the crew as they arrived and Lieutenant Buckley called the group to order about ten minutes before the hour. Checking the names off on a clipboard, roll call was over in less than a minute. After a few remarks about special chores that the lieutenant wanted addressed, the men scattered to fill their lockers and prepare for the day.

The first order of business was Squad A's truck. It was a bright red American-LaFrance ladder truck with a completely open cab. The only thing protecting the driver from the weather was a ten-inch-tall pane of glass, the width of the cab. This windshield was held in place with a steel frame and filling the space between the bottom of the glass and the engine cowling was a simple piece of canvas. The four tires on the vehicle were almost three feet in diameter but narrow, necessitating the use of chains on the back wheels all winter long.

On each side of the truck were mounted ladders and both chemical and water fire extinguishers. The top section of the truck held numerous 50-foot sections of cotton-jacketed hose in diameters from 2 ½' to 4". Long-tailed helmets and fire-retardant jackets hung all over the apparatus, waiting for the firefighters to slip into them. Fully loaded, the engine could transport two firemen in the front seat and four others standing on the fantail. It was no secret to the men of Squad A that 25 percent of all firefighters' deaths occurred while riding to and from fires.

After stowing their personal gear in the lockers on the second floor, the five men from Squad A concentrated on readying the engine for its next outing. The fire company had plenty of extra hose so hanging the wet ones was a low priority. The truck was completely wiped down and all of the extinguishers refilled. A few more dry hoses were added to the unused hoses on the truck.

Only after the engine was completely readied did the men relax a bit. At this point, the younger firemen took the wet hoses to the back of the firehouse and prepared to hang them up in the drying tower.

The work was invigorating although the first floor of the station was only heated enough to keep the water in the pumpers from freezing. Unfortunately, the maintenance work on the Squad A truck was the only serious work they did all day. This particular Sunday was an exasperatingly slow day. After the 6:54 A.M.

alarm—responded to by the previous crew at Squad A—there were no calls for the rest of the morning, afternoon and evening. This was extraordinary for a weekend in March. Usually a homeowner could be counted on for a grease fire while cooking bacon or notice smoke coming from the furnace. At the very least, someone would decide to use a fireplace that had not been used in a decade and, within a few minutes of ignition, the alarm would be ringing off the wall at the firehouse. But not this day.

The hours crawled by as men swept the firehouse and mended their personal gear. When they talked to each another, they gazed out onto Pleasant Street as if expecting to be called out in the middle of the next sentence. By late afternoon, the whole company was ready for a good long nap while they awaited Eddie Hogan's spaghetti and meatballs. With the alarm bell as silent as could be, a few sparkies appeared at the firehouse to chew the fat and help move the hands of the clock along. Finally, the men began to assemble in the second floor dining room for supper.

This Sunday, there were twenty-two people sitting around the big table when Eddie emerged from the kitchen with two big bowls of spaghetti. Several more times he dipped into the kitchen to retrieve meatballs, sauce, salad and garlic bread. Most of the firemen drank coffee with a few of the younger ones preferring milk or soda. There were two beat cops and three sparkies joining the regular firemen for dinner. The sparkies were an interesting bunch of hangers-on. While most of them were harmless enough, they all had one thing in common—an unnatural love of fire. They could never be ruled out as potential arsonists. Thus, it was far wiser to befriend them and have them safely hanging around the firehouse than wandering about the city itching for a thrill. In that sense, the sparkies misread the firefighters comradeship completely. They thought they were being accepted into a special brotherhood when in fact they were spending their days under a powerful microscope. They, of course, never understood.

After a leisurely meal that thankfully was not interrupted by an alarm, men splintered off into groups to talk, read the papers or play Forty Fives. Some just dozed in the lounge's easy chairs.

Almost without exception though, the men piled into the radio room and pulled their chairs closer to the strange contraption for their favorite Sunday night shows, broadcast over WEEI in

Boston. At 7, *Jack Benny* came on with Mary Livingston, Don Wilson and "Rochester." At 7:30, *Bandwagon* filled a half hour while they waited for *Edgar Bergen and Charlie McCarthy*. Eight-thirty brought *One Man's Family*, followed by *Manhattan Merry-Go-Round* at 9. After 9:30, it was all orchestra music until the war news from Europe at midnight, but no one stayed up for the final broadcast of the evening. After the *All Girl Orchestra* completed their selections at 10:30, slowly the games of Forty Fives wound down and everyone headed for bed.

In early 1941, the talk the fire station was almost exclusively about Hitler and the Boston Red Sox. Many of the firemen had all of the same concerns for their sons that Denis Murphy had for his. But there was nothing anyone could do about it. For many of the firemen, it was a subject best avoided while on duty. Instead, they did what all men do to wile away the time, they talked about meaningless matters—like sports.

Unlike the Italian immigrants, who organized bocce clubs, the Irish brought no sports with them from the old country. True, there were a few young hardheads who insisted on playing the ancient and violent Irish game of hurling on their days off, but it was far too brutal for men whose families depended on them for a weekly paycheck. A broken limb meant privation.

As a result—and as a further acculturating feature—baseball became the spectator sport of the Irish-Americans in the Boston area. The National League Boston Braves were the club of the upper classes while the American League Red Sox were the favorite of the working class Brocktonians. In 1940, Ted Williams had completed his second year with the team, batting a strong .344. The other two outfielders, Doc Cramer and Dom DiMaggio batted .303 and .301, respectively. The hot pitcher for the Sox was Lefty Grove with an ERA of 3.99. Ted Williams was clearly the star of the team, expected to do great things for the Red Sox in the years ahead. (Williams batted .406 in the 1941 season.)

At 9:45, almost three hours after they had finished eating, an alarm sounded, but it was only a small oil stove fire on Galen Street, in the eastern part of the city. Engine No. 4 took the call. Such a small fire would not require the assistance of Squad A, Engine No. 1 or Ladder No. 1. The men at Engine No. 4 handled it by themselves and were back at their eastside station within the hour.

By 11 P.M., the Central Fire House was locked up tight and the men were all in bed with their "night hitches" bunched up next to their bunks.

The winter had not been especially cold, but the wind blew from the east endlessly and the temperature at night dipped down to the low twenties. Spring seemed a long way off. Still, the weather had not kept people from enjoying a night at the movies. *The Philadelphia Story* played at the Brockton Theatre with Katherine Hepburn, Cary Grant and Jimmy Stewart. Rosalind Russell and Melvyn Douglas starred in *This Thing Called Love* at the Colonial. At the Modern, W. C. Fields tore up audiences with his comedy, *The Bank Dick*, and Judy Garland starred at the Rialto in *Little Nellie Kelly*. There were three other theaters in the downtown area with the Park showing *A Bill Of Divorcement* and the Keith running *The Mark of Zorro* with Tyrone Powers.

The Strand Theatre, on School Street, was one of the oldest movie houses in town. Its marquee blazed *Mickey Rooney— Hoosier Schoolboy* and *Secret Evidence*.

The Depression years were tough on the shoe industry and, in predictable ripple fashion, the other businesses experienced slow times too. The newer theaters—that could afford the best new movies—bucked the trend. Older places like the Strand had it rough. The Strand's tenant, Proven Pictures, remodeled the building in 1937, installing the finest new camera equipment available and introduced a novel enticement—female usherettes. On Saturday afternoons, youngsters flocked to the theater to see Tom Mix and Hoot Gibson movies. The Strand even offered 10¢ passes, which were bartered around the city like scrip on a military base. These coupons were in fairly short supply and the general public was usually faced with a choice between a first run movie at the Brockton Theatre for 50¢ or a second run movie at the Strand for 35¢. More often than not, people chose J.J. Cahill's offering at the Brockton Theatre.

The Strand Theatre introduced Brockton to the talking picture with *The Jazz Singer*. The movie house was part of the Washburn Block, a collection of almost all brick buildings, owned by Mrs. Ella P. Gurney, of 49 Newbury Street, and Mrs. Maybelle C.

Gurney, of 1315 Main Street. These two women were the widows of Merton and Sanford Gurney who ran a jewelry and optical company on Main Street—Gurney Brothers. Plowing their profits into real estate, they left their widows very well fixed indeed. The women leased the theater to Boston's Proven Pictures.

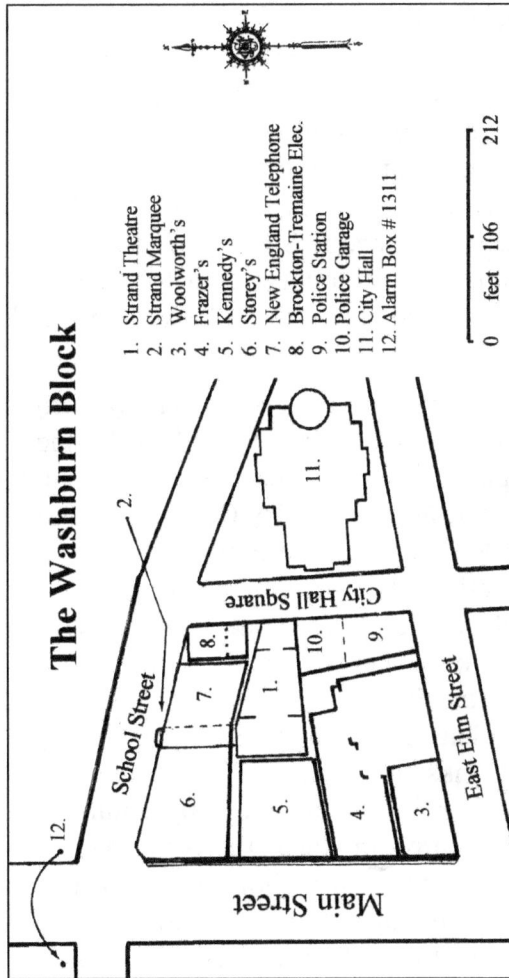

The Washburn Block

1. Strand Theatre
2. Strand Marquee
3. Woolworth's
4. Frazer's
5. Kennedy's
6. Storey's
7. New England Telephone
8. Brockton-Tremaine Elec.
9. Police Station
10. Police Garage
11. City Hall
12. Alarm Box # 1311

0   feet   106   212

City Hall Square

School Street

East Elm Street

Main Street

On Main Street—to the west of the Strand—sat Storey's, an upscale women's clothing store and Kennedy's, another clothier, who carried a broader line of clothes for both men and women. Between these two buildings ran a long alley that offered theatergoers a shortcut from Main Street to the west entrance of the Strand. The last building that fronted Main Street on the Washburn Block was Woolworth's 5¢ & 10¢, to the south of Kennedy's.

The north side of Storey's ran down School Street about 120 feet to the entrance of the Strand. The movie house's huge marquee resembled a shoe box in that it was rectangular. It hung over the sidewalk about eight feet, running twenty feet along School Street. It stood six feet tall and had a white finger-like projection, which shot into the sky another twenty feet. In black, stacked letters, this extension spelled out the word STRAND. Next to the Strand's entrance, on the east, was Stanley's Package Store and the offices of the New England Telephone Company. The last business on School Street was the Brockton-Tremaine Electric Company, an electrical contractor. Their offices were in the only wooden building on the block, a place smaller than a Cape Cod style house.

The land where the Strand Theatre sat was originally occupied by Sheedy's Theatre, which first opened for business in 1900. The first theater operator was Michael Sheedy, a Fall River native, who later moved to New York. By October 1913, the theater, now Atty. Stewart McLeod's Empire Playhouse, was leased to John L. Sullivan (the retired heavyweight boxing champion) of West Abington. Sullivan had won the bare-knuckles heavyweight championship by knocking out Paddy Ryan of Troy, New York in 1882. The "Boston Strong Boy" had a widow-maker of a punch and a swashbuckling, garrulous personality, but was one of the all-time meanest drunks that ever lived. His bigger-than-life persona made him the recipient of an unending round of free drinks in America's hotel barrooms and the spit-and-sawdust joints he loved. By closing time, he was thoroughly sloshed and the owners grew increasingly anxious. It was touch and go; either Sullivan would head for another saloon or destroy the place. Even for the most avid fight fan, it was definitely preferable to worship "The Great John L." from afar.

The Empire Playhouse fared no better under the stewardship of John L. Sullivan than the bars that he dismantled over the years. Rather suspiciously, in the early morning hours of Saturday, April 7, 1915, it burned to the ground.

The Strand Theatre was the successor of the Empire Playhouse and was completed in March 1916, the brainchild of Brockton architect W. F. Barlow Jr. The new Strand was the largest playhouse in the city with a seating capacity of 1685. Insofar as architecture went, it conformed to no school at all. Wedged tightly in place, it was almost completely surrounded by other large buildings. The Strand Theatre's marquee and entrance were on School Street, a side street that ran east off Main. The entrance though was actually only the mouth of a tunnel-like foyer that was about 100 feet long. After purchasing a ticket, a long walk and a quick turn to the left put a patron at the back of the auditorium—about 105 feet from the movie screen. At the back of the stage—over which the movie screen hung—was a 32-foot wide brick wall that abutted a small street—Town Hall Square. Here, and only here, the theater finally met with a public thoroughfare.

The building was 139 feet long and of varying widths. It stood 60 feet tall. However, all these numbers are misleading because the building was built to conform to the structures around it, which were almost all parallelograms. Their unusual shapes were necessitated by School Street's irregular connection to Main. While almost every other street formed a traditional 90° intersection, School Street connected to Main Street at a 77° angle. The Strand, in turn, was designed as a five-sided building to accommodate the surrounding structures. In 1916, construction costs ran a scant $30,000. Dennis J. Gorman and Samuel Stone of the Stone Leather Company, Henry L. Alexander of Alexander's Fashion Shop, and Constantine Condikey were the owners of the new showplace. They chose "Strand" because New York's first true motion picture palace, built in 1914, bore that name.

John W. Sullivan (no relation to John L.) was the first manager of the Strand but, in May of 1916, J.J. Cahill took his place. Alex H. Hurwitz of Brockton became the manager just as extensive refurbishing was completed in August 1937. The new tenant was Frederick E. Lieberman of Proven Pictures.

Chapter 5

Strand Theatre Fire

The sparse Sunday night crowd left the Strand Theatre by 11:30 and the manager, Frank Clementa, had the building completely locked up by midnight. At 12:30 A.M. (March 10), the Strand's house officer, Sanford Alger, and custodian, Patrick Moore, started cleaning up the theatre for the next day's performances. But as soon as the two men swung the door to the theater open, the acrid smell of smoke hit them. Then Patrick Moore noticed flames in the back of the balcony. Sanford Alger quickly ran across Main Street to pull the handle of alarm box #1311 on the corner of High Street. (The same box is still there.)

At 12:38 A.M., on the second floor of the Central Fire House, the seventeen firefighters were sound asleep when the call came in. Throwing back their bedcovers, they swung their feet toward their "night hitches" and slipped the heavy bunker pants up over their long underwear. Scrambling for the brass fire pole, one by one they slid down to the first floor, grabbed their fire jackets, leather "New Yorker" helmets, and jumped onto the fire trucks. Easing out of the station house onto Pleasant Street, the trucks turned south on Main Street. The Strand Theatre was only four blocks away. Denis Murphy rode to the fire on the back of the Squad A truck.

At the first alarm, Squad A, Engine No. 1 and Ladder No. 1 were all dispatched from the Central Fire House. Owing to the density of the buildings in the area of the Strand Theatre—and because of the mention of open flame—two other engine companies were also sent to the fire—No. 4 from the east side and No. 5 from the west side.

When the fire crew arrived at the scene, the two men who worked at the Strand—Sanford Alger and Patrick Moore—were back inside the building. Immediately, a blaze was seen just inside one of the doors. This door allowed patrons to use an alley to enter or leave the theater from Main Street. Looking up, Patrick Moore could see flames through a ventilator in the balcony. Events were moving apace. By this time, the theater was filled with smoke and visibility was deteriorating rapidly.

The first firefighters on the scene figured out quickly that the fire had begun in the basement. The men found flames just inside the lobby and cut a hole in the floor to get at them. Water was directed at the flames, with limited results. Running for more hose, the firefighters brought in a booster line, but again to little avail. It was the most peculiar fire because as one fire fighter put it, "The more water we put on it, the hotter the flames burned."

Unlike the other firemen, Captain Carroll, first saw flames outside, coming through a fire exit door—on the south wall of the theater. A line of water was directed to that spot from the ground to keep the flames from leaping onto Frazier's Dry Goods next door. Captain Carroll, now noticing flames in a number of different places, knew instinctively that he was quickly losing control of the conflagration. Taking no chances, he called in a second alarm. From the same alarm box, at the corner of Main and High Streets, he changed the designation to a four-alarm fire, bringing Engine No. 2 and Ladder No. 2 in from Campello (two miles down Main Street). This second alarm at 12:44 A.M., also alerted the skeleton crew at the *Brockton Enterprise*. Arriving at the scene in no time were Connie Lyons, a night reporter, and Stanley Bauman, an *Enterprise* photographer.

Even after the second alarm had been called in, firefighters didn't realize how bad the situation had gotten. Stanley Bauman of the *Enterprise* remembered, "Firefighters in the balcony, and on the main floor, were pouring water on the balcony's smoking back wall. Others, waiting for more hose, were standing around or sitting on the balcony seats. On the stage at the other end of the auditorium, a few firemen and some sparkies were watching the firefighters work . . . Someone came in and said, 'Fire's breaking through the roof.'"[159]

There was so much smoke in the theater that Stanley Bauman couldn't get any pictures. A helpful fireman told him to walk out onto the balcony fire escape and he might be able to get a shot of the fire as it pushed out of the building. This helpful advice saved Bauman's life. No sooner had he walked onto the fire escape than the roof of the theater let go.

Just like any other escalating blaze, smoke and flames showed themselves in other places. Captain Carroll wasted no time. He strode over to the alarm box on Main Street at 1:19 A.M. and changed the Strand Theatre Fire to a general alarm. This final call brought out Engine No. 3 from the Montello Station and Ladder No. 3 from the Battles Street Station (a mile north of the scene). At the same time, aid was requested from the surrounding towns of Stoughton, Abington and West Bridgewater.

Meanwhile, the flames kept growing in size on the south side of the theater until the entire sky was lit up wildly. Firemen standing on a roof nearby were almost drawn into the flames.

Now hopelessly out of control, the only chance of fighting the blaze appeared to be some odd maneuver to get water inside the theater and up in the balcony—where the fire seemed most intense. In order to reach that area, firefighters walked the long entrance from School Street to the theater proper. Passing through the openings in the back wall—which led to the seats—there were two sets of stairs to the balcony. These stairs were attached to the north and south sidewalls of the theater. Moving as quickly as possible, hoses were laid from a hydrant on School Street and into the theater proper. Eventually more than a dozen firefighters were up on the balcony playing water on the southwest corner. Simultaneously, there were firefighters on the first floor dousing the back wall where the balcony connected.

Without the heat seeking equipment of a later era, the firemen did not know that between the plaster ceiling and the flat roof at the very top of the sixty-foot high structure was a series of ten-foot tall steel trusses, running from side to side (north to south). As they worked to extinguish the flames on the sidewalls, fire roared madly out of control in the ten-foot open space above the plaster ceiling.

The fire had started in the basement and found its way up to the roof inside the wall near the back of the theater. Only then did it jump into the space above the ceiling and begin to consume the wooden ceiling joists running between the steel trusses. The fire could well have been burning in this area even before the firefighters arrived at the theater. As the fire superheated the confined space, it began to force out the brick sidewalls of the building. Eventually the ends of the trusses had nothing to sit on. All they could do was collapse.

No one knows the exact moment when the roof of the theater gave way. Retired Chief Kenneth Galligan, who has studied the Strand Theatre Fire at least as much as anyone else, believes the roof collapsed about an hour after the first alarm. That would be 1:38 A. M. (March 10). Chief Galligan also believes that film canisters exploding in the projection room cause the roof to buckle. "At first, the fire in the projection room burned with a yellow flame," he told an *Enterprise* reporter the day after the fire. "I heard a loud boom. The roof definitely went up before it came down."[160]

The Strand Theatre After The Fire.

The combined weight of the brick chimney, roofing materials, wood sheathing, steel roof trusses, wooden ceiling joists, and plaster caused the whole roof to suffer structural fatigue. In fires, roof trusses are particularly vulnerable to early collapse because of the large surface-to-mass ratio of truss systems.

When the roof collapsed, some firemen were crushed and died instantly in the balcony while twenty others were tossed into the flames, smoke and water in the auditorium below. All together, thirteen firemen died—twelve instantly, including Denis Murphy—and one in the hospital a few days later. It was such a mess of twisted rubble that the firefighters could not be extricated. The cries of the trapped fireman—who were pinned but not crushed by the debris—could be heard out on School Street.

In reconstructing the events of that night, men who understand fires and their fiendish ways, believe that the falling ceiling and roof crushed the firefighters first and any burns received were post mortem.

From outside of the building—except for a "whoosh" and a burst of sparks and flames—bystanders and firemen alike had no indication that the roof had collapsed. Nonetheless, when the roof caved in, it took the cantalevered center part of the balcony down with it.

Another man who just barely escaped death was Larry Johnson, a twenty-four-year-old rookie firefighter with Engine No. 1 at the Central Fire House. As with every other business, rookies are practically worked to death, and in the Brockton Fire Department, it was no different. Larry Johnson had been sent out for more hose. When Johnson got back inside the theater, he began to climb the balcony stairs with the hose draped over his shoulder. It was then that the roof let go. The impact knocked him back down the stairs. He lay there semi-conscious and buried in debris. As he regained his wits, Lieutenant Bill Bussey yelled at him, "Don't go up there. It's bad up there."[161]

After the roof collapsed, firefighters, policemen, sparkies, and newspapermen all jumped into the mess in an effort to pull the trapped firemen to safety. One of the first men they tried to help was Lt. John Buckley of Engine No. 1, whose legs were pinned under the front edge of the balcony. At first, they could not budge the heavy balcony. The situation was so desperate that Father Morrisroe of St. Patrick's Church gave Buckley Last Rites. The flames, debris and screaming was so terrifying that Buckley begged his would-be rescuers to cut off his legs at the knees and get him out of there. Fortunately, cooler heads prevailed and finally enough men were assembled to lift the balcony just enough to tug him out from under its incredible weight.

"I helped carry out two bodies," said hoseman George Brady. "One was Billy Murphy and I think the other was Ray Mitchell. I took them outside and laid them on the sidewalk. Then, Chief Dickinson sent me to Hickey's Funeral Parlor to make arrangements . . . ."

Firemen, policemen, newsmen, and sparkies continued to extricate downed firefighters. Many men escaped death by a few feet. In the process of moving debris, many more firemen were injured. Policemen helping at the scene were also injured. Reports of injuries suffered at the fire were made by three police officers to their superior, Sergeant Harry Swartz. Patrolman John Brides complained of a shoulder injury, while officers Nelson and Vaughn each suffered leg injuries. The three were treated and reported for duty the following day.

The Strand Theatre Balcony That Killed Men Above and Below.

At 2:05 A.M., the Brockton Police Department called the State Police headquarters in Bridgewater for help. In response, a detail of men and four ambulance cruisers were dispatched to the Strand Theatre. At 2:07 A.M., an engine from Stoughton Fire Company arrived. There was precious little they could do inasmuch as the four streets surrounding the block—Main, East Elm, School Streets, and City Hall Square—were already clogged with every piece of Brockton's firefighting equipment. All together, the firefighters had laid fourteen hoses into the burning building. Ambulances and fire engines were double parked on East Elm Street.

Many firefighters awaited orders from Captain Carroll, but the orders never came. Captain Carroll was one of three firefighters at the northwestern corner of the balcony when the roof collapsed. He died instantly. The nearby firemen were able to get to the captain fairly quickly and his body was removed from the building.

The grim work continued through the early morning hours of Monday, March 10. As the temperature dropped during the night to 25 degrees, firefighters tried to extinguish the blaze and rescue their coworkers at the same time. All night long, police headquarters was besieged with telephone calls from law enforcement and newspaper people outside the city seeking information as to the condition of the hospitalized firemen. Police headquarters—just southeast of the theater—also acted as a triage unit, as injured firefighters were brought there all night. Telephone traffic was so extensive that Madeline (McCarthy) Davis was awakened by her supervisor and asked to report to New England Telephone Company on School Street to run the switchboard. She worked more than twenty-four hours straight.[162]

In a startling coincidence—because his life had always been so inextricably intertwined with Mary (Sullivan) Murphy and her family—at 5 o'clock in the morning, J.J. Cahill's car caught fire in the driveway of his home at 131 Moraine Street. (Ten years earlier, the Cahills had moved from Highland Terrace to Moraine Street.) The Brockton Fire Department couldn't help so they passed the call along to the Abington Fire Department.

J.J. Cahill first learned of the blaze at the Strand Theatre when he called the Brockton Fire Department. The *Brockton Enterprise* made special note of the fact that ordinarily J.J. Cahill was a bit of a sparkie himself, usually making an appearance at all of the cities larger fires. Compounding the otherworldly qualities of the incident was J.J. Cahill's stint as manager of the Strand Theatre from 1916 to 1925.[163]

For a man who routinely worked until the early hours of the morning, it does seem odd that J.J. Cahill's automobile would catch fire at 5 o'clock in the morning, though car fires were fairly common in 1941. Perhaps J.J. had breakfast or coffee at an all-night diner after his Brockton Theatre closed?[164]

When the water lines were shut off shortly before 6 A.M. and Chief Dickinson felt that there would not be another cave-in, firemen, policemen and civilians went to work in the debris. Except for the bodies of Captain Carroll and William Murphy—which were taken from the fire scene early—the others bodies were not taken out until after 6 A.M. There were so many bodies that the workers at Hickey's had to move their vehicles out of the garage so that it could be used for storage of the fallen firefighters.

After the water was shut off at 6 A.M., employees of Creedon & Cronin, a house moving company, arrived with massive jacks and cranked up the balcony. Once this was completed, the bodies lying beneath were recovered. The state police ambulance units left the fire at 8 A.M., having spent the night ferrying injured firefighters to Brockton Hospital. The local ambulances could handle the remaining bodies.

As one firefighter's body were removed from the charred theater, Chief Dickinson stopped the litter bearers. The men stood there patiently while Father Morrisroe administered the Last Rites of the Church. As the bodies came out, they were placed in baskets and borne away to Hickey's Funeral Parlor. Deputy Chief Lynch's driver, Axel Larsen, made tentative identification at the undertaking parlors. He and Medical Examiner Leavitt had left the Strand at 8 A.M. At Hickey's, the bodies of four of the firemen were identified, but the fifth proved more difficult. It was Denis Murphy and he was finally identified by his wedding ring and his badge—No. 78. Although the badge would seem to be identification enough, the possibility that one fireman—in the rush to leave the station—might have grabbed another man's coat by mistake could not be ruled out. The wedding ring was the only positive means of identification.

As a final insult, a small fire rekindled at 9 o'clock Monday morning in the upper northwest corner of what had been the balcony. Firemen put a heavy stream of water on the flame from the roof, but were unable to extinguish it because of the debris. Finally, a small line was run in through one of the fire exits in the balcony and the fire was extinguished.

The body of the last fallen fireman was located and removed at 10 A.M. Firefighters kept searching the debris for the rest of the day—hoping either that they would find someone alive or that all the victims were already found.

The *Brockton Enterprise* was getting so many telephone calls that they finally typed up a list of the dead and taped it in their front window on Main Street. They were working feverishly to get out a special edition, but were not able to do so until after 10 A.M. As passersby gathered to study the names on the list in the front window, a large crowd gathered. People saw the name of a friend or loved one and broke down. Finally, the *Enterprise* got out an "extra," and it sold 4,625 copies in a few hours.

Monday afternoon, firemen silently walked the theater's haunted aisles. Water still dripped from the collapsed balcony, and the choking smell of smoke still hung in the air like a mourning cloak. The middle aisle's red carpet was still wet. Seats were tipped back. High above, through the roof's jagged hole, the winter sky showed.

The balcony that had caused the deaths of thirteen firemen, and brought misery and suffering to so many others, was a mass of crumpled building materials. Yet the ticket booth out in the foyer of the theater was unscathed. The pretty blonde could still be selling tickets, without anyone thinking she was out of place.

Also out in the foyer—just thirty steps from the spot where tickets were taken— stood the untouched candy counter. Even its little tinsel lamp was undamaged. Under the glass of the confections case sat row upon row of candy bars, unharmed in any way by the mayhem of the preceding ten hours.

As one walked into the body of the theater, the farthest aisle (on the south) ended in a pile of beams, bricks, and sheets of wrinkled steel. On the stage, Captain Charles Bell was leaning against a piano and talking to a man who wanted to know what happened. The captain talked without taking his eyes off the balcony. The fat little footlight bulbs, that had once blinked excitement onto the stage, lay shattered on the hardwood floor.

By noon Monday, all the firemen had been positively identified. On Monday afternoon, William G. Green, superintendent of buildings in the City of Brockton, posted warning notices on the Strand Theatre's walls. These signs read, "Notice is hereby given that this building is in a dangerous condition, in that it is officially unsafe because of fire. This notice is affixed by me as inspector of buildings for the City of Brockton under the provision section six of Chapter 143 of the commonwealth . . . ."

From the roof of the Kennedy building on Main Street, Chief Dickinson gathered with State Fire Marshall Stephen Garrity, Brockton Building Superintendent William G. Green and Fire Chiefs David Tierney of Arlington and Seiden Allen of Brookline. From there, they could look down inside the Strand Theatre and examine the wreckage.

Late Monday afternoon, police roped off the entrance to the theater. Although nothing could be seen from the outside of the building, on Monday afternoon, huge crowds of curious spectators visited Centerville to view the scene. Since the burned building had no structural integrity, police kept the crowds at a distance. Thousands of cars circled the square and then drove slowly along School Street. Many were surprised at how little damage was visible from the outside.

Mayor Rowe proclaimed Wednesday (March 12) as a day of mourning. All schools, public buildings, and places of entertainment remained closed until 6 o'clock at night.

Meanwhile, men from the funeral homes worked feverishly Monday afternoon to make arrangements. Many residents thought that a single mass made the most sense, but Mayor Rowe dismissed the idea. Instead, the funerals were held separately on Wednesday and Thursday. Captain Carroll, William Murphy and Mathew McGeary were the only three who had open caskets. All of the other firemen's bodies were so badly crushed and charred that their caskets were buttoned up tight before they left the funeral homes.

On Monday, the dean of Tufts College sent for Joe and Bob Murphy. They were to go home immediately because their "father was hurt." After getting into their best clothes, they took the MTA to Ashmont Station, where they caught a bus to Brockton. The bus dumped them right on the corner of Main Street and School Streets, near the Strand Theatre marquee. A short distance to the north, they could see a large crowd in front of the *Brockton Enterprise* building, at the corner of Main and Centre Streets. Walking up Main Street, they could see that the front windows of the building were papered over—from the inside—with stories of the fire and the names of the dead firemen. There, pushed shoulder to shoulder with silent residents, they saw their father's name. They had traveled from Medford to Brockton so that they could read the tragic and incomprehensible news of their father's death through smudged glass, surrounded by strangers. They immediately went to 551 Warren Avenue.

On Tuesday evening, March 11, Denis P. Murphy's closed casket rested in the front parlor of 551 Warren Avenue, while family, friends, and other firefighters paid their respects. In this room was a long sofa that fit into the area created by the wide bay window facing the street. Next to the sofa was a tall chintz floor lamp with a shade made of tiny glass beads on strings. When a person passed, the slight movement was enough to make the beads touch together, creating an eerie tinkling sound. The beads tinkled well into the nighttime hours as well wishers moved slowly past Denis Murphy's casket.

At 9 A.M. on Wednesday, March 12, 1941, a solemn high Mass of Requiem was said at St. Patrick's Church by Denis Murphy's thirty-four-years-old cousin, Rev. Thomas J. Murphy, S.J. Assisting on the alter was Father Lawrence Morrisroe, who annointed the deceased and gave him Last Rites when his body was finally extricated from the debris after sunrise on Monday morning.

Present were persons from all walks of life. Friends of the young fireman in social and church life, and businessmen who had learned to respect him as he made fire inspections throughout the center of the city. The Sisters of Charity from the convent of St. Anne on Bartlett Street were there as well. Mayor Rowe and City Marshall Humphreys represented the City of Brockton.

Besides being a member of the Massachusetts Permanent Firemen's Benefit Fund and Fire Fighters Union #144, Denis Murphy was also a member of the Seville Council Knights of Columbus, the Ancient Order of Hibernians, the Oko Club (a firefighters association), and the Firemen's Relief Organization.

Denis Murphy was interred in Calvary Cemetery next to his brother, Father Thomas J. Murphy, who died in the 1918 Spanish Influenza.[165] In the same family plot were Denis's father and

196

mother, Daniel and Catherine Murphy, and Annie C., his youngest sister who died as an infant in 1902.

Perhaps because Denis Murphy was only fifty-one when he pulled up his "night-hitch" in the early morning hours of Monday, March 10, 1941, his death reverberated for many decades among those he left behind. His three sons rarely mentioned it.

The Inquest

As is normal in conflagrations and disasters, an inquest was held to determine culpability and to fix judgments where applicable. Sitting on the inquest panel were State Fire Marshal Stephen Garrity, Assistant Marshal Edward Murtagh, Fire Chief Franklin Dickinson and Building Inspector William Green. Ten witnesses were called to testify. Among them were theater manager Frank Clementa; two stagehands, Andrew Butler and Israel Baker; the janitor, Patrick Moore; the motion picture operator, Ray Shattuck; the house officer, Sanford Alger; the custodian of the Strand Theatre property, William Fencer; the relief cashier, Miss Dorothy Chubbuck; the candy girl, Miss Tanya Washuck; and an officer with Proven Pictures, Frederick Lieberman. Although Proven Pictures was the operator of the Strand Theatre, Frederick Lieberman had not been summoned.

There was of course plenty of talk. Massachusetts' Assistant State Fire Marshal Edward Murtagh said flatly, "In my opinion, the Strand Theatre Fire was incendiary."

The *Brockton Enterprise* ventured, "Cutting across the photos taken from the roof of the Kennedy Building is the steel beam that buckled, thereby weakening the snow-covered roof. It is claimed that this steel beam was released when the weak supports were burned away. Another possibility was that the intense heat forced one of the supports out from under the girder, allowing it to collapse. These angles were studied closely by State Fire Marshal Garrity, Asst. Marshal Murtagh, Chief Dickinson, Building Inspector Green and others, and the photographs probably had a strong bearing on their reports."[166]

The final cause of the blaze did not come down for months and, although some members of the committee—including Assistant State Fire Marshal Edward Murtagh—remained convinced that it was arson, the wording of the final decision was ambiguous and no one was ever charged with setting the fire.

Chapter 6

Firemen's Disaster Relief Fund

Even before the firemen were buried, talk of a firemen's relief fund was underway. The *Brockton Enterprise* was good enough to print the existing town regulations—

"Under the provisions of the law, widows of the dead Brockton firemen will receive half of a fireman's base pay. Since that amounts to $1850 in this city, each widow will be paid $925 a year.

"The law says that in no case shall the compensation paid to a wife be more than $1000. For each child under 18 years of age, the wife will receive $200 yearly. But the total, regardless of how many children there are in the family, cannot be more than the father earned while living, or $1850.

"In the case of a single man, the law provides that compensation be paid to his father or mother if they were dependant on him for support at the time of his death.

"Should one of the widows remarry, her compensation stops. But the $200 for each child goes on and is increased by $60, making it $260 for each one under 18.[167]

The secretary of the Massachusetts Permanent Firemen's Benefit Fund, John J. Kelly, said immediately after the fire that the firemen were all probably members and insured for $1000.[168]

The thirteen foremen who died in the 1941 Strand Theatre Fire in Brockton represented the largest number of firemen to die in a single building fire in the United States for the next sixty-one years. The attack on the World Trade Center on September 11, 2001—at which 343 firemen lost their lives—surpassed the Brockton mark. With increased security, sprinkler systems and smoke alarms, firemen's lives should never be at such risk again.

Immediately, Brockton's Mayor Fred D. Rowe established a relief fund. To run it, he appointed Edward A. Dinneen, the manager of the Brockton office of an insurance company. Four donation centers were designated—the mayor's office, the Brockton National Bank, the Home National Bank, and the *Brockton Enterprise*.

The New York Fire Department sent $5,781; Athens, Georgia mailed in $74.50; Kansas City responded with $225; and, even Eleanor Roosevelt sent $100. Two Brockton boys, Francis Ennis, 8, and Lawrence Tormey, Jr., 10, put on a homemade movie and sent in 1,420 pennies. A truck driver sent 25¢ and a local dairyman donated a quart of milk a day for a year to each family.

In the aftermath of the tragedy in Brockton, there were tag sales, and basketball games. One contest pitted the Class A and B South Shore High School Tournament winners; another game was between the Holy Cross and Boston College *football* teams—in a basketball game. Just eight days after the fire, donations had already reached $66,500. Within thirty days, the fund was up to $125,000. After the 1941 All-Star Game at Briggs Stadium in Detroit—where Ted Williams electrified the crowd by hitting a game winning 3-run homer in the bottom of the ninth inning—the Red Sox traveled to Eldon B. Keith Field, Brockton, and played an exhibition game with the soldiers from Fort Edwards to raise money. (The Red Sox beat the Fort Edwards irregulars, 7-4.)

It was reported later in the *Brockton Enterprise* that each family received an annuity of $1,000 a year, but that was probably money received from the Massachusetts Permanent Firemen's Benefit Fund and/or the Firemen's Relief Organization. No matter. Thirteen families were in real financial straits.

The idea of a relief fund and the donations received were heartening, but the administration of the fund left a bad taste in the mouths of the beneficiaries as the years went by. The fund was designated strictly for the widows. If the widow of a fireman died, no money at all would accrue to the children of the men who died in the fire. Fred Kelley's widow, Margaret, died a short time after the fire, having received almost nothing. Her two sons, Robert and Frederick, were over eighteen and ineligible to collect from the fund. George Collins' widow, Bess, died about a year after the fire, and she received almost nothing. She left one son Howard, who also could not collect from the fund.

The case of fireman Daniel O'Brien illustrated how poorly the fund was managed. His widow, Alice, died about seven years after the disaster. During that time, she received $4,000 (two checks of $2,000). Within days of her passing, her daughter Margaret was told by an attorney that the family could no longer participate in the fund. Margaret and her brother, Daniel, received nothing more.

When Ray & Clayton Mitchell's mother, Junie, died in 1944, she received no more money from the fund. However, her son Clayton received money until his eighteenth birthday.

As if the management of the fund wasn't a big enough problem, some of the widows objected to the exclusion of the children and brought the matter to court. One poor widow almost had a nervous breakdown because she dreaded the thought of testifying in court. (This woman, by the way, was disarmingly honest and had nothing to worry about). The court action was the reason why the second payment lagged the first by several years. Of course, one can't help but wonder how the fund administrators' attorneys were paid.

Obviously, if the money were not distributed in a timely fashion, then there would be fewer widows to pay later. Just for the sake of discussion, let's assume that the fund finally totaled $130,000 and that at the end of the first year all of the thirteen widows received $2,000. Adding in simple interest of 2 $\frac{3}{4}$ percent (which a number of Brockton banks were paying at the time), the fund would have increased to approximately $133,575 and then $26,000 would have been paid to the widows. That leaves $107,575 in the fund. Sadly, two widows died before the next installment could be made and the fund continued to grow at 2 $\frac{3}{4}$ percent. By the time the next installment was made in 1945, the money had benefited from three more years of interest and would have grown to $116,696. Another $2,000 payment was made to the eleven remaining widows, reducing the fund by $22,000, but still leaving a healthy $94,696. In 1948, when Alice O'Brien died, no more payments had been made, so the fund should have benefited from three more years of interest and rested at $102,725.

If the money were finally divided among the remaining ten widows, each would have received $10,272, but no one knows if any of them received this money or not.

As a wonderful illustration of human nature, at least one family in Brockton thought the money in the fund was used to send the three Murphy boys to college and medical school. In fact, the three young men in question received no money of any kind from family or the relief fund. In the case of all three Murphy boys, the United States Armed Services footed the lion's share of the bill. The only groups in Brockton who helped, in a small way, was the Ancient Order of Hibernians and the Massachusetts Catholic Order of Foresters, who held small fund raisers to help with educational expenses.

Mary Murphy received half of Denis Murphy's salary until he would have reached retirement age. She also received his pension for the rest of her life, as did all the other widows of the Strand Theatre Fire. At one point, the City of Brockton tried to end her payments; she was forced to hire an attorney to fight that initiative at city hall.

Within the extended Murphy family, there were those who believed that Mary Murphy got very little from the fund and others who calculated her final payout at $13,000. As they say, no amount of money could have reimbursed those who lost a loved one in the Strand Theater Fire. Mary Murphy never talked about the matter.

Chapter 7

School Days & World War II

As the population of the city grew, Brockton High School was expanded periodically to accommodate the mushrooming student body. The original high school at Warren Avenue and West Elm Street was completed in 1906 and accepted 1000 pupils. An extension was built in 1911 and double sessions were instituted to handle the student explosion. A second building opened in January 1918, and the student population pushed still higher to 2,200. By the time Joe Murphy graduated in 1939, there were almost 2500 pupils at the school.

Though Brockton High School has always been one of the biggest secondary schools east of the Mississippi River, in the late 1930s and early 1940s, it operated no differently than any other school. The old Warren Avenue building wasn't torn down until 1974, after a new facility opened its doors on Crescent Street a couple of years earlier.

Joe and Bob Murphy had talked about becoming doctors although, in complete fairness, the profession seemed out of reach for them. Denis Murphy's wages were so small. True, during the Depression—when shoe workers only got thirty-five weeks pay a year—policemen and firemen seemed to be doing well. But when this money was compared with the cost of medical school tuitions, and other assorted costs, the money was paltry. Truth told, Denis Murphy enjoyed the wonderful security of a city job, in exchange for extreme danger and a *little* better-than-average wages.

Looking at the families living in the Foster Street Gang section of Centerville, a trend emerges. Almost none of the Brockton High students' fathers were involved directly in the shoe business. There was a pressman, salesman, electrician, photographer, fireman, engraver, and superintendent of the Brockton Water Works. All of these occupations were more stable than those in the shoe business. If a man could arrange a good job outside the shoe factories, he owed it to his family to take it.

Another interesting fact about Brockton High was that by the end of the 1930s, 57 percent of the graduates were women. During the tough Depression years, young men were expected to bring some money home, so they got to work as quickly as possible. Lest we forget, Brockton was about shoe production. The more enlightened factory owners devised recreation programs, picnics and the like, but Brockton still meant shoes. And that sacred shoe production began to slowly fall again in 1940. If not for the United States' entry into World War II in December 1941, the industry may have collapsed sooner than it did. The United States' recovery from the Great Depression and its entrance into World War II boosted the national economy *and* shoe production. The war created a huge demand for all kinds of military shoes and boots. In 1940, Brockton held steady at 27 shoe factories.

In the late 1930s, Bob Murphy badgered his mother into buying an automobile. Mary Murphy said, "Do you think that I'm made of money?" She had no interest in a car, but Bob persisted. A friend had a 1935 Chevrolet that could be had for $250. (It cost $400 new.) Finally, Mary Murphy drew the line at $200. Bob Murphy countered that his friend wouldn't take $200. Throwing her open palm downward, she said, "Oh. Too bad about him!" (The extra $50 was eventually paid out of Bob Murphy's savings—*without* his mother's knowledge.)

Mary Murphy registered the automobile, but it still wasn't of much value because nobody in the family had a driver's license. Not even Denis Murphy. He used the car to pull the Taylor's camper out to Cape Cod, but without a license. The car spent the winter in the Murphy's wobbly garage. In the spring, the boys pushed the car back and forth in the driveway in a futile effort to get it running. Even after the engine started sputtering, they did nothing with the car. It was simply a case of not understanding one's real needs and wants.[169]

Between high school, caddying, and ushering, school days for Joe and Bob Murphy flew by. With Mary Murphy watching closely, they banked whatever they could.

As early as 1885, Brockton High School held its graduation exercises at the Opera House on Elm Street. The city paid $75 to use the place—plus $4 for the orchestra. This venue met with general approval until 1925 when J.J. Cahill's new Brockton Theatre took over the graduation exercises—through 1939. In 1940, the ceremonies were held outdoors for the first time at Eldon B. Keith Field (behind Brockton High) and that tradition continued until the new high school was completed in 1970.[170]

In June 1939, Joe Murphy put on a cap and gown and marched into J.J. Cahill's Brockton Theatre for his graduation ceremony. The elaborate spectacle, featuring 250 students, essentially welcomed 90 percent of the boys into the shoe industry. Come September, Joe Murphy would start the pre-med program at Tufts College in Medford. By the time Joe Murphy was ready to begin college, he had saved $2000. In those days, $400 paid for a year's tuition at Tufts; room and board money came from odd jobs. Among many other gigs, Joe Murphy sold programs at football games and later taught freshman biology. When Joe's brother Bob got to Tufts, he ushered at the Boston Opera House, and washed dishes at Delta Upsilon, the fraternity he joined.

Bob Murphy's 1940 entry in the *Brocktonian* read—

Robert Daniel Murphy
Bob

College L. A. . . . Act, Student Council 2, Dramatic Club 3 (Executive Committee), Swimming 2,3,4, Class Ring Committee 3, Senior Class Party 4, Junior Usher, Class President 4. Interest: Hi-Y, swimming, dancing, golf, reading, theater, ushering. Future: Tufts (medicine)

Bob Murphy graduated from Brockton High School in 1940. On Eldon B. Keith Field, behind the school, a wooden platform, only a foot off the ground, held all the usual dignitaries, plus the class president and orator Bob Murphy. Dressed in his best clothes, including a new set of white bucks, Bob Murphy gave a dignified speech and, soon enough, the ceremony concluded. Given the immigrant masses in Brockton, one must keep in mind that at least some of the graduating seniors were the first person in their families to ever finish high school.

A summer of caddying, ushering, and assorted odd jobs kept Bob Murphy busy until he left in September for Tufts College. Joe Murphy was now a sophomore at Tufts, but the two brothers did not see much of each other on campus.

Since Massachusetts was the cradle of leather tanning and shoemaking in America, it's not surprising that Tufts College was founded on the leather tanning fortune of Charles Tufts. Another donor, Silvanus Packard—originally from North Bridgewater (Brockton)—established himself in business on the Central Wharf in Boston, conducting an import-export business that specialized in cotton goods. Many of his relatives remained in Brockton to pursue careers in the shoe manufacturing business.

By the middle of the 1800s, the major Protestant denominations controlled most of the colleges and universities in New England. Governing boards were comprised of ministers and deeply religious civic leaders who considered education and religious training two sides of the same coin. In 1840, the Universalists set out to establish a non-sectarian school. In Tufts College, they accomplished this goal masterfully.

The original incorporators consisted of businessmen and ministers from Charlestown, Somerville, and Boston. Charles Tufts donated twenty acres atop Walnut Hill, straddling the Medford-Somerville line. This original grant was valued at $20,000 and Charles Tufts gifted another 80 acres—and also financial assistance—during his lifetime.

Charles Tufts was a farmer and brick manufacturer, with slight features, a high voice and a gentle disposition. Tufts and his wife, Hannah, never had children, but were married for fifty-five years.

In 1850, Packard bequethed $20,000 to Tufts College, and when he died in 1866, he gifted a further $300,000.

Tufts College was the perfect school for three Murphy brothers. Instead of enduring the elitist ways of some of the other colleges in Boston, all three passed through Tufts with very little made of their Irish Catholic backgrounds. Dennis Ryan, the social

206

historian, who chronicled the progress of Irish Catholics in Boston, noted, "By the early years of the twentieth century, Irish Catholic attorneys were very active in politics although they were slow to be seated on the state's higher courts." Similarly, Irish Catholic doctors were the exception in colleges and medical schools in the first half of the 1900s. The medical profession was still almost the exclusive province of the old-line Yankees. So said, by mid-century, the barriers had fallen away. First, talent and achievement cannot be denied forever. At some point, the person doing the discriminating begins to look like a fool. Second, World War II was such an all-encompassing national emergency that petty prejudices disappeared.

When Joe and Bob Murphy first got to Tufts College, they both found the class work twice as hard as at Brockton High. Classes at Tufts were only on Mondays, Wednesdays and Fridays, but the amount of material that they had to read, understand and memorize was more than they had ever seen before. Nevertheless, they buckled down and earned good grades.

One summer, Joe and Bob worked at the Fore River Shipyard in Quincy, Massachusetts. Shipyard jobs paid well, but ran seven days a week, with one Sunday off a month. The Lend-Lease Act was passed in March 1941 and the allies needed ships badly. Working beside all that sun-baked steel made men sweat like racehorses, and they took plenty of water and salt pills to compensate for the loss of bodily fluids and nutrients. If the temperature got to eighty degrees, they took one pill during a ten-hour shift, and for each five degrees above that, they took another pill—with a maximum of four per day. Shipbuilding was some of the hardest work that men performed during the early 1940s.

The Japanese bombed Pearl Harbor on December 7, 1941, and the Murphys' world turned upside down for the second time in nine months. Now the armed services needed doctors badly. Pre-med students joined the services and finished college in three years by going year round. The same aggressive approach was used at the nation's medical schools. Now the government was picking up the tab and even giving monthly allowances for room and board.

Joe Murphy was a Clydesdale when it came to studying and he was accepted at Yale Medical School after a brief interview. He traveled to New Haven for a 10 A.M. appointment with Miss Daisy (real name), who sent him to see a doctor in the pediatrics unit. When Joe Murphy returned, Miss Daisy asked what he thought. Joe lauded the program and she said that he was accepted. This was at 2 o'clock in the afternoon!

At Yale, Joe joined the navy and they helped with his tuition bills. His wife Muriel (McCarthy) Murphy remembered that she and Joe paid for the first and last six months of Yale Med and the navy paid the rest. Joe graduated from Yale Med in 1945, a few months after V-E day and was able to begin his internship at Hartford Hospital (1846-47) within a month. He followed with three years of obstetrics at Quonset Point Naval Station in Rhode Island. Finally he did his residency at Children's Hospital in Boston. At long last, in July 1952—at almost thirty-one years of age—Joe opened his first office on West Elm Street, opposite Eldon Keith Field in Brockton.

Joe Murphy married Muriel McCarthy on September 8, 1945. Together they had six children.[171]

When her sons married, Mary Murphy morphed into an obstructionist madwoman. Joe was the first to announce his plans to wed, completely unaware that his younger brother Bob, and his fiancée, Mary Foss, had planned to wed just a week later. The idea of losing two sons in two weeks was more than Mary Murphy could handle and she promptly announced that she would not be attending either wedding. She was particularly adamant in the case of the oldest son, Joe, because—until Muriel (McCarthy) Murphy got to middle age—Joe's mother thought the younger woman was too affected for her own good.[172]

Muriel's parents, Charles and Katherine McCarthy, brought their daughters up as ladies of the first water. They always behaved properly and regarded themselves in the best light. At least in the eyes of the penurious Mary Murphy, the McCarthy girls put on airs and consequently Muriel was an unacceptable mate for Joe. In truth, no one could have been more acceptable.[173]

As promised, the day of the wedding, Mary Murphy began her housekeeping chores as usual, with no intention at all of going to the wedding. (She had bought a new dress, but told no one.) She was horribly conflicted about the matter though and, after everyone left for church, she got dressed and walked the few blocks to St. Patrick's Church, with the intention of sneaking into the last pew when nobody was looking. Her two other sons, acting as ushers, saw her though and coerced her to take her seat at the front of the church as decorum dictated. She did so reluctantly.[174]

After a beautiful and trouble free ceremony, she announced her departure. Again, her sons persuaded her to go with them to the reception for a few minutes and say hello to everyone. Sensing that her indecorous behavior might blossom into an irreparable rift, she agreed. Nevertheless, at the reception she refused to leave the ladies' room. Finally, someone brought in a plate of food—and with her head held high—she ate it there. Until the end of the reception, Mary Murphy manned the ramparts of the *loo*. She would never have understood the word *adamantine*, but what does it matter at this late date?[175]

After Tufts College pre-med, Bob Murphy joined the Army Specialist Training Program (ASTP) and Uncle Sam helped enormously with his medical school costs. Typically, the government paid 85 percent of the tuition and gave students a stipend of $65 a month. For the recipients of Uncle Sam's largesse, the program was a godsend. The original purpose of the army and navy STP courses was to keep colleges and universities from going bankrupt. A secondary benefit was the financial help given to land grant colleges whose male student bodies had been decimated by the draft of 14 million students. Incidentally, these programs also softened university resistance to lowering the draft age from twenty to eighteen.[176]

After three years at Tufts College, Bob Murphy spent three years at Tufts Med. His last year ran about sixteen months to allow for a June graduation. At the time, tuition at Tufts Med ran about $1300 a year.[177]

Originally, Tufts College School of Medical was located in a three-story building at 188 Boylston Street, Boston. When Bob Murphy started Tufts Med, it was located on Huntington Avenue, and at this campus, he completed his studies in 1946. In the intervening years, the med school moved to a new facility on Harrison Avenue, in the southern part of Chinatown. The old property was bought by Boston University and ultimately turned into a parking garage.

Even with a year round program, Bob Murphy did not finish med school until 1946, which posed a small problem. Since World War II technically ended on September 2, 1945, when the Japanese signed the Instrument of Surrender on the *USS Missouri* in Tokyo Bay, the army wanted to stop funding medical students immediately. Leveler heads prevailed though, and the government continued to help students with small monthly stipends. Bob Murphy augmented this by working in the Infectious Disease Unit of Boston City Hospital and teaching freshman anatomy classes. Still, the government had picked up the bulk of his tuition costs. By working at Boston City Hospital, and picking up a number of other jobs, Bob Murphy was able to finish Tufts Med. There were 125 students in his class when he started; only 85 finished.[178]

Bob Murphy married Mary Cecelia Foss of Milton, Massachusetts, on September 15, 1945. They had eight children.[179]

Mary Murphy was little better at the wedding of her second son. Sensing the animosity toward her, the new Muriel (McCarthy) Murphy sat in the last pew of the church while her husband, Joe, performed his duties as best man. His younger brother, Ed, had the duty of seating his mother when she arrived at the church. As Ed brought his mother past the last pew, he stopped. Putting out his other elbow, he asked Muriel to come along and he would seat the two women together. Such was the relationship between the two women for the next twenty years. Mary Murphy disliked Muriel for marrying her oldest boy and Muriel was content to stay away from the older woman. In later life, Muriel was extraordinarily kind to Mary Murphy, taking her shopping, and in fairness, acted as her most important caregiver. The thawing process was the emotional equivalent of the end of the last great ice age, but was inevitable because the two women both loved T. J. (Joe) Murphy.[180]

It seemed logical that Bob Murphy would go back to Massachusetts to do his internship and residency, but he was lured to Hartford by a gentlemanly, old school surgeon, Jim Cullen. He was a dapper man who loved boats and rented a huge cabin cruiser for the whole month of August each year. Dr. Cullen was the most affable of men and tops in the field of general surgery, but in the operating room, he was something of a despot. The operating room nurses called him "the magnificent bastard."

Bob Murphy did his internship and residency at St. Francis Hospital in Hartford, and later entered into the practice of internal medicine in Wethersfield, Connecticut.

Ed Murphy—so young when his father died—changed his name several times in an effort to carry forward something that he could not bring himself to admit was gone. When he graduated from High School, the *Brocktonian* yearbook showed him as Edward Denis Murphy, exchanging his given middle name, Francis, for his father's first name. Sometimes he used E. Denis Murphy. By the time he married on January 22, 1955, he was once again Edward Francis Murphy, the extra talisman leaving him along with the memories of that awful Monday morning in 1941, when he awoke to find his world shattered.

At Brockton High, Ed Murphy took the college course, but also played basketball for a couple of years and football in his freshman, sophomore, and senior years. He sat on the student council, and was involved in many other pursuits.

By January of his senior year—with the war still raging in Europe—Ed Murphy finally talked his mother into signing the papers that would allow him to join the navy. He left Brockton High for his basic training in New York and in June got a weekend pass so he could to return to Brockton High and graduate with his friends in the Brockton High School, Class of 1945. Later he was assigned to Casco Bay Naval Station in Maine.[181]

While Ed was in the Navy, he had a large tattoo emblazoned on his large and powerful forearm. It was a fouled anchor overlaid by a bald eagle in flight. A ribbon trailing from the eagle's beak read: Death Before Dishonor. Tattoos were so rare in the 1950s that young Murphy children from all the different branches of the family asked endlessly to see the tattoo. Though Ed was accommodative, he actual hated the tattoo. It reminded him of a night when he was in his cups and did something stupid. All of us make mistakes, but few of us have to be reminded of our foolishness daily.

After the war, Ed used the GI Bill to attend Tufts College. In 1939 when his older brother, Joe, had applied for admission, less than 10 percent of the young men in America earned bachelor's

211

degrees from four-year colleges. The GI Bill shot that number to 18 percent. Right after the war, more than 50 percent of the students at all colleges and universities in America were veterans.

Even with the increased competition, Ed Murphy managed to enter Tufts College and graduated in 1951. Med school was next, or so he thought.

In March 1951, Ed Murphy felt his future was set, when a nasty letter arrived from the government. He was scheduled to start med school in a few months and, suddenly, Uncle Sam wanted him again. By remaining in the Naval Reserves after the Second World War, Ed thought he'd been pretty clever. For doing little or nothing, another check would arrive each month. Who, at the time, could have conceived of more combat after the fifty-six million deaths of the Second World War? The check he received was puny, and looking smaller by the minute, as he contemplated his next move. The so-called "police action" in Korea was threatening to derail everything. He was to report to the navy yard just below South Station in Boston.

One hears unfathomable stories from time to time about guardian angels, but few take note. So said, what happened to Ed Murphy at the navy yard beggars belief.

Ed knew he had no choice but to report, as required, to the navy yard on the appointed April day. While there, he buttonholed an aging officer to explain his predicament. The old sailor was a red-faced, cigar-chomping Irishman, who on his tiptoes stood a shade under five feet. The man listened intently to Ed's story, nodding his head the whole time. With his eyes darting quickly around the navy yard, he told Ed to follow him.

A stone's throw away, the two stepped into a Quonset hut and found a large office with a window overlooking the yard. The man acted in a conspiratorial manner, shooting quick glances out of the window at regular intervals while he rummaged through the desk drawers.

Finally, a rubber stamp and an inkpad appeared. After another sidelong glance out the window, the paper was stamped, dated and initialed with a reassuring flourish. Through a cloud of pungent cigar smoke, the old salt wished Ed well in medical school and told him to disappear. Recognizing instantly the import of the old

Irishman's chicanery, Ed thanked him profusely and beat a hasty retreat.

Ed had manners though. Recognizing the huge debt that he owed the old timer, he found a drugstore and bought a box of *Muniemakers*. When Ed returned to the navy yard, the old sailor was nowhere to be found. Ed asked around, but still nothing. It was as if the fellow had disappeared in a cloud of his own cigar smoke. Ed left the base, shaking his head.

Ed Murphy always believed that something much more grand than navy sloppiness delivered him from the clutches of the government and allowed him to start medical school. To the end of his life, Ed never stopped marveling at the old-timers machinations on that April day in the Boston Navy Yard.

During his first semester in medical school, the sheer weight of the workload precluded any outside employment. Money was tight, and there was nothing from home.

During the second semester of his first year, Ed landed a dream job at Boston City Hospital—on Harrison Avenue with Tufts Med only a mile to the north. He worked for the Surgery Department starting intravenous drips, drawing blood, supervising the lab data and checking patient's charts. For an hour and a half of work each morning, he received room and board plus a stipend of $50 a month. He was "House Officer, Edward F. Murphy,"

Owing mostly to his own diligence, he was able to complete his work at Boston City Hospital, and walk the mile to Tufts in time for his 8 A.M. class. It was a long day, for classes did not end until 5 P.M. and evenings were strictly for studying.

Ed Murphy was shocked at how intense the regimen was at Tufts Med. He wisely buckled down like never before. Building up the knowledge base of a physician has always been a daunting task. Students at Tufts were reduced to using mnemonic devices for memorizing long lists of body parts. For example, the bones of the hand—Distal end, Trochlea, Tubercle, Pisiform, and so forth—became "Don't Touch Tilley's Panties, Mother May Come Home."

Also, toward the end of their time at Tuft's Med, the students were called to a special evening session and administered the Hippocratic Oath. Having always believed the first paragraph said, "First, do no harm," Ed was surprised to find that the oath said nothing of the kind. The oath itself was divided into six paragraphs and the first merely asks the new physician to uphold the oath. The second paragraph asks the new doctor to revere his teachers as his parents and "to impart a knowledge of the art of medicine to others." It is the third paragraph that deals with the doctor's responsibilities to his patients. It reads, "I will follow that method of treatment, which according to my ability and judgment, I consider for the benefit of my patient and abstain from whatever is harmful and mischievous. I will neither prescribe nor administer a lethal dose of medicine to any patient even if asked nor counsel any such thing and maintain the utmost respect for every human life from fertilization to natural death and reject abortion that deliberately takes a unique human life." (The Hippocratic Oath forbids abortion?)

In Ed Murphy's last year of medical school, another important matter blossomed. While performing his duties at Boston City Hospital, he met a young nursing student, Claire MacLeod, from Islington, Massachusetts (a village within the town of Westwood). At the time of their meeting, she was a statuesque, dark-haired, nineteen-year-old girl of French-Canadian and Irish stock. Her father, Raymond MacLeod, was a fireman as had been Ed's father, a point of mutual interest. They went out for the first time in 1953, continued dating all through 1954 and married on Saturday, January 22, 1955, two weeks after Claire's twenty-first birthday.[182]

When Ed and Claire married, the young doctors were in and out of the church tending to flu-struck children, but the ceremony went off without a hitch. And wonder of wonders, Mary Murphy behaved herself.[183]

214

Chapter 8

Grammy Murphy

Mary Murphy knew that she had to work after her husband's death. M. A. Packard Shoes was located at 583 Warren Avenue (corner of Foster Street, and just a block south of the Murphy home). Denis Murphy had worked for Packard in the same building from 1907 to 1918. One day, Mary applied for a job and soon thereafter started in the stitchery department.

Mary Murphy stayed at Packard until it burned down in 1948. (Pachard was actually a division of Knapp Shoes toward the end.) Next, she worked for a die maker on Warren Avenue, where she lost the tip of her index finger in an accident. By now she was fifty-six, and found an easier job at Golka Leather on Warren Avenue (south of Bartlett Street). The company was later known as New England Handicraft. Golka Leather was not a shoemaker, but more in the findings end of the industry. For example, they sold small leather loops that could be hooked together to make belts and other ornamental items.[184]

After Denis Murphy died tragically in March 1941, the two oldest boys continued in pre-med at Tufts College and it was Ed who was left to care for his mother. As Bob Murphy once said, "It was Ed who saved Grammy Murphy."[185]

Ed Murphy got the worst of it in many ways. Later in life, when he got in his cups, he would complain to his brothers that he never had anyone take him to the movies when he was a kid. As a forty-year-old man, Ed bought one of the first Sony Betamax recorders in Connecticut and diligently set about recording old movies from the television. In the middle of the night, while he and his children slept, the machine in the basement recaptured for him Garbo, Harlow, Chaplin, Gable, Cagney, Bogart—all of the wonderful movie actors and actresses of an earlier time—that he missed altogether. The movies were the gold in his own personal Fort Knox.[186]

Oddly enough, he almost never watched them. He labeled them meticulously and filed them neatly in tall metal cabinets that he managed to snare from the local hospitals as they upgraded their utility rooms. The tapes sat mostly untouched, but protected from the elements, until long after his death in 1994.[187]

In retrospect, it's downright ridiculous that all three Murphy boys took the college course at Brockton High, when Mary Murphy refused to give them a dime for their educations. She always made it clear that if the boys wanted to go to college, they had to pay for it themselves. She would not help. Both Joe and Bob Murphy used their savings for tuition and worked continuously to pay their room and board. Ed had the GI Bill for part of his education at Tufts College, and two older brothers who *probably* helped him with part of his medical school tuition in the early 1950s. The remainder of the tuition, plus room and board, he managed himself. (Can you hear the sound of the fiddle music in the clachan?)

Mary Murphy was often a target of resentment, as mothers often are, for she was the impossible taskmaster, complaining of A's on report cards, as if they weren't good enough. But she was also the one who gave her sons their brains. She was the accountant, the scrivener, the bookkeeper, a position so typical in the households of the Boston Irish. She was the one who was as tight with her affections as she was with her purse strings, playing the achievements of one son against those of the others. She was the one who expected levels of accomplishment that were just beyond the horizon. But who better?

While he was alive, people loved Denis Murphy. He was a strong, quiet, good-looking man, stoic by nature and slow to anger, but unfortunately he didn't possess the intellectual abilities of his wife and sons. It was Mary Murphy's genes that delivered the gift of intelligence. How was it that a girl raised in an overcrowded, dirt-floored, stone cottage in the dismal reaches of County Mayo, Ireland—with only a sixth grade education—could be the fountainhead of intelligence? God only knows.

Beyond the gift over which she had no control, she was the one who taught them to scrape and save for the future. Her frugal ways had rankled the women that might have otherwise been her friends, but she airily dismissed their backbiting, "Oh. Too bad about them."

Some of them accorded her the same combination of envy and loathing reserved for people like Hetty Green, the Witch of Wall Street. This was extreme because Mary Murphy's idea of dazzling financial footwork was to save until it hurt and then watch as simple bank interest grew the money—ohhh, so slowly. Her method was the way of the Irish housewife who saved by doing without, squirreling away money for bad times, and in the process, forgetting what money was—a means of exchange whereby lives can be enriched. Still, for all of her eccentric ways, she had watched her sons fight their way through college and medical school in her own inimical way—by withholding encouragement and compliments even more fiercely than the clachan Irish. "If they want it, then they can get it themselves," she hammered.

The Saturday that Ed Murphy graduated from Tufts Medical School—June 11, 1955—was the conclusion of Mary Murphy's own personal hat trick. Mary Murphy—the pleasant but flint-hearted woman from Mayo—had engineered it all by refusing encouragement, by offering nothing.

Not surprisingly, she had a way of showing so little interest that one might reasonably ask why she bothered to attend the graduation. Almost completely without her interest or encouragement, her youngest son proudly accepted his diploma, the culmination of almost a decade of hard work and sacrifice.

The early 1940s were an ugly, empty time for Mary Murphy, but she got through it. When Ed Murphy married, Mary Murphy's two older boys had been married for ten years and the world hadn't come to an end. In fact, Mary Murphy was a grandmother eleven times over and she actually relished her new position as Grammy Murphy, the matriarch. When her sons needed a short vacation, she acted *in loco parentis*, and got to know her grandchildren from infancy. She changed diapers again; she cooked; she did the laundry; she settled disputes. Grammy Murphy was absolutely unflappable and capably met the needs of eight children at a time—sixteen hours a day! She could pack a bag in a heartbeat and never seemed flummoxed by any situation.

(Seated l. to r.) Mary Murphy, Grammy Murphy
(Standing l. to r.) Dr. Robert D. Murphy, Dr. Edward F. Murphy,
Kate Murphy, Muriel Murphy, Dr. Thomas J. (Joe) Murphy

Even in her eighties, she seemed to relish the call from her sons. Who would have guessed that Grammy Murphy would develop into a woman that wanted to be needed? When she was young, she loved to say, "Oh. . . too bad about them," but she didn't say that anymore. True, she was still an immigrant, but the designation meant nothing. Her three sons were medical doctors.

Grammy Murphy developed a little heart trouble in her late seventies, but kept active all the same. As she got older, she'd get up from the dinner table and fart all the way to the bathroom, laughing like a lunatic at life's little indignities and everyone's reaction to them. After all, she'd changed the diapers of everyone in the room. What did she care?

From 1946 until about 1975, she floated from house to house—sometimes to baby-sit, sometimes for a holiday gathering, and sometimes to help when someone was sick. As she mellowed, the devil still ran through her. The oldest girl in each family was her favorite. So said, at Christmas she bought a fabulous gift for the oldest girl and gave the second in line a used set of nylons (with the seam down the back). She could really bring out the tears when she was feeling ornery. Of course, her sons took turns pulling her aside and telling her that if she ever did that again, she would no longer be invited to family gatherings. Fortunately, she remained a quick study all her life.[188]

Mary Murphy kept the house at 551 Warren Avenue until early 1958, when she sold it to a Greek man named Deftos—without telling a soul. One day, the man telephoned to say that he'd found a box of money in the wall. It contained $300-$400. Mary said, "It must have be Katherine's." (Presumably the money was returned to her sister Katherine.)[189]

Mary Murphy subsequently moved into an apartment at Central Square and remained there for a couple of years. The place was substandard. When Joe Murphy saw the place, he said, "My mother cannot live here."[190]

In the summer of 1961, Joe Murphy built himself a new medical office at 990 Pleasant Street, a quiet residential section of western Brockton. Wisely, with an eye toward resale, he designed it to look like a Cape Cod style house. The second floor was laid out as a comfortable apartment, but could be converted to bedrooms for a nominal fee. After the traditional pleading, Mary Murphy agreed to move into the small apartment above her son's medical office.[191]

In April 1977, she fell and fractured her pelvis, necessitating a move into St. Joseph's Manor, a short-term rehabilitation facility. She remained there a whole year (paid for by her sons) and then relocated to the Braemore Nursing Home on Pearl Street, near Joe Murphy's medical office. She was there from March 1978 until she died on September 3, 1980. After the traditional funeral mass, she was interred next to her husband, Denis P. Murphy, in the family plot at Calvary Cemetery.[192]

To be continued . . .

Author's Notes

[1] Cornelius Murphy of Ross (Ross Island townland) and Catherine Lyne of Ross (Ross Island townland) were married in Killarney (townland) on 20 Apr. 1919. The witnesses to the marriage were the bride's parents, Timothy and Catherine Lyne. Cornelius Murphy was born in 1790 and died in 1870 at Killarney. He was 80. Catherine Lyne was born in 1802 and died in 1875 at Killarney. She was 73. (FamilySearch.org)

Maurice Murphy was born 17 Feb 1820 (www.irishgenealogy.ie) and died in Killarney in 1871 (FamilySearch.org). His death certificate records that he was 53, when he was only about 51. The children of Cornelius Murphy and Catherine Lyne were:

Maurice, born Killarney, Killarney Civil Parish, 17 Feb 1820; died 1871
Timothy Murphy, born Killarney, Killarney Civil Parish, 30 Dec 1821
John Murphy, Born Teernaboul Townland, Killarney Civil Parish, 19 May 1824
Cornelius Murphy, born Teernaboul Townland, Killarney Civil Parish, 8 Jun 1829
Mary Murphy, born Killarney, Killarney Civil Parish, 14 Aug 1836
Thomas Murphy, born Killarney, Killarney Civil Parish, 3 Dec 1837

Killarney Townland
Killarney Civil Parish
Magunihy Barony
Killarney Poor Law Union (PLU)
Munster Province
County Kerry
Ireland

[2] The townlands of Ireland are frequently altered based on a variety of variables. For example, Cornelius Murphy and Catherine Lyne recorded their townland on their marriage license as simply "Ross" when the townland is Ross Island. Later we will see that Honora McCarthy recorded that she was from Ballagh, when the townland is Ballaghcommane. Some of Honora's siblings were born in East Ballagh, while others were born in West Ballagh, all the while referring to Ballaghcommane. This was simply the parlance of the day.

[3] Birth, marriage and death information of all of Cornelius and Catherine Murphy's children. (FamilySearch.org)

[4] Ibid.

[5] *Royal Commission of Inquiry, Primary Education, Ireland*, Vol. VI, Educational Census Returns. Number of children actually present in each primary school on 25 June 1868.
http://eppi.dippam.ac.uk/documents/15444 (download pdf doc.)

[6] Pigot, 1824, 273-275. Regarding the term "well-paved"—People confuse cobblestones with setts. Cobblestones are small, round stones that are injurious to working horses' ankles. A workhorse on cobblestones only lasts about two years. "Setts" are flat, roughly rectangular, quarried granite paving stones that are laid in regular patterns. The picture in this chapter of Boherkeale Lane offers an example of setts.

[7] *Slater's Directory,* 1881

[8] Ibid.

[9] Ibid.

[10] Jones, 1906, 286-294.

[11] Ibid.

[12] Ibid.

[13] Miller, 1985, 20-22; Sullivan, 1881, 40-51.

[14] Ibid.

[15] Bartlett, 2010, 127-132; Miller, 1985, 20-22.

[16] Miller, 1985, 20-22; Sullivan, 1881, 40-51.

[17] Bartlett, 2010, 127.

[18] Cronin, 2001, 71-73.

[19] MacLysaght, p.229

[20] Letters of Recommendation to Daniel Murphy from Lord Bishop of Kerry, John Hiffin, dated July 4 and July 5, 1877. The history of "The Palace" and its tenants can be gleaned from this website:
http://www.killarneyholidayvillage.com/st-marys-cathedral-things-you-mightnt-know/ (Accessed October 4, 2013)

[21] Killarney's population in 1861 was 5,187.
Library Ireland, "Kerry County and Borough Directory 1862" (Accessed October 4, 2013)
http://www.census.nationalarchives.ie/exhibition/kerry/main.html (Accessed October 14, 2013)
" . . .only 5,137 people . . . ." By 2011, Killarney had a population of about 9,000.

[22] Clachan Project, Summary of Findings of the Project, What is a Clachan? . . .
http://www.antrimhistory.net/clachan-project/summary-of-findings-of-project/books-articles-on-clachans-and-rundale/ (Accessed November 29, 2013)
The clachan project was conducted by the Glens of Antrim Historical Society to study the remnants of the clachens before they were gone forever. The project ran from 2004 to 2007, and incorporated first hand study of the clachens in the Glens of Counties Antrim and Down in Northern Ireland, coupled with the writings of Estyn Evans (1939), Desmond McCourt (M.A. thesis 1947), and the work of their many students.

[23] Lloyd, 2011, 71-73; Miller, 1985, 27, 28.

[24] Ibid.

[25] Cusack, M. F. (1871) "Maurice Murphy. Merchant tailor, 3 Main-street" is listed as one of the subscribers of M. F. Cusack's *A History of the Kingdom of Kerry*. Since Maurice's father, Cornelius, was a merchant tailor on Main Street in Killarney, it is logical that Maurice worked with him in the same shop.

[26] The largest cathedral in Ireland is Immaculate Conception in Sligo, with a seating capacity of 4,000. St. Mary's Cathedral in Killarney—with its narrow nave—was modeled after the Salisbury Cathedral in England, which seats only 1,900. Killarney Cathedral (St. Mary's) seating capacity is about the same.

[27] Griffith Valuation (1848-1864). Griffith's Valuation of 1853 (County Kerry). Richard Griffith lists all of the properties in Killarney with the lessee, lessor, property description, and valuation. When the Griffith's Valuation (Kerry) concluded, there were no churches or chapels on Chapel's Lane, and only a "R. C. Chapel" on Upper New Street. The Chapel was so small—and dare one say nondescript—that Rt. Rev. Dr. Egan's rectory house had a higher valuation.

[28] The National Archives of Ireland, "What was County Kerry Like in the 20th Century?" http://www.census.nationalarchives.ie/exhibition/kerry/main.html (Accessed October 17, 2013)

[29] There could be many reasons why family members did not act as witnesses to the nuptials between Maurice Murphy and Honora McCarthy. However, because Maurice Murphy's family had done everything possible to reduce their status to that of outsiders in Killarney—not to mention the big age difference between Maurice and Honora—it is possible that there was enmity between the two clans or a perception that the union was a mésalliance.

[30] Honora McCarthy was born on April 30, 1837 and Marice Murphy was born February 17, 1820, making Maurice seventeen years older than his new bride. Honora McCarthy's siblings were:

Mary McCarthy, born East Ballagh, Killarney Civil Parish, 19 Dec 1821
Margaret McCarthy, born West Ballagh, Killarney Civil Parish, 9 Mar 1823
Catherine McCarthy, born Ballagh, Killarney Civil Parish, 29 Jun 1825
Bridget McCarthy, born West Ballagh, Killarney Civil Parish, 5 Aug 1827
Gobinet McCarthy, born West Ballagh, Killarney Civil Parish, 27 Feb 1830
Julia McCarthy, born West Ballagh, Killarney Civil Parish, 17 Jun 1832
Johanna McCarthy, born Ballagh, Killarney Civil Parish, 6 Jan 1835
Honora McCarthy, born Ballagh, Killarney Civil Parish, 30 Apr 1837
Ellen McCarthy, born Ballagh, Killarney Civil Parish, 8 Dec 1839
Elizabeth McCarthy, born Ballagh, Killarney Civil Parish, 22 May 1842
Dermot McCarthy, born Ballagh, Killarney Civil Parish, 1 Dec 1844

[31] Maurice Murphy & Honora McCarthy's children were:

Daniel Maurice Murphy, born Killarney Townland, Killarney Civil Parish, 12 Oct 1856
Thomas J. Murphy, born Killarney Townland, Killarney Civil Parish,, 19 Aug 1858
Mary Murphy, born Killarney Townland, Killarney Civil Parish, 10 Jul 1860
Denis A. Murphy, born Killarney Townland, Killarney Civil Parish, 7 Oct 1861
Mary Murphy, born Killarney Townland, Killarney Civil Parish, 4 Apr 1864
Mary Ellen Murphy, born Killarney Townland, Killarney Civil Parish, 11 May 1865
Maurice Murphy, born Killarney Townland, Killarney Civil Parish, 10 Nov 1867
Mary Ann Murphy, born Killarney Townland, Killarney Civil Parish, 2 May 1870

The first Mary was born on July 12, 1860 and died in 1863. (http://records.ancestry.com/Mary_Murphy_records.ashx?pid=169068942) (Accessed October 24, 2013). The second Mary, born in 1864, died the same year. (FamilySearch.org). Honora McCarthy's last two attempts to name a child after her mother were: Mary Ellen (b. May 10, 1865) and Mary Ann (b. May 2, 1870). Both girls survived, emigrated, and married their husbands in Brockton, Massachusetts.

[32] Irish Ancestors, http://www.irishtimes.com/ancestor/index.htm (Accessed December 5, 2013)

[33] www.irishgenealogy.ie

[34] Resume letter composed by Daniel Murphy. (*see* pg. 61) Though not dated, it is clear that the letter was written by Dan Murphy shortly after 1893 in America. In it, he mentions taking work at R. B. Grover Shoes in Brockton, Massachusetts. This autobiographical letter was probably used to get a better job after Dan Murphy had been at R. B. Grover Shoes for a time.

[35] Ibid.

[36] FamilySearch.org; Since Maurice's father lived to be eighty and Maurice died at fifty-one, one wonders what felled him. The typical Irishman of the time ate almost no meat and very few dairy products, surviving instead on grains and vegetables. Based on this, the possibility of "sudden death" is ever present. However, the strong religious background of the family augers against this. In any event, due to the outright quackery of nineteenth century medicine, the cause of death on Maurice Murphy's death certificate probably would not be accurate anyway.

[37] Resume letter composed by Daniel Murphy. (*see* pg. 61)

[38] Recorded interview by Dr. Ed Murphy of Father Thomas Murphy S. J. and his maiden sisters, Theresa and Peg, at 404 Wolcott Hill Road, Wethersfield, CT, 1982.

[39] Ibid.

[40] Miller, 1985, 355.

[41] Hyde, 1975, *passim.*

[42] Ibid.

[43] Cunard enjoyed a lucrative relationship with the Lords of the Admiralty—and its coveted mail contract—until 1867 when it went back to the post office and ultimately out to bid. Truth be told, Cunard couldn't depend on the mail contract at all after 1867.

[44] In his scholarly text, *Between the Dollar-Sterling Gold Point: Exchange Rates, Parity, and Market Behavior,* Lawrence Oliver points out that for almost a century (1837-1931), the dollar / pound rate settled at the 'famous' 4.8665635 point. Standard deviation fell to less than .5 percent after 1871 and less than .2 percent between 1901 and 1914.

[45] Hyde, 1975, *passim.*

[46] Schrier, 1958, 94; Miller, 1985, 72.

[47] *Titanic* and other White Star Ships, Technical Facts. http://www.titanic-whitestarships.com/MGY_Tech_Facts.htm (Accessed December 7, 2013)

[48] Kingman, 1866, Chapter XX, "Misc. History."

[49] Carroll, 1989, 52

[50] Carroll, 1989, 53.

[51] To attach shoe uppers to soles, the McKay machines crudely ran two parallel lines of stitches—about 2" apart—down the center of the shoe. With plenty of glue, the result was fantastic, although the shoes were real "clodhoppers."

[52] Carroll, 1989, 62.

[53] Tom Murphy (b. Aug. 19, 1858) and Nel Kelly (b. Oct 28, 1870) were married in 1888 and their children were:

Mary (Molly) K. Murphy, born Brockton, MA, Dec 1864
Grace M. Murphy, born Brockton, MA, Apr 1891
Eileen (Ellen) Murphy, born Brockton, MA, Oct 1892
Ann F. Murphy, born Brockton, MA, Sept. 1894
Maurice V. Murphy, born Brockton, MA, Jul 1896
Margaret V. Murphy, born Brockton, MA, Oct 1897
John J. Murphy, born Brockton, MA, Mar 1900
Teresa J. Murphy, born Brockton, MA, 16 Mar 1902
Thomas J. Murphy, S. J., born Brockton, MA, 8 Oct 1906; Boston College '28; Joined Jesuits '28; Weston College, Weston, MA; Ordained '39; Fairfield University (about 40 years); died 18 Nov 1999.

[54] U.S. Census Records, 1900, 1910, 1920; Brockton City Directories; Kane, 1983, 21-22

[55] Nellie Sullivan is listed as such on her marriage license, although she preferred Ellen in later life.

[56] Dinny and Ellen (Nellie) Murphy's children were:

Nora F, born in Brockton, Massachusetts, Sept 1886
Maurice J. (Beechie), born in Brockton, Massachusetts, Aug 1888
Mary, born in Brockton, Massachusetts, Apr 1891
John B. (Tuckie), born in Brockton, Massachusetts, Aug 1897
Ellen E., born in Brockton, Massachusetts, 27 Nov 1905

[57] Kane, 1983, 10-22

[58] Catherine (Sullivan) Murphy's Massachusetts death certificate dated July 7, 1915 lists her age as 51. That is not correct. Catherine Sullivan was born on 15 Aug 1860 (irishgenealogy.ie) and died on 7 Jun 1915, making her 54. Denis Sullivan and Mary Herlihey of Park Lane, Killarney had six children. They were:

Patrick Sullivan, born Killarney townland, Killarney Civil Parish, 27 Feb 1845
Julia Sullivan, born Killarney townland, Killarney Civil Parish, 4 Dec 1848
Mary Sullivan, born Killarney townland, Killarney Civil Parish, 2 Dec 1849
Ellen Sullivan, born Killarney townland, Killarney Civil Parish, 4 Jul 1854
John Sullivan, born Killarney townland, Killarney Civil Parish, 9 Mar 1856
Catherine Sullivan, born Killarney townland, Killarney Civil Parish, 15 Aug 1860

A last word about Catherine (Sullivan) Murphy's chronic valvular disease: "Data are presented in 400 autopsy patients, each over fourteen years of age with functionally severe valvular cardiac disease. Of 139 patients with anatomically isolated aortic valvular disease, 6 per cent had positive histories of acute rheumatic fever (ARF) or chorea, none had Aschoff bodies, nearly all had histologically normal atrial walls, and 72 per cent of the 105 patients with AS and 26.5 per cent of the thirty-four patients with pure AR had congenitally malformed aortic valves. In contrast, of 235 patients with anatomic mitral disease with or without anatomic involvement of other valves, 68 per cent had positive histories of ARF or chorea, twelve (5 per cent) had Aschoff bodies, nearly all had histologically abnormal left atrial walls, and only two patients (<1 per cent) had congenitally malformed valves. It is concluded that anatomically isolated aortic valve disease is of non-rheumatic etiology and most frequently the consequence of a congenital malformation. (The American Journal of Medicine, Volume 49, Issue 2 , Pages 151-159, August 1970).

[59] Catherine Sullivan's mother's last name is a trial. "Herlihey" is spelled in so many different ways on birth and wedding records, we will never know the correct spelling. For what it's worth, her husband Daniel Murphy listed Mary A. Herlihey as his wife's mother on Catherine's death certificate, dated June 7, 1915.

[60] Resume letter composed by Daniel Murphy. (*see* pg. 61)

[61] Keeping in mind that Maurice and Honora Murphy's first two Marys died young, did Mary Ellen (Nellie) and Mary Ann (Annie) choose not to use the name because of superstition?

[62] Dan Murphy's letter of recommendation on Charles Meagher & Son stationary dated July 8, 1893.

[63] Miller, 1985, 9

[64] Ibid.

[65] Rollyson, 2013, 20.; "The Lusitania's Passengers and Crew, May 7, 1915," http://homepages.rootsweb.ancestry.com/~lusilist/LusitaniaPassengerList.htm l (Accessed October 28, 2013)

[66] Another example of the cost of children's tickets versus those of adults: Steerage tickets on the *RMS Titanic* in 1912 cost £7 ($34), while children sailed for £3 ($14.60).

[67] Pierce, 1905, 7-9

[68] Ibid, 9-11, 17-18.

[69] Listed oldest to youngest, the children of Daniel and Catherine Murphy were:

Mary A., born Killarney townland, Ire., 24 Aug 1885; died Brockton, MA, 1972
Thomas J., born Killarney townland, Ire., 11 July 1887; died Brockton. MA, 11 Nov 1918
Denis P., born Killarney townland, Ire., 16 Aug 1889; died Brockton, MA, 10 Mar 1941
Honora F. (Nonie), born Killarney townland, Ire., Nov 1893; died Brockton, MA, 1975
Helena (Lena), born Brockton, MA, 1897; died Plymouth, MA, late 1970s.
Annie C., born Brockton, MA, 1900; died Brockton, MA, 31 Mar 1902

[70] Raymond and Helena (Murphy) Girard were married in 1827 and moved to Plymouth, Massachusetts. Ray was born in 1897, as was Helena, and he passed away in July 1967. Helena outlived Ray and died in Plymouth in the late 1970s.
Dan Murphy died of Acute Dilation of the Heart and Chronic Myocarditis. For the record, Dan's obituary in the Brockton Enterprise reads as follows:

Daniel M. Murphy

The funeral of Daniel M. Murphy took place this morning from the home of his son, Denis Murphy, 248 Forest Avenue, with solemn high mass of requiem at St. Patrick's Church celebrated by Rev. Dr. Irving L. Gifford, with Rev. Jeremiah Minihan as deacon and Rev. Fr. O'Brien as sub-deacon. The bearers were Frank O'Neil, Dr. A.C. Grogan, and George MacDonald, representing St. Thomas Court, M.C.O.F. (Massachusetts Catholic Order of Foresters), Daniel

Murphy, J.P. Sullivan, and Thomas Healey. Interment was in St. Patrick's Cemetery.

As explained in the text, Daniel Murphy named his two sons after Thomas and Denis, who were his only hope of emigrating from Ireland. One suspects Daniel eventually adopted Maurice as his middle name—perhaps to finally show the proper respect for his father—or maybe out of superstition.

[71] Recorded interview by Dr. Ed Murphy of Father Thomas Murphy S. J. and his maiden sisters, Theresa and Peg, at 404 Wolcott Hill Road, Wethersfield, CT, 1982.

[72] Recorded interview by Dr. Ed Murphy of Father Thomas Murphy S. J. and his maiden sisters, Theresa and Peg, at 404 Wolcott Hill Road, Wethersfield, CT, 1982.

Nellie Clifford's husband John died in his middle forties—between 1904 and 1910— leaving her with nine children, ages 24 to 5. Their names were:

Thomas, born Brockton, Massachusetts, Apr 1885
Michael, born Brockton, Massachusetts, Sept 1887
Nora, born Brockton, Massachusetts, Jan 1890
Mary, born Brockton, Massachusetts, Oct 1891
Nellie, born Brockton, Massachusetts, Sept 1897
Jeremiah, born Brockton, Massachusetts, Sept 1895
Annie, born Brockton, Massachusetts, May 1897
Maurice, born Brockton, Massachusetts, 1900 ?
John, born Brockton, Massachusetts, 1905 ?

[73] Ibid.; Re: Women lying about their ages—even on important documents— Annie Murphy was born on 2 May 1870 and married Patrick James Lucey in Brockton on 22 June 1901, making her thirty-one at the time. On the marriage license, she listed her age as twenty-nine. (FamilySearch.org)

[74] Recorded interview by Dr. Ed Murphy of Father Thomas Murphy S. J. and his maiden sisters, Theresa and Peg, at 404 Wolcott Hill Road, Wethersfield, CT, 1982.

[75] FamilySearch.org; irishgenealogy.ie; 1900, 1910, 1920, and 1930 U.S Census Reports; Recorded interview by Dr. Ed Murphy of Father Thomas Murphy S. J., and his maiden sisters, Theresa and Peg, at 404 Wolcott Hill Road, Wethersfield, CT, 1982.

[76] FamilySearch.org; U.S. Census Records, 1900.

[77] Family gravestone at Calvary Cemetery, Brockton, MA.; Interviews with Madeline (McCarthy) Davis and Muriel (McCarthy) Murphy on September 6, 2001 and October 22, 2001, respectively. Regarding Nonie's salary. The 1940 U.S. Census makes it clear that in 1939, Denis P. Murphy made $1800 while Nonie made $800. There were compensations though. Nonie and Mary

were allowed to rent the third floor of 551 Warren Avenue for $20 a month, while rents in the neighborhood ranged between $24 and $30 a month.

[78] Brockton City Directories.

[79] Copy of letter from Father Bartholomew Killilea, dated September 26, 1910.

[80] Copies of original documents passed down through the years. Catherine's death date is taken from her Massachusetts death certificate.

[81] Interview by Dr. Ed Murphy of Father Thomas Murphy S. J. and his maiden sisters, Theresa and Peg, at 404 Wolcott Hill Road, Wethersfield, CT, 1982.

[82] "Recombination in the Hemagglutinin Gene of the 1918 "Spanish Flu," *Science* magazine, September 7, 2001. http://www.sciencemag.org/content/293/5536/1842 (Accessed November 14, 2013)

[83] Carroll, 1989, 71.

[84] Various letters, printed programs, report cards, sales receipts and other information collected over the years concerning Rev. Thomas J. Murphy's short life. One item not included in the text: There was a life insurance policy on Rev. Thomas Murphy and The Equitable Life Assurance Society of the United States, on November 11, 1918, paid out $2,030.25 on his death.

[85] Brockton City Directories; U.S. Census Records; and family interviews.

[86] Miller, 1985, 28.

[87] Lodge, 1789, 201.

[88] Ibid.

[89] Schrier, 1958, 119; Miller, 1985, 390; There are many different ways to state the outcome of the Wyndham Act and the subsequent land purchases in Ireland, but the important fact remains: Landlordism was crushed by this act in 1903, and the Free Irish State was born.

[90] Keenan, 2006, 66-67.

[91] Jordan, 1994, 134.

[92] Jordan, 1994, 69.

[93] Irish Ancestors, http://www.irishtimes.com/ancestor/index.htm

[94] Ballyhaunis district, deaths; 1901 Census, Derrylea; Ballyhaunis district RC marriages; Annagh RC parish cemetery.

[95] Thomas and Catherine (Kate McGarry) Sullivan of Coolougrhra township, County Mayo, were married on February 21, 1867 in the Ballyhaunis RC church. Thomas was born in 1836 and Catherine in 1848. Catherine was the daughter of Patrick McGarry and the Sullivan children were:

Honoria Sullivan, born Derrylea, County Mayo, 30 May 1868; m. Stephen Greenin of Laughhill townland, County Mayo, 13 Mar 1892
Thomas Sullivan, born Derrylea, County Mayo, 24 Mar 1870
Patrick Sullivan, born Derrylea, County Mayo, 6 Jan 1872
John Sullivan, born Derrylea, County Mayo, 25 Jan 1874
Bridget Sullivan, born Derrylea, County Mayo, 7 Nov 1875
Catherine Sullivan, born Derrylea, County Mayo, 9, Sept 1887
Michael Sullivan, born Derrylea, County Mayo, 3 Aug 1879

Andrew Sullivan, born Derrylea, County Mayo, 18 Dec 1881
Mary Ann Sullivan, born Derrylea, County Mayo, 20 Nov 1883
Winifred Sullivan, born Derrylea, County Mayo, 8 Nov 1885
Agnes Sullivan, born Derrylea, County Mayo, 3 Mar 1888

Darby Sullivan died before 1856—probably more like 1851—while his wife
Bridget was born in 1826 and died 14 Jul 1895 (age 69). Their children were:

Michael Sullivan, born Derrylea, County Mayo, 1842; m. Bridget Agnes
Lyons of Clagnagh, County Mayo at the Ballyhaunis RC Church on 13 Apr
1886; died 11 May 1926. Bridget was the daughter of Patrick Lyons, She was
born in 1855 and died 29 Mar 1946. The children of Michael and Bridget
Sullivan were:

Mary Sullivan, born Derrylea, County Mayo, 31 May 1887; died 25 Jan 1890
Bridget (Dehlia) Sullivan, born Derrylea, County Mayo, 15 Dec 1888;
Katherine Sullivan, born Derrylea, County Mayo, 25 Aug 1890
Mary Ann Sullivan, born Derrylea, County Mayo, 24 Jan 1892; died 3 Sept
1980
Norah Sullivan, born Derrylea, County Mayo, 2 Sept 1894
Patrick Sullivan, born Derrylea, County Mayo, 19 Jan 1896; died 13 Jun
1948.
Ellen (Helen) Sullivan, born Derrylea, County Mayo, 26 May 1898; died 10
Sept 1994.
Michael Thomas Sullivan, born Derrylea, County Mayo, 18 Jan 1902

Mary Sullivan (Michael Sullivan's younger sister), born Derrylea, County
Mayo, c. 1850; m. Patrick Finegan of Derrintogher townland, County Mayo,
3 Apr 1884, at Ballyhaunis RC Church. Mary died 19 Aug 1890 (age 40).

[96] Irish Census Reports 1841, 1851.; Decline in the Population of Ireland,
www.libraryireland.com (Accessed October 20, 2013)
[97] Gray, 1995, n.p.
[98] Ask About Ireland, "Soils in Ireland,"
http://www.askaboutireland.ie/enfo/irelands-
environment/biodiversity/definitions/soils-in- ireland/ (Accessed October 21,
2013)
[99] Miller, 1985, 9
[100] Ireland's History in Maps, Ireland: The Famine Years
http://www.rootsweb.ancestry.com/~irlkik/ihm/ire1841.htm (Accessed
October 21, 2013)
[101] Jones, Plummer F. Deserted Ireland: An acccount how the Irish abandon
Ireland to become Americans, and the consequences to Ireland. The World
Today, February 1906. p. 286-294, Chicago: The World Today Company, 67
Wabash Ave., Chicago, IL. (Heart's International, Vol. 10, 2-5).

[102] Patrick Lyons, born c 1830, died 28 Apr 1892, aged 60, of Clagnagh townland and his wife Honor (née Lyons; born c 1825; died 28 Dec 1895, aged 70) had the following children:

Bridget, born in Clagnagh, County Mayo, 1 Dec 1855
James, born in Clagnagh, County Mayo, 1 Aug 1857
David, born in Clagnagh, County Mayo, 1 Aug 1861
Mary, born in Clagnagh, County Mayo, 20 Feb 1865
Patrick, born in Clagnagh, County Mayo, 3 Dec 1866
Michael, born in Clagnagh, County Mayo, 10 Sept 1869

[103] Michel Sullivan's mother Bridget was born about 1826 and died July 14, 1895 (age 69). Michael Sullivan's younger sister, Mary Sullivan, married the farmer Patrick Finegan of Derrintogher townland—son of John Finegan—on April 3, 1884. Mary died on August 19, 1890 (age 40). (Ballyhaunis District, deaths.)

[104] Griffith's Valuation of 1856, Census of Ireland 1901, Ship's Manifest for the Cunard Liner *SS Ivernia* that landed in Boston in April 1908.

[105] Caryle Murphy's interview of Mary Ann (Sullivan) Murphy, Aug. 1974.

[106] Ibid.

[107] Ibid.

[108] Sullivan, 1881, 129-135.

[109] *Irish Times,* Friday, April 10, 1908, 11.

[110] Hyde, 1975, *passim.*

[111] Ibid.

[112] Caryle Murphy's interview of Mary Ann (Sullivan) Murphy, Aug. 1974.

[113] *Boston Daily Globe*, April 17, 1908, 10.

[114] Caryle Murphy's interview of Mary Ann (Sullivan) Murphy, Aug. 1974.

[115] Laxton, 1996, *passim.*

[116] Caryle Murphy's interview of Mary Ann (Sullivan) Murphy, Aug. 1974.

[117] 1908 Brockton City Directory

[118] "Trolleys vs. Jitneys," *Hartford Courant,* December 8, 1919, 10.

[119] Institute For Historical Study Newsletter, 7.

[120] 1880, 1900, 1910, 1920 U.S. Census Records.

[121] US Census Records, 1940

[122] In 1867, the Lords of the Admiralty gave the mail contract back to the post office and it was put out to bid. That is why Norah Sullivan's ship was called the *RMS Laconia* in 1912. Since the designation was so coveted, the White Star Line owners made sure that they had a mail contract too in 1912, and that their new unsinkable ship was christened the *RMS Titanic.*

[123] Cleveland McGee was born in Augusta, Maine on 31 Mar 1893. He died in Falmouth, Massachusetts, 1 Nov 1969. Cleveland and Nora (Sullivan) McGee's children were:

Kathryn, born Rockland, Massachusetts, 1919

Harriet, born Rockland, Massachusetts, 1921
Elfreda, born Rockland, Massachusetts, 1922
Joseph, born Rockland, Massachusetts, 1927
Eloise, born Rockland, Massachusetts, 1928
Cleveland, Jr., born Rockland, Massachusetts, 7 Feb 1931; d. 1 Jan 2010

[124] FamilySearch.org
[125] 1930, 1940 U.S. Census Records.
[126] Telephone interview with Jennifer McGee Martin, June 18, 2006.
[127] Patrick and May Sullivan's three sons were:

Eamon, born Ireland
Oliver, born Ireland
Porraigh (Patrick), born Ireland

[128] 1930, 1940 U.S. Census; FamilySearch.org
[129] The children of Pat and Dehlia Moran were:

Peggy, born Derrylea, County May, Ireland; m. Pat Devanny
Pat, born Derrylea, County May, Ireland; m. Eileen
David born Derrylea, County May, Ireland; m.Nora,
Dehlia, born Derrylea, County May, Ireland; m. Tom Glynn, Sr.

[130] Caryle Murphy's interview of Mary Ann (Sullivan) Murphy, Aug. 1974.
[131] Schrier, 1958, 107.
[132] "Paying By Check," *Hartford Courant,* March 4, 1910, 8.
[133] Caryle Murphy's interview of Mary Ann (Sullivan) Murphy, Aug. 1974.
[134] WWI Draft Registration card; Brockton city directories; Interviews with Bob
   Murphy, Joe Murphy, Muriel Murphy and Madeline Davis; Caryle Murphy's
   interview of Mary Ann (Sullivan) Murphy, Aug. 1974. Ed Murphy's
   interview with Father Tom Murphy S.J. of Fairfield, CT and his sisters,
   Teresa and Peg, at 404 Wolcott Hill Rd., Wethersfield, CT in 1982.
[135] http://www.careercast.com/career-news/most-stressful-jobs-2013-firefighter
[136] Terkel, 1972, 586-89.
[137] Ibid.
[138] Ibid; Tele-interview with Muriel (McCarthy) Murphy; October 12, 2001.
[139] Ibid.
[140] Caryle Murphy's interview of Mary Ann (Sullivan) Murphy, Aug. 1974.;
   Interview by Dr. Ed Murphy of Father Thomas Murphy S. J., and his maiden
   sisters, Theresa and Peg, at 404 Wolcott Hill Road, Wethersfield, CT, 1982.
[141] Brockton City Directories; Brockton Business Directories; Boot and Shoe
   Industry Statistics, 1946 ED., Dept. of Commerce, Washington D.C.
[142] Denis Murphy's 1917-1918 draft registration card can be viewed at
   FamilySearch.org.
[143] Caryle Murphy's interview of Mary Ann (Sullivan) Murphy, Aug. 1974.

[144] Plymouth County Registry of Deeds, 50 Obery St., Plymouth, MA. Vol. 1575, p. 518-19.

In order to pay off the $5000 in 37 months, Denis and Mary Murphy had to come up with $136.24 per month—on average. In addition to Denis Murphy's salary as a city fireman (about $112 a month), the couple also had rents coming in from the second and third floor apartments (perhaps a total of about $48 a month) and were therefore able to save a great deal of money. Based on the fact that they were able to pay off a $5000 note in just under 37 months, one can assume that by the time their firstborn son was ready for college in September of 1939, they had amassed almost $12,000 in savings. But the oldest boy, Joe, had saved $2000 from caddying and ushering at Brockton Theatre and was able to pay for Tufts himself.

[145] Stacy, Adams was at the NE corner of Warren Avenue and Dover Street. The company moved from 69 Montello Street to 80 Center Street and then to 33 Dover in 1932. Rocky Marciano would have been nine at the time of the last move, and this is probably where his father worked until his son began winning prizefights.

[146] "The Progress of Prohibition," *Hartford Courant,* January 15, 1924, 14.

[147] Telephone interview with Muriel (McCarthy) Murphy; October 12, 2001.

[148] "Six Brocton Races," *Hartford Courant,* October 8, 1909, 15.

[149] Telephone interview with Madeleine McCarthy Davis; September 6, 2001.

[150] M. A. Packard had become a division of Knapp Shoes before it burned down in 1948. Carroll, 1989, 77-80.

[151] Ibid.; "Brockton Shoe Plants Will Reopen Today," *Hartford Courant,* October 4, 1933, 18.

[152] "Day's Business," *Hartford Courant,* November 4, 1939, 13.

[153] Kingman, 1866, Chapter XVI, "Fire Department,"; "Automobile Fire Wagon," *Hartford Courant,* September 2, 1909, 16.

[154] Telephone interview with Brockton's Larry Noonan; August 6, 2001 and September 3, 2001.

[155] Telephone Interview with Brockton's Larry Noonan, Sept. 3, 2001; Draft Registration card, Aug. 14, 1918.

[156] U.S. Census Records, 1880, 1900, 1910, 1920, 1930, 1940; Massachusetts Marriage Records; Brockton City Directories; Telephone interview with Larry Noonan of Brockton; August 6, 2001.

[157] Lockport, New York was the first town to use mechanical voting machines in 1892. Rochester took up the gauntlet four years later. By 1920 the gear and lever voting machine was in use throughout Massachusetts and sixteen other states. Ten years later, they were in use in every major city in the United States. However, even as late as 1996, only 20.7 percent of the vote in the nation was tallied by mechanical voting machines.

[158] US Census Records, 1880, 1900, 1910, 1920, 1930, 1940; FamilySearch.org., WWI Draft Registration Cards; *Some Vital Statistics of Brockton Veterans of World War I* (Brockton Library).

[159] Brockton Enterprise, March 11, 1941.

[160] Ibid.

[161] *Brockton Enterprise*, March 11, 1941.

[162] Telephone interview with Madeline (McCarthy) Davis; September 6, 2001.

[163] *Brockton Enterprise*, March 11, 1941.

[164] The *Enterprise*, March 10, 1941, wrote the story this way—J. Joseph Cahill, manager of the Brockton Theatre, usually on the scene at big local fires, first learned of the Strand Theatre tragedy shortly after 5 o'clock this morning (Monday) when calling the fire department for aid in fighting a blaze in his own car. Though short of apparatus, the department managed to provide the required aid, saving his car from serious damage.

[165] *Brockton Enterprise,* March 12, 1941.

[166] *Brockton Enterprise*, March 11, 1941.

[167] *Brockton Enterprise*, March 11, 1941.

[168] *Brockton Enterprise,* March 10, 1941.

[169] State of Massachusetts, Motor Vehicle Department, Ms.Lillian Laro, September 5, 2001 (email); Interview with Bob Murphy; September 15, 2001.

[170] *Brockton City Expenses*, 1897.

[171] Joe Murphy (b. 27 Sept 1921; d. 26 Mar 1994) married Muriel Kathryn McCarthy (b. 7 Jan 1921; d. 9 Sept. 2013) on 8 Sept 1945. Their children were:

Carole (Caryle) Marie, b. 16 Nov 1946
Karen (Kerry) Anne, b. 22 Oct 1948
Colin Denis, b. 7 Apr 1951
Kevin Joseph, b. 1 Oct 1953
Kenan Charles, b. 1 Nov 1954
Coleen Mary, b. 25 Jun 1958

[172] Telephone interview with Muriel (McCarthy) Murphy; October 12, 2001; Telephone interview with Madeline (McCarthy) Davis; September 6, 2001.

[173] Ibid.

[174] Ibid.

[175] Ibid.

[176] Interview with Bob Murphy; September 15, 2001

[177] Ibid.

[178] Interview with Bob Murphy; September 15, 2001.

[179] Bob Murphy (b. 30 Mar 1923; d. 18 May 2007) and Mary Cecelia Foss (b. 24 Nov 1923) were married on September 15, 1945. Their children were:

Judith Ann, b. 11 Apr 1947
Denis Philip, b. 17 Jun 1948
Kevin James, b. 29 Jul 1949
Kathleen Marie, b. 8 Jun 1951
Brendan John, b. 30 May 1952; d. 5 Apr 2012
Marilyn, b.23 Oct 1954

Barbara Jean, b. 26 Nov 1955
Maureen Elizabeth, b. 25 May 1957

[180] Telephone interview with Muriel (McCarthy) Murphy; October 12, 2001
[181] Interview with Kate Murphy; summer 1986.
[182] Edward Murphy (b. 9 Apr 1927; d. 1 Feb 1994) married Claire Jeanne
MacLeod (b. 8 Jan 1934; d. 9 Mar 1963) in Jan 1955. Their children were:

Michael Raymond, b. 12 Nov 1955
Susan Catherine, b. 12 Oct. 1956
Ruth Elizabeth, b. 12 Nov 1957
Daniel Patrick, b.29 Dec. 1958

Ed Murphy's wife, Claire Jeanne (MacLeod) Murphy died unexpectedly in
March 1963. Eleven years later, Ed Murphy married Catherine "Kate"
Elizabeth Munns Murphy (b. 13 Aug 1929) on 28 Sept 1974. Kate brought
two children to the marriage:

Eugene Sean, born 19 May 1951
Jerry Beth, born 31 Oct 1958

[183] Dr. Brendan Fox, who was in the same Tufts Med School class as Ed
Murphy, supplied all the educational and some of the personal information
about Dr. Edward F. Murphy. Dr. Fox also offered an enormous amount of
information about Tufts Med School in the early 1950s. Dr. Fox allowed the
author to interview him for an afternoon at his home in Black Point (Niantic),
CT, on September 28, 2001.
[184] Telephone interview with Muriel (McCarthy) Murphy; October 12, 2001;
Interview with Brockton resident Vinnie Hayes; August 28, 2001.
[185] Interview with Bob Murphy; September 15, 2001.
[186] Information from Ed Murphy to Kevin James Murphy; summer of 1986.
[187] Ibid.
[188] Interview with Kerry Murphy; summer 2001.
[189] Telephone interview with Muriel (McCarthy) Murphy; October 12, 2001.
[190] Ibid.
[191] Ibid.
[192] Ibid.

Glossary

Act of Union -This took effect in 1801 and was a British effort to merge all Irish institutions with those of England. The English never tired of trying to kill Catholicism and this was the ultimate goal of the Act of Union.

Battle of the Boyne - Fought in 1690 between two rival claimants of the English, Scottish, and Irish thrones The battle pitted the Catholic King James and the Protestant King William of Orange. The battle took place on July 1, 1690 and William's army defeated James's followers.

Bogs - One-sixth of Ireland consists of bogland. These bogs tend to be in the midlands and the far west. The peat cut from the bogs was for centuries the main fuel supply for most of the population.

Brehon Laws - Pre-conquest Gaelic Irish pandect.

Catholic Emancipation -The Battle of the Boyne was in 1690, and the most serious Penal Laws followed over the next three decades. More than a century later, the British finally realized that the Irish would never accept the Church of Ireland (Protestant), and never become "little Englishmen." The most important relaxation of the Penal Laws was the Catholic Emancipation of 1829.

Church of Ireland - Anglican Church designed to replace Catholicism in Ireland. To placate Catholics, Prime Minister Gladstone outlawed the Church of Ireland in 1869, but the protestant church remained in place.

Clachan - A haphazard cluster of a half-dozen to several hundred farmhouses that lacked shops, markets, or churches.

Cottier - Small subsistence farmer.

Demesne - Common lands.

Easter 1916 - Easter Monday and a group of nationalist revolutionaries took over the General Post Office in Dublin's O'Connell Street, and held the city for several days. This revolt led eventually to Irish independence.

Emigration - The leaving of Ireland for greener pasture in America, Canada, Australia, and the Mediterranean. Impartible inheritance left most of the

237

children in a family without any land and they had little choice but to leave Ireland.

Fairies - Imaginary little people (both good and bad).

Famine - Generally refers to the Great Hunger from 1845-1851. However, there were many famines before the Great Hunger, and a number afterwards.

Fenians - Members of the Irish Republican Brotherhood, a secret society, emerging in the late 1850s.

Hedge Schools - The Penal Laws were passed in the late 1600s and early 1700s, and outlawed Irish schools. The Irish responded by holding classes wherever they could—even behind hedges. Thus the name hedge schools.

Killarney - One of the biggest tourist towns in all of Ireland, because it is the gateway to one of the most beautiful lakes regions in Ireland. Just southwest of the town is MacGillycuddy's Reeks, the highest peak in Ireland.

Land Act of 1870 - Prime Minister William Gladstone's first feeble effort to compensate the Irish for improvements made on the land. This first land act led ultimately to the Wyndham Land Act of 1903, ensuring that the Irish would again own Ireland.

Laster - In the shoe business, a laster is a person or, later a machine, that attached the upper part of the shoe to the sole.

Norman Invasion of Ireland - The Norman invasion of Ireland was a twelfth century effort—beginning in County Wexford—to recapture the kingdom of Diarmait MacMurchada. In 1171, Henry II landed a much bigger army in Waterford to cement control.

Penal Laws - Laws (passed from 1607 to 1714) designed to eliminate Catholic land ownership. These laws were exhaustive in scope.

Poor Law Act (1838) - The basis of the Poor Law Unions (PLUs), which built workhouses all over Ireland.

Potatoes - At one point in Irish history, the poorer Irish people survived almost entirely on potatoes, which first came to Ireland in the 1600s.

Poteen - indicates any spirituous liquor distilled illegally. The British banned the substance in 1831.

Protestant Ascendancy - English idea of converting Ireland to an all-English Protestant land.

Rundale - Communal system whereby each household was given scattered, unfenced acreage for tillage and pastureland. The terms clachan and rundale can almost be used interchangeably because clachan was the cluster of huts and rundale was the system the residents lived by.

Sciving - Cutting upper leather, especially, to a thin edge, in the cutting or stitching department.

Saints and Scholars - Barbarians overran Europe from about 500 to 1000 A.D. This period is called the Dark Ages. Thanks to Ireland's isolation, friaries and monasteries were able to squirrel away the books and written materials that mattered.

St. Patrick - The patron Saint of Ireland, who arrived in 432 A.D.

Tara - Site of the ancient kings of Ireland in County Meath, and one of traditional Ireland's most sacred symbols.

Temperance Movement - In 1838. a priest in Cork began the Irish Temperance Movement. By 1845—when the total population of Ireland was 8.2 million—about 5 million Irish men and women had taken the pledge.

Wake - At an Irish wake, neighbors dropped by to commiserate with the relatives, drink, eat, talk, play music, and sometimes dance. The wake lasts several days.

Wyndham Land Act of 1903 - named after George Wyndham, who became chief secretary of the Irish Parliament in 1900, is regarded as the last piece of the complex legislation aimed at revolutionizing the property ownership of Ireland. The Irish people were allowed to buy back the land they now worked, with loans from the English government. In short, the treasury of England would be used to, once and for all, return land that had been stolen by Oliver Cromwell's Ironsides in the middle of the 1600s.

Bibliography

City Directories

City of Brockton, City Directories, 1880 to 1960.

Yearbooks

The *Brocktonian* (Brockton High School Yearbook) 1939, 1940 and 1945

Newspapers

Boston Globe
Brockton Enterprise
Hartford Courant
New York Times

Magazines

Jones, Plummer F. *Deserted Ireland: An acccount how the Irish abandon Ireland to become Americans, and the consequences to Ireland. The World Today,* February 1906. p. 286-294, Chicago: The World Today Company, 67 Wabash Ave., Chicago, IL. (Heart's International, Vol. 10, 2-5)

Libraries, &c.

Boston Public Library
Copley Square
Boston, MA

Boston City Archives
Mr. John McColgan
Boston City Archives

Brockton Public Library
Main Library Temporary Location
155 W. Elm Street
Brockton, MA 02301

Brockton Historical Society Museum
(Includes Shoe Museum and Fire Museum)
Pleasant Street
Brockton, MA

National Archives & Research Administration
NARA- Boston Branch
380 Trapelo Road
Waltham, MA 02452

Massachusetts Archives at Columbia Point
Office of the Secretary of State
220 Morrissey Blvd.
Boston, MA

Mayo County Library
The Mall
Castlebar
County Mayo, Ireland

Ballyhaunis Library
Clare Street
Ballyhaunis
County Mayo, Ireland

South Mayo Family Research Center
Main Street, Ballinrobe,
County Mayo, Ireland.

County of Plymouth
Registry of Deeds
Main Recording Department
10 Obery Street
Plymouth, MA 02360-2199

VIDEO CASSETTES

Out Of Ireland: The Story of Irish Emigration To America, Written and
Directed by Paul Wagner, Produced by Paul and Ellen Casey Wagner,
Shanachie Entertainment Corporation, 1995, (Narrated by Kelly McGillis.)

BOOKS

Adams, William Forbes. *Ireland and Irish Emigration to the New World: from
1815 to the Famine.* New York: Russell & Russell, 1932.

Albion, Robert; Baker, William; Labaree, Benjamin & Brewington, Marion,
New England And The Sea, Middletown, CT: Wesleyan University Press (for
The Marine Historical Association, Inc. Mystic Seaport, 1972.

Allen, Frederick J. *The Shoe Industry*. New York: Henry Holt & Co., 1922.

Bartlett, Thomas. *Ireland: A History*. Cambridge: Cambridge University Press, 2010.

Black, Charles. *Black's Guide to Ireland* (12th Edition). London: A. & C. Black, publishers, 1906.

Blewett, Mary H. *Men, Women, and Work: Class, Gender, and Protest in the New England Shoe Industry, 1780-1910*, Urbana and Chicago: University of Illinois Press, 1990.

Brown, Thomas N. *Irish-American Nationalism: 1870-1890*, New York: J. B. Lippincott Company, 1966.

Bryant, Seth. Shoe and Leather Trade of the Last Hundred Years, s.p. Ashmont, publisher, 1891.

Butman, Arthur B. *Shoe & Leather Report,* Washington: Government Printing Office, 1907.

Byrne, Stephen. *Irish Emigration to the United States*. New York: Arno Press & New York Times, 1969.
Carroll, Walter F. *Brockton: From Rural Parish to Urban Center*. Northridge, California: Windsor Publications, 1989.

Carse, Robert. *The Twilight of Sailing Ships*. New York: Grosset & Dunlap, 1965.

Cusack, M. F. *A History of the Kingdom of Killarney*. London: Longmann, Green & Co., 1871.

Davis, Horace B. *Shoes: The Workers and the Industry*. New York: International Publishers, 1940.
De Breffny, Brian (editor). *The Irish World: The Art and Culture Of The Irish People*, New York: Harry N. Abrams, Inc., Publishers, 1977.

Eagleton, Terry. *The Truth About Irish History*: New York, St. Martin's Press, 1999.

Esson, D. M. R. *The Curse of Cromwell: The History of the Ironside Conquest of Ireland, 1649-53*. Totowa, NJ: Rowman & Littleton, 1971.

Flexner, Abraham. *Medical Education in the United States and Canada: A Report to the Carnegie Foundation for the Advancement of Teaching.* New York: Arno Press, 1972.

Foster, R. F. (editor). *The Oxford Illustrated History of Ireland.* Oxford, New York: Oxford University Press, 1989.

Gill Pub. *Three Hundred Years of Shoe and Leather Making in Massachusetts.* Boston: compiled by Gill Publications, 1930.

Gray, Peter. *The Irish Famine.* Harry N. Abrams, Inc., New York, 1995.

Greeley, Andrew M. *The Irish Americans*, New York: Harper & Row, 1981.

Greenhill, Basil & Giffard, Ann. *Traveling By Sea in the Nineteenth Century: Interior Design In Victorian Passenger Ships.* New York: Hastings House Publishers, 1974.

Handlin, Oscar. *The Uprooted*, Boston: Little Brown & Company, 1951,1973.

Hyde, Francis E. *Cunard And The North Atlantic: 1840 – 1973, A History of Shipping and Financial Management,* Humanities Press, Atlantic Highlands, N.J., 1975

Joy, Arthur F. *Shoe City: Growing Up In Brockton, Massachusetts In The Roaring 20s.* South Wellfleet, MA: Saturscent Publishing, 1978.

Jordan, Donald E. *Land and Popular Politics in Ireland: County Mayo from the Plantation to the Land War.* London: Cambridge University Press, 1994.

Kane, Robert A. *The Brockton Irish: From the Tip To the Bush.* s.p., 1983.

Kane, Robert A. *The Brockton Irish: From The Tip To The Bush...AND BACK! Vol. II*, s.p., 1984.

Kee, Robert. *Ireland: A History.* Boston: Little Brown & Co., 1980.

Keenan, Desmond. *Post-Famine Ireland: Social Structure: Ireland As It Really Was.* Xlibris Corp. 2006.

Kingman, Bradford. *The History of North Bridgewater, Plymouth County Massachusetts, From Its Settlement to the Present Time*, Boston, s.p. 1866.

Laing, Alexander. *American Sail: A Pictorial History*, New York: E. P. Dutton & Company, 1961.

Landers, Warren P. *Brockton and its Centennial: 1821-1921*, Published by the City of Brockton, 1921.

Landstrom, Bjorn. *The Ship: An Illustrated History.* New York: Doubleday & Co., 1961.

Laxton, Edward. *The Famine Ships: The Irish Exodus To America.* New York: Henry Holt & Co., 1996.

Lloyd, David. *Irish Culture and Colonial Modernity 1800-2000: The Transformation of Oral Space.* Cambridge: Cambridge University Press, 2011.

Lodge, John. *The Peerage of Ireland.* London: Oxford University, 1789.

MacLysaght, Edward (ed.). *The Kenmare Manuscripts.* Dublin: Irish University Press, 1942.

Maddocks, Melvin. *The Atlantic Crossing.* Alexandria, VA: Time-Life Books, 1981.

Mensoian, Michael G., Robert L. Turner, Winfred E. A. Bernhard, *Massachusetts*, Discovery Channel School, original content provided by World Book Online, http://www.discoveryschool.com/homeworkhelp/ worldbook/atozgeography/m/348140.html

Miller, Kerby A. *Emigrants and Exiles: Ireland and the Irish Exodus to North America.* New York: Oxford University Press, 1985.

Mitchell, Nahum. *History of the Early Settlement of Bridgewater in Plymouth County, Massachusetts*, s.p. Kidder and Wright, Boston, 1840. Reprinted by Henry T. Pratt, Bridgewater, MA 1897.

O'Brien, Jacqueline & Harbison, Peter. *Ancient Ireland: From Prehistory to the Middle Ages.* New York: Oxford University Press, 1996.

O'Connor, Thomas H. *The Boston Irish: A Political History.* Boston: Back Bay Books, 1995.

Officer, Lawrence H. *Between the Dollar / Sterling Gold points: Exchange Rates, Parity, and Market Behavior.* Cambridge: Cambridge University Press, 1996.

Pierce, Rev. Albert F. D.D. *History of the Brockton Relief Fund: Aid Of Sufferers From The R. B. Grover & Co. Factory Fire. Brockton, Mass., March 20, 1905*, Boston: The Fort Hill Press, 1905.

Pigot, James. *Provincial Directory of Ireland*. Manchester, England: Pigot & Co., 1824.

Rebman, Renee C. *Life on Ellis Island,* San Diego: Lucent Books, 2000.

Rollyson, Carl. *Amy Lowell Anew: A Biography*. Lanham, Maryland: Rowman & Littlefield, 2013.

Schrier, Arnold. *Ireland and the Irish Emigration: 1850-1900*. Chester Springs, PA, 1997.

Sullivan, M. F. *Ireland of Today: The Causes and Aims of Irish Agitation*. Philadelphia: J. C. McCurdy & Co., 1881.

Tavernier, Bruno. *Great Maritime Routes : An Illustrated History,* (Translated by Nicholas Fry), New York: The Viking Press, 1970.

Terkel, Studs. *Working*. New York: Pantheon Books, 1972.

Tunis, Edwin. *Oars, Sails And Steam: A Picture Book of Ships*. New York: World Publishing Company, 1952.

Woodman, Richard. *The History of the Ship: The comprehensive story of seafaring from the earliest times to the present day*. New York: The Lyons Press, 1997.

Map & Photo Credits

Maps

The maps in this book were drawn by the author from his own extensive collection of maps. The only exception to this is the map of Killarney which was redrawn by the author from the original Griffith Valuation Ordinance Survey of 1863. This map has been in the public domain since 1863.

Photographs

The photographs in this books were contributed almost exclusively by family members, including but not limited to, Robert and Mary Murphy, Joe and Muriel Murphy, Ed and Kate Murphy, Kenan Murphy, Kerry (Murphy) Burke, Jennifer McGee Martin, Stanley Bauman, and Chief Kenneth Galligan.

Beyond the foregoing special mention, all of the photographs in this book came from out-of-print books of the period—the Connecticut State Library and/or U.S. government sources. The author is grateful to all those who helped obtain the necessary photographs.

Acknowledgements

Many people contributed to this genealogical text and a tribute to them is in order.

First, I would like to acknowledge the great debt that I owe to my parents, Bob and Mary Murphy, for all that they have given me. Much of life is random, but my birth and education were planned and my parents deserve credit for the sacrifices therein.

This book was only possible with the help of Muriel (McCarthy) Murphy and Madeline (McCarthy) Davis, who gave interviews that brought Denis and Mary Murphy's lives into sharp focus. They shed a great deal of light on all of the Murphys and Sullivans who emigrated from Ireland and made their homes in Brockton.

A special thanks goes to my aunt Kate (Munns) Murphy, the widow of Ed Murphy, who filled in many gaps in Ed's school years before and after World War II.

Dr. Brendan Fox—who roomed with Ed Murphy at Tufts Med School and graduated with him in 1955—deserved special thanks. Dr. Fox knew Ed well and was kind enough to allow me to interview him for an afternoon at his home in Black Point (Niantic), CT.

Laurene and Steve Frederick did research for me in Brockton—and Calvary Cemetery—and also offered much needed encouragement. Thank you.

Regarding recorded interviews, I would like to thank Caryle Murphy for interviewing Grammy Murphy in 1974 at Tara II, and offer a word of gratitude to the late Ed Murphy for interviewing Father Tom Murphy S.J., along with his sisters Teresa and Peg, in Wethersfield, CT in 1982.

The details of Dan Murphy's days in Killarney were made possible by Ed Murphy, who salvaged Dan Murphy's personal papers. Similarly, the personal papers of Father Thomas Murphy and his mother, Catherine, were preserved by Ed Murphy as well.

In Brockton, Windsor, Wethersfield, Northern California, and Florida, I would like to thank all of the family members who were kind enough to share information and photos that are now part of this book. Their names are in this text already, so . . . 'nuff said.

In Brockton, there were many folks who contributed a great deal: Lucia Shannon and Daniel McCormack, at the Brockton Public Library, were models of professionalism as I spent days digging through their files; former fire chiefs Kenneth Galligan and Ed Burrell, and others—Larry Noonan, William Donovan and Larry Johnson—all very knowledgeable retirees of the Brockton Fire Department; Vinnie Hayes, retired shoe worker and walking encyclopedia of Brockton and the shoe industry. Lastly, Stanley

Bauman, photographer of the *Enterprise,* was kind enough to share information and photos of the Strand Theatre Fire. Many Thanks to all.

A tip of the hat goes to Peggy (O'Brien) Moore who helped with information about the Firemen's Relief Fund. (Her father, Daniel O'Brien, died in the Strand Theatre Fire.)

Gerard M. Delaney of the Mayo Family History Center was enormously helpful. By gathering all of the important documents of the Sullivans of Derrylea, he made my work much easier. Gerard Delaney also answered a number of questions regarding the railroads of Ireland and emigration details that the average genialogist might miss. I am enormously grateful for the help.

As usual, historical and genealogical contributions were made by the able staff of the Connecticut Historical Society—Diana McCain, Barbara Austen, Nancy Finlay, Cindy Harbeson, Sierra Dixon, and Richard C. Malley. For their help, I will always be indebted.

At the Connecticut State Library, I would like to thank Jeannie Sherman, Mel Smith, Carol Ganz, Carolyn Picciano, Bonnie Linck, Steve Rice, Kristi Finnan, Jerry Seagrave, Kevin Johnson, and Bruce Stark. A special word of thanks is reserved for Connecticut State Librarian Kendall F. Wiggin and Curator Dave Corrigan of the Museum of Connecticut History at the Connecticut State Library.

This, I'm afraid, is only a representative collection of the people who contributed to *A Few Murphys From Brockton.* For those I may have inadvertently missed, rest assured that this book would never have come together without your help. Many thanks.

Index

Kerry, County, 15, 21, 22, 27-28, 30, 33, 73, 76, 79, 127, 132
Kilfoyle, Bridget, 77-78, 86
Kilfoyle, Agnes, 86-89, 126
Killarney Cathedral (*see* St. Mary's Cathedral)
Killarney Union, 22, 31-32, 52
Killilea, Rev. Bartholomew, 66
Knights of St. Crispin, 42

Laconia, SS, 119-121
Limerick, County, 19, 21, 34, 89-90
Liverpool, 34-37, 83, 86, 92, 118
Lucey, Annie (Murphy), 30, 37, 54-55, 62-63
Lucey, Patrick, 63
Lunatic Asylum, 32, 33
Lyne, Catherine, 15-16
Lynn, 33, 39, 111, 155
Lusitania, SS, 57, 125

McKay machines, 40, 47, 103
Marciano, Rocky (Rocco Francis Marchegiano), 144-145
Massachusetts Catholic Order of Foresters, 127, 200
Mayo, County, 21, 24, 51, 69, 71, 79-88, 102, 106, 127, 145, 164, 184, 195, 198, 215
McCarthy, Denis, 52
McCue & Cahill, 106, 111-113
McGee, Cleveland, 121-123
McGee, Norah (Sullivan), 82, 119-122
Meagher, Charles & Son, 56
Meath, County, 240
Midland & Great Western train, 88-89
"Monstry of the Brothers" (Presentation Brothers Monastery), 28
Morrisroe, Rev. Lawrence, 189, 192, 196
Murphy, Bob, (Dr.), 124, 144, 148, 154, 167, 182, 194, 201-214
Murphy, Catherine (Sullivan), 52, 60, 62, 65-66, 68, 157, 194
Murphy, Cornelius, 15-16, 23-26, 29
Murphy, Daniel (Dan), 26, 30-33, 37, 48, 52-54, 59-69, 135, 167
    autobiographical resume letter, 61
Murphy, Ed, (Dr.), 140-141, 154, 173, 208-216
Murphy, Joe, (Dr.), 139, 144, 148-149, 154, 167, 182, 192, 201-210, 216, 218
Murphy, Denis (Dinny), 17, 31-37, 48-63, 138, 166
Murphy, Denis P., 30-31, 48-59, 62, 66-70, 108, 116, 123, 132-149, 155-218
Murphy, Honora (Nonie), 56, 57, 59, 65, 68, 139, 144
Murphy, Honora (McCarthy) "Gramma Murphy," 23, 26-69
Murphy, Mary (Sullivan), 70, 81-95, 99-133, 140-157, 201-218
Murphy, Mary A., 57, 65, 68

Murphy, Mary C. (Foss), 208
Murphy, Maurice, 15-17, 23-33, 48-49, 62-63
Murphy, Maurice, Jr., 67-69
Murphy, Maurice, judge (Beeshie), 48
Murphy, Thomas (Tom), 33-48, 52-55, 60-62, 67-69, 166
Murphy, Rev. Thomas J. (Father Tom of Fairfield, CT), 194
Murphy, Thomas J, Rev., 67-70, 140, 194
Moore, Archie, 145
Moran, Dehlia (Sullivan), 80-85, 92, 100-107, 118-120, 124, 127
Moville Londonderry, 34

National Lines, 35, 58
National schools, 16, 86, 133
Newell, Daniels, 42
Noodle's Island, 59, 99-100
Norman Invasion, 19

Oko Club, 196
Old Colony Street Railroad, 37, 50, 59, 100, 102, 105
"Old School, The," 50
Onset Beach, 130, 139

Packard, M.A. Shoes, 41, 69, 104, 133-134, 154, 157, 173, 213
"Paddy Lane," 50-51
Palace, The, 33
Pavonia, SS, 56
Penal Laws, 20-21, 27
Pigot's 1824 *Provincial Directory of Ireland,* 16
Pilot, The, 127-128
Poor Law Unions, 22, 31-32, 52, 75
population figures
        Brockton, 111, 103-104, 140
        Ireland, 22-24, 75, 103
Port of Boston Immigration Facility, 59, 99
Presentation Brothers, 28
Presentation Brothers Monastery, 28
Presentation Convent, 28
Presentation Sisters, 28
Pugin, Augustus, 33
Proven Pictures, 179, 180, 182, 195

Queenstown (see also Cobh), 19, 23, 34, 35, 56-59, 83-92, 103, 118-121

Red Willy, ix
Reilly, Katie, 48

Roman Catholic Chapel (R. C. Chapel), 28
Roscommon, County, 78-79
Ross Island townland, 15
Royal Mail contract, 35
rundale, 25, 73

Saxonia, SS, 58, 93-94, 125
Seccombe, Capt, William S., 57
Seville Council Knights of Columbus, 194
Sirius, 34
Slater's Directory (1881), 17
South Station, Boston, 37, 59, 100, 102, 210
Southern Massachusetts Telephone & Telegraph, 105
Spanish Influenza, 67-68
sparkies, 173-174, 177-178, 186, 189-190, 192
Spillane family, 17
St. Colman's Cathedral, 35, 90
St. Crispin, 42
St. Joseph, Chapel of, 28
St. Margaret's Roman Catholic Church, 170
St. Mary's Cathedral, 18, 27, 28, 30, 33, 52
St. Patrick's Church, (Ballyhaunis R. C. Church, County Mayo, Ireland), 79-81
St. Patrick's Church, 48-52, 60-63, 66, 79, 119, 137, 153, 173-175, 194, 207
St. Patrick's Church (old), 52
St. Patrick's School, 52, 69, 167
St. Patrick's School (old), 52, 133
Stacy, Adams, 134, 144, 173
steamships
    cost of passage to America, 36, 55
    steerage, 36, 53-54, 58, 90, 93-94, 99
    third-class, 36, 58, 100, 120-121
    typical passengers, 58
Strand Theatre, 178-200
Sullivan, Bridget, 75, 80-83
Sullivan, Darby & Bridget, 76-79
Sullivan, Denis, 52
Sullivan, Ellen (Nel), 48
Sullivan, Helen, 82, 123
Sullivan, John L., 181
Sullivan, Mary (Herlihey), 52
Sullivan, Mary (Michael Sullivan's sister), 80
Sullivan, Michael, 74-75, 77-92
Sullivan, Michael T. (Uncle Mike), 82, 123-124
Sullivan, Patrick (Honora McCarthy's oldest sibling), 52
Sullivan, Patrick, 82-83, 123

www.ingramcontent.com/pod-product-compliance
Lightning Source LLC
Chambersburg PA
CBHW060303100426
42742CB00011B/1850